# Hands-On Graph Neural Networks Using Python

Practical techniques and architectures for building powerful graph and deep learning apps with PyTorch

**Maxime Labonne**

BIRMINGHAM—MUMBAI

# Hands-On Graph Neural Networks Using Python

**Group Product Manager**: Gebin George

**Publishing Product Manager**: Dinesh Chaudhary

**Senior Editor**: David Sugarman

**Technical Editor**: Devanshi Ayare

**Copy Editor**: Safis Editing

**Project Coordinator**: Farheen Fathima

**Proofreader**: Safis Editing

**Indexer**: Tejal Daruwale Soni

**Production Designer**: Joshua Misquitta

First published: April 2023

Production reference: 1240323

Published by Packt Publishing Ltd.
Livery Place
35 Livery Street
Birmingham
B3 2PB, UK.

ISBN 978-1-80461-752-6

www.packtpub.com

# Contributors

## About the author

**Maxime Labonne** is a senior applied researcher at J.P. Morgan with a Ph.D. in machine learning and cyber security from the Polytechnic Institute of Paris. During his Ph.D., Maxime worked on developing machine learning algorithms for anomaly detection in computer networks. He then joined the AI Connectivity Lab at Airbus, where he applied his expertise in machine learning to improve the security and performance of computer networks. He then joined J.P. Morgan, where he now develops techniques for solving a variety of challenging problems in finance and other domains. In addition to his research work, Maxime is passionate about sharing his knowledge and experience with others through Twitter (*@maximelabonne*) and his personal blog.

# About the reviewers

**Dr. Mürsel Taşgın** is a computer scientist with a Ph.D. He graduated from the Computer Engineering Department of Middle East Technical University in 2002. He completed his master of science and Ph.D. in the Computer Engineering Department of Bogazici University. During his Ph.D., he worked in the field of complex systems, graphs, and ML. He also worked in industry in technical, research, and managerial roles (at Mostly.AI, KKB, Turkcell, and Akbank). Dr. Mürsel Taşgın's current focus is mainly on generative AI, graph machine learning, and financial applications of machine learning. He also teaches **artificial intelligence (AI)**/ML courses at universities.

*I would like to thank my dear wife Zehra and precious son Kerem for their support and understanding during my long working hours.*

**Amir Shirian** is a data scientist at Nokia, where he applies his expertise in multimodal signal processing and ML to solve complex problems. He received his Ph.D. in computer science from the University of Warwick, England, after completing his bachelor of science and master of science degrees in electrical engineering at the University of Tehran, Iran. Amir's research focuses on developing algorithms and models for emotion and behavior understanding, with a particular interest in using graph neural networks to analyze and interpret data from multiple sources. His work has been published in several high-profile academic journals and presented at international conferences. Amir enjoys hiking, playing 3tar, and exploring new technologies in his free time.

**Lorenzo Giusti** is a Ph.D. student in data science at La Sapienza, University of Rome, with a focus on extending graph neural networks through topological deep learning. He has extensive research experience as a visiting Ph.D. student at Cambridge, as a research scientist intern at NASA, where he supervised a team and led a project on synthesizing the Martian environment using images from spacecraft cameras, and as a research scientist intern at CERN, working on anomaly detection for particle physics accelerators. Lorenzo also has a master of science in data science from La Sapienza and a bachelor of engineering in computer engineering from Roma Tre University, where he focused on quantum technologies.

# Table of Contents

# Part 3: Advanced Techniques

# 9

## Defining Expressiveness for Graph Classification 145

# 10

## Predicting Links with Graph Neural Networks 163

# 11

## Generating Graphs Using Graph Neural Networks 183

# 12

## Learning from Heterogeneous Graphs                                          199

# 13

## Temporal Graph Neural Networks                                             219

# 14

## Explaining Graph Neural Networks                                           241

# Part 4: Applications

## 15

## 16

## 17

# 18

# Preface

In just ten years, **Graph Neural Networks** (**GNNs**) have become an essential and popular deep learning architecture. They have already had a significant impact various industries, such as in drug discovery, where GNNs predicted a new antibiotic, named halicin, and have improved estimated time of arrival calculations on Google Maps. Tech companies and universities are exploring the potential of GNNs in various applications, including recommender systems, fake news detection, and chip design. GNNs have enormous potential and many yet-to-be-discovered applications, making them a critical tool for solving global problems.

In this book, we aim to provide a comprehensive and practical overview of the world of GNNs. We will begin by exploring the fundamental concepts of graph theory and graph learning and then delve into the most widely used and well-established GNN architectures. As we progress, we will also cover the latest advances in GNNs and introduce specialized architectures that are designed to tackle specific tasks, such as graph generation, link prediction, and more.

In addition to these specialized chapters, we will provide hands-on experience through three practical projects. These projects will cover critical real-world applications of GNNs, including traffic forecasting, anomaly detection, and recommender systems. Through these projects, you will gain a deeper understanding of how GNNs work and also develop the skills to implement them in practical scenarios.

Finally, this book provides a hands-on learning experience with readable code for every chapter's techniques and relevant applications, which are readily accessible on GitHub and Google Colab.

By the end of this book, you will have a comprehensive understanding of the field of graph learning and GNNs and will be well-equipped to design and implement these models for a wide range of applications.

## Who this book is for

This book is intended for individuals interested in learning about GNNs and how they can be applied to various real-world problems. This book is ideal for **data scientists**, **machine learning engineers**, and **artificial intelligence** (**AI**) professionals who want to gain practical experience in designing and implementing GNNs. This book is written for individuals with prior knowledge of deep learning and machine learning. However, it provides a comprehensive introduction to the fundamental concepts of graph theory and graph learning for those new to the field. It will also be useful for researchers and students in computer science, mathematics, and engineering who want to expand their knowledge in this rapidly growing area of research.

# What this book covers

*Chapter 1, Getting Started with Graph Learning,* provides a comprehensive introduction to GNNs, including their importance in modern data analysis and machine learning. The chapter starts by exploring the relevance of graphs as a representation of data and their widespread use in various domains. It then delves into the importance of graph learning, including different applications and techniques. Finally, the chapter focuses on the GNN architecture and highlights its unique features and performance compared to other methods.

*Chapter 2, Graph Theory for Graph Neural Networks,* covers the basics of graph theory and introduces various types of graphs, including their properties and applications. This chapter also covers fundamental graph concepts, such as the adjacency matrix, graph measures, such as centrality, and graph algorithms, **Breadth-First Search (BFS)** and **Depth-First Search (DFS)**.

*Chapter 3, Creating Node Representations with DeepWalk,* focuses on DeepWalk, a pioneer in applying machine learning to graph data. The main objective of the DeepWalk architecture is to generate node representations that other models can utilize for downstream tasks such as node classification. The chapter covers two key components of DeepWalk – Word2Vec and random walks – with a particular emphasis on the Word2Vec skip-gram model.

*Chapter 4, Improving Embeddings with Biased Random Walks in Node2Vec,* focuses on the Node2Vec architecture, which is based on the DeepWalk architecture covered in the previous chapter. The chapter covers the modifications made to the random walk generation in Node2Vec and how to select the best parameters for a specific graph. The implementation of Node2Vec is compared to DeepWalk on Zachary's Karate Club to highlight the differences between the two architectures. The chapter concludes with a practical application of Node2Vec, building a movie recommendation system.

*Chapter 5, Including Node Features with Vanilla Neural Networks,* explores the integration of additional information, such as node and edge features, into the graph embeddings to produce more accurate results. The chapter starts with a comparison of vanilla neural networks' performance on node features only, treated as tabular datasets. Then, we will experiment with adding topological information to the neural networks, leading to the creation of a simple vanilla GNN architecture.

*Chapter 6, Introducing Graph Convolutional Networks,* focuses on the **Graph Convolutional Network (GCN)** architecture and its importance as a blueprint for GNNs. It covers the limitations of previous vanilla GNN layers and explains the motivation behind GCNs. The chapter details how the GCN layer works, its performance improvements over the vanilla GNN layer, and its implementation on the Cora and Facebook Page-Page datasets using PyTorch Geometric. The chapter also touches upon the task of node regression and the benefits of transforming tabular data into a graph.

*Chapter 7, Graph Attention Networks,* focuses on **Graph Attention Networks (GATs)**, which are an improvement over GCNs. The chapter explains how GATs work by using the concept of self-attention and provides a step-by-step understanding of the graph attention layer. The chapter also implements a graph attention layer from scratch using NumPy. The final section of the chapter discusses the use of a GAT on two node classification datasets, Cora and CiteSeer, and compares the accuracy with that of a GCN.

*Chapter 8, Scaling up Graph Neural Networks with GraphSAGE*, focuses on the GraphSAGE architecture and its ability to handle large graphs effectively. The chapter covers the two main ideas behind GraphSAGE, including its neighbor sampling technique and aggregation operators. You will learn about the variants proposed by tech companies such as Uber Eats and Pinterest, as well as the benefits of GraphSAGE's inductive approach. The chapter concludes by implementing GraphSAGE for node classification and multi-label classification tasks.

*Chapter 9, Defining Expressiveness for Graph Classification*, explores the concept of expressiveness in GNNs and how it can be used to design better models. It introduces the **Weisfeiler-Leman (WL)** test, which provides the framework for understanding expressiveness in GNNs. The chapter uses the WL test to compare different GNN layers and determine the most expressive one. Based on this result, a more powerful GNN is designed and implemented using PyTorch Geometric. The chapter concludes with a comparison of different methods for graph classification on the PROTEINS dataset.

*Chapter 10, Predicting Links with Graph Neural Networks*, focuses on link prediction in graphs. It covers traditional techniques, such as matrix factorization and GNN-based methods. The chapter explains the concept of link prediction and its importance in social networks and recommender systems. You will learn about the limitations of traditional techniques and the benefits of using GNN-based methods. We will explore three GNN-based techniques from two different families, including node embeddings and subgraph representation. Finally, you will implement various link prediction techniques in PyTorch Geometric and choose the best method for a given problem.

*Chapter 11, Generating Graphs Using Graph Neural Networks*, explores the field of graph generation, which involves finding methods to create new graphs. The chapter first introduces you to traditional techniques such as Erdős–Rényi and small-world models. Then you will focus on three families of solutions for GNN-based graph generation: VAE-based, autoregressive, and GAN-based models. The chapter concludes with an implementation of a GAN-based framework with **Reinforcement Learning (RL)** to generate new chemical compounds using the DeepChem library with TensorFlow.

*Chapter 12, Learning from Heterogeneous Graphs*, focuses on heterogeneous GNNs. Heterogeneous graphs contain different types of nodes and edges, in contrast to homogeneous graphs, which only involve one type of node and one type of edge. The chapter begins by reviewing the **Message Passing Neural Network (MPNN)** framework for homogeneous GNNs, then expands the framework to heterogeneous networks. Finally, we introduce a technique for creating a heterogeneous dataset, transforming homogeneous architectures into heterogeneous ones, and discussing an architecture specifically designed for processing heterogeneous networks.

*Chapter 13, Temporal Graph Neural Networks*, focuses on Temporal GNNs, or Spatio-Temporal GNNs, which are a type of GNN that can handle graphs with changing edges and features over time. The chapter first explains the concept of dynamic graphs and the applications of temporal GNNs, focusing on time series forecasting. The chapter then moves on to the application of temporal GNNs to web traffic forecasting to improve results using temporal information. Finally, the chapter describes another temporal GNN architecture specifically designed for dynamic graphs and applies it to the task of epidemic forecasting.

*Chapter 14, Explaining Graph Neural Networks,* covers various techniques to better understand the predictions and behavior of a GNN model. The chapter highlights two popular explanation methods: GNNExplainer and integrated gradients. Then, you will see the application of these techniques on a graph classification task using the MUTAG dataset and a node classification task using the Twitch social network.

*Chapter 15, Forecasting Traffic Using A3T-GCN,* focuses on the application of Temporal Graph Neural Networks in the field of traffic forecasting. It highlights the importance of accurate traffic forecasts in smart cities and the challenges of traffic forecasting due to complex spatial and temporal dependencies. The chapter covers the steps involved in processing a new dataset to create a temporal graph and the implementation of a new type of temporal GNN to predict future traffic speed. Finally, the results are compared to a baseline solution to verify the relevance of the architecture.

*Chapter 16, Detecting Anomalies Using Heterogeneous GNNs,* focuses on the application of GNNs in anomaly detection. GNNs, with their ability to capture complex relationships, make them well-suited for detecting anomalies and can handle large amounts of data efficiently. In this chapter, you will learn how to implement a GNN for intrusion detection in computer networks using the CIDDS-001 dataset. The chapter covers processing the dataset, building relevant features, implementing a heterogenous GNN, and evaluating the results to determine its effectiveness in detecting anomalies in network traffic.

*Chapter 17, Recommending Books Using LightGCN,* focuses on the application of GNNs in recommender systems. The goal of recommender systems is to provide personalized recommendations to users based on their interests and past interactions. GNNs are well-suited for this task as they can effectively incorporate complex relationships between users and items. In this chapter, the LightGCN architecture is introduced as a GNN specifically designed for recommender systems. Using the Book-Crossing dataset, the chapter demonstrates how to build a book recommender system with collaborative filtering using the LightGCN architecture.

*Chapter 18, Unlocking the Potential of Graph Neural Networks for Real-Word Applications,* summarizes what we have learned throughout the book, and looks ahead to the future of GNNs.

## To get the most out of this book

You should have a basic understanding of graph theory and machine learning concepts, such as supervised and unsupervised learning, training, and the evaluation of models to maximize your learning experience. Familiarity with deep learning frameworks, such as PyTorch, will also be useful, although not essential, as the book will provide a comprehensive introduction to the mathematical concepts and their implementation.

| Software covered in the book | Operating system requirements |
| --- | --- |
| Python 3.8.15 | Windows, macOS, or Linux |
| PyTorch 1.13.1 | Windows, macOS, or Linux |
| PyTorch Geometric 2.2.0 | Windows, macOS, or Linux |

To install Python 3.8.15, you can download the latest version from the official Python website: `https://www.python.org/downloads/`. We strongly recommend using a virtual environment, such as `venv` or `conda`.

Optionally, if you want to use a **Graphics Processing Unit** (**GPU**) from NVIDIA to accelerate training and inference, you will need to install **CUDA** and **cuDNN**:

CUDA is a parallel computing platform and API developed by NVIDIA for general computing on GPUs. To install CUDA, you can follow the instructions on the NVIDIA website: `https://developer.nvidia.com/cuda-downloads`.

cuDNN is a library developed by NVIDIA, which provides highly optimized GPU implementations of primitives for deep learning algorithms. To install cuDNN, you need to create an account on the NVIDIA website and download the library from the cuDNN download page: `https://developer.nvidia.com/cudnn`.

You can check out the list of CUDA-enabled GPU products on the NVIDIA website: `https://developer.nvidia.com/cuda-gpus`.

To install PyTorch 1.13.1, you can follow the instructions on the official PyTorch website: `https://pytorch.org/`. You can choose the installation method that is most appropriate for your system (including CUDA and cuDNN).

To install PyTorch Geometric 2.2.0, you can follow the instructions in the GitHub repository: `https://pytorch-geometric.readthedocs.io/en/2.2.0/notes/installation.html`. You will need to have PyTorch installed on your system first.

*Chapter 11* requires TensorFlow 2.4. To install it, you can follow the instructions on the official TensorFlow website: `https://www.tensorflow.org/install`. You can choose the installation method that is most appropriate for your system and the version of TensorFlow you want to use.

*Chapter 14* requires an older version of PyTorch Geometric (version 2.0.4). It is recommended to create a specific virtual environment for this chapter.

*Chapter 15*, *Chapter 16*, and *Chapter 17* require a high GPU memory usage. You can lower it by decreasing the size of the training set in the code.

Other Python libraries are required in some or most chapters. You can install them using `pip install <name==version>`, or using another installer depending on your configuration (such as `conda`). Here is the complete list of required packages with the corresponding versions:

- `pandas==1.5.2`
- `gensim==4.3.0`
- `networkx==2.8.8`
- `matplotlib==3.6.3`

- `node2vec==0.4.6`

- `seaborn==0.12.2`

- `scikit-learn==1.2.0`

- `deepchem==2.7.1`

- `torch-geometric-temporal==0.54.0`

- `captum==0.6.0`

The complete list of requirements is available on GitHub at `https://github.com/PacktPublishing/Hands-On-Graph-Neural-Networks-Using-Python`. Alternatively, you can directly import notebooks in Google Colab at `https://colab.research.google.com`.

**If you are using the digital version of this book, we advise you to type the code yourself or access the code from the book's GitHub repository (a link is available in the next section). Doing so will help you avoid any potential errors related to the copying and pasting of code.**

## Download the example code files

You can download the example code files for this book from GitHub at `https://github.com/PacktPublishing/Hands-On-Graph-Neural-Networks-Using-Python`. If there's an update to the code, it will be updated in the GitHub repository.

We also have other code bundles from our rich catalog of books and videos available at `https://github.com/PacktPublishing/`. Check them out!

## Download the color images

We also provide a PDF file that has color images of the screenshots and diagrams used in this book. You can download it here: `https://packt.link/gaFU6`.

## Conventions used

There are a number of text conventions used throughout this book.

`Code in text`: Indicates code words in text, database table names, folder names, filenames, file extensions, pathnames, dummy URLs, user input, and Twitter handles. Here is an example: "We initialize two lists (`visited` and `queue`) and add the starting node."

A block of code is set as follows:

```
DG = nx.DiGraph()

DG.add_edges_from([('A', 'B'), ('A', 'C'), ('B', 'D'), ('B',
'E'), ('C', 'F'), ('C', 'G')])
```

> **Tips or important notes**
> Appear like this.

# Get in touch

Feedback from our readers is always welcome.

**General feedback**: If you have questions about any aspect of this book, email us at customercare@packtpub.com and mention the book title in the subject of your message.

**Errata**: Although we have taken every care to ensure the accuracy of our content, mistakes do happen. If you have found a mistake in this book, we would be grateful if you would report this to us. Please visit www.packtpub.com/support/errata and fill in the form.

**Piracy**: If you come across any illegal copies of our works in any form on the internet, we would be grateful if you would provide us with the location address or website name. Please contact us at copyright@packt.com with a link to the material.

**If you are interested in becoming an author**: If there is a topic that you have expertise in and you are interested in either writing or contributing to a book, please visit authors.packtpub.com.

## Share your thoughts

Once you've read *Hands-On Graph Neural Networks Using Python*, we'd love to hear your thoughts! Scan the QR code below to go straight to the Amazon review page for this book and share your feedback.

https://packt.link/r/1-804-61752-0

Your review is important to us and the tech community and will help us make sure we're delivering excellent quality content.

# Download a free PDF copy of this book

Thanks for purchasing this book!

Do you like to read on the go but are unable to carry your print books everywhere?

Is your eBook purchase not compatible with the device of your choice?

Don't worry, now with every Packt book you get a DRM-free PDF version of that book at no cost.

Read anywhere, any place, on any device. Search, copy, and paste code from your favorite technical books directly into your application.

The perks don't stop there, you can get exclusive access to discounts, newsletters, and great free content in your inbox daily

Follow these simple steps to get the benefits:

1. Scan the QR code or visit the link below

https://packt.link/free-ebook/9781804617526

2. Submit your proof of purchase
3. That's it! We'll send your free PDF and other benefits to your email directly

# Part 1: Introduction to Graph Learning

In recent years, graph representation of data has become increasingly prevalent across various domains, from social networks to molecular biology. It is crucial to have a deep understanding of **Graph Neural Networks** (**GNNs**), which are designed specifically to handle graph-structured data, to unlock the full potential of this representation.

This first part consists of two chapters and serves as a solid foundation for the rest of the book. It introduces the concepts of graph learning and GNNs and their relevance in numerous tasks and industries. It also covers the fundamental concepts of graph theory and its applications in graph learning, such as graph centrality measures. This part also highlights the unique features and performance of the GNN architecture compared to other methods.

By the end of this part, you will have a solid understanding of the importance of GNNs in solving many real-world problems. You will be acquainted with the essentials of graph learning and how it is used in various domains. Furthermore, you will have a comprehensive overview of the main concepts of graph theory that we will use in later chapters. With this solid foundation, you will be well equipped to move on to the more advanced concepts in graph learning and GNNs in the following parts of the book.

This part comprises the following chapters:

- *Chapter 1, Getting Started with Graph Learning*
- *Chapter 2, Graph Theory for Graph Neural Networks*

# 1

# Getting Started with Graph Learning

Welcome to the first chapter of our journey into the world of **graph neural networks** (**GNNs**). In this chapter, we will delve into the foundations of GNNs and understand why they are crucial tools in modern data analysis and machine learning. To that end, we will answer three essential questions that will provide us with a comprehensive understanding of GNNs.

First, we will explore the significance of graphs as a representation of data, and why they are widely used in various domains such as computer science, biology, and finance. Next, we will delve into the importance of graph learning, where we will understand the different applications of graph learning and the different families of graph learning techniques. Finally, we will focus on the GNN family, highlighting its unique features, performance, and how it stands out compared to other methods.

By the end of this chapter, you will have a clear understanding of why GNNs are important and how they can be used to solve real-world problems. You will also be equipped with the knowledge and skills you need to dive deeper into more advanced topics. So, let's get started!

In this chapter, we will cover the following main topics:

- Why graphs?
- Why graph learning?
- Why graph neural networks?

## Why graphs?

The first question we need to address is: why are we interested in graphs in the first place? **Graph theory**, the mathematical study of graphs, has emerged as a fundamental tool for understanding complex systems and relationships. A graph is a visual representation of a collection of **nodes** (also called **vertices**) and **edges** that connect these nodes, providing a structure to represent entities and their relationships (see *Figure 1.1*).

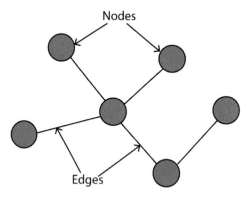

Figure 1.1 – Example of a graph with six nodes and five edges

By representing a complex system as a network of entities with interactions, we can analyze their relationships, allowing us to gain a deeper understanding of their underlying structures and patterns. The versatility of graphs makes them a popular choice in various domains, including the following:

- Computer science, where graphs can be used to model the structure of computer programs, making it easier to understand how different components of a system interact with each other

- Physics, where graphs can be used to model physical systems and their interactions, such as the relationship between particles and their properties

- Biology, where graphs can be used to model biological systems, such as metabolic pathways, as a network of interconnected entities

- Social sciences, where graphs can be used to study and understand complex social networks, including the relationships between individuals in a community

- Finance, where graphs can be used to analyze stock market trends and relationships between different financial instruments

- Engineering, where graphs can be used to model and analyze complex systems, such as transportation networks and electrical power grids

These domains naturally exhibit a relational structure. For instance, graphs are a natural representation of social networks: nodes are users, and edges represent friendships. But graphs are so versatile they can also be applied to domains where the relational structure is less natural, unlocking new insights and understanding.

For example, images can be represented as a graph, as in *Figure 1.2*. Each pixel is a node, and edges represent relationships between neighboring pixels. This allows for the application of graph-based algorithms to image processing and computer vision tasks.

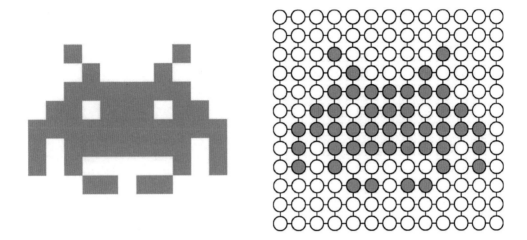

Figure 1.2 – Left: original image; right: graph representation of this image

Similarly, a sentence can be transformed into a graph, where nodes are words and edges represent relationships between adjacent words. This approach is useful in natural language processing and information retrieval tasks, where the context and meaning of words are critical factors.

Unlike text and images, graphs do not have a fixed structure. However, this flexibility also makes graphs more challenging to handle. The absence of a fixed structure means they can have an arbitrary number of nodes and edges, with no specific ordering. In addition, graphs can represent dynamic data, where the connections between entities can change over time. For example, the relationships between users and products can change as they interact with each other. In this scenario, nodes and edges are updated to reflect changes in the real world, such as new users, new products, and new relationships.

In the next section, we will delve deeper into how to use graphs with machine learning to create valuable applications.

# Why graph learning?

Graph learning is the application of machine learning techniques to graph data. This study area encompasses a range of tasks aimed at understanding and manipulating graph-structured data. There are many graphs learning tasks, including the following:

- **Node classification** is a task that involves predicting the category (class) of a node in a graph. For example, it can categorize online users or items based on their characteristics. In this task, the model is trained on a set of labeled nodes and their attributes, and it uses this information to predict the class of unlabeled nodes.

- **Link prediction** is a task that involves predicting missing links between pairs of nodes in a graph. This is useful in knowledge graph completion, where the goal is to complete a graph of entities and their relationships. For example, it can be used to predict the relationships between people based on their social network connections (friend recommendation).

- **Graph classification** is a task that involves categorizing different graphs into predefined categories. One example of this is in molecular biology, where molecular structures can be represented as graphs, and the goal is to predict their properties for drug design. In this task, the model is trained on a set of labeled graphs and their attributes, and it uses this information to categorize unseen graphs.

- **Graph generation** is a task that involves generating new graphs based on a set of desired properties. One of the main applications is generating novel molecular structures for drug discovery. This is achieved by training a model on a set of existing molecular structures and then using it to generate new, unseen structures. The generated structures can be evaluated for their potential as drug candidates and further studied.

Graph learning has many other practical applications that can have a significant impact. One of the most well-known applications is **recommender systems**, where graph learning algorithms recommend relevant items to users based on their previous interactions and relationships with other items. Another important application is **traffic forecasting**, where graph learning can improve travel time predictions by considering the complex relationships between different routes and modes of transportation.

The versatility and potential of graph learning make it an exciting field of research and development. The study of graphs has advanced rapidly in recent years, driven by the availability of large datasets, powerful computing resources, and advancements in machine learning and artificial intelligence. As a result, we can list four prominent families of graph learning techniques [1]:

- **Graph signal processing**, which applies traditional signal processing methods to graphs, such as the graph Fourier transform and spectral analysis. These techniques reveal the intrinsic properties of the graph, such as its connectivity and structure.

- **Matrix factorization**, which seeks to find low-dimensional representations of large matrices. The goal of matrix factorization is to identify latent factors or patterns that explain the observed relationships in the original matrix. This approach can provide a compact and interpretable representation of the data.

- **Random walk**, which refers to a mathematical concept used to model the movement of entities in a graph. By simulating random walks over a graph, information about the relationships between nodes can be gathered. This is why they are often used to generate training data for machine learning models.

- **Deep learning**, which is a subfield of machine learning that focuses on neural networks with multiple layers. Deep learning methods can effectively encode and represent graph data as vectors. These vectors can then be used in various tasks with remarkable performance.

It is important to note that these techniques are not mutually exclusive and often overlap in their applications. In practice, they are often combined to form hybrid models that leverage the strengths of each. For example, matrix factorization and deep learning techniques might be used in combination to learn low-dimensional representations of graph-structured data.

As we delve into the world of graph learning, it is crucial to understand the fundamental building block of any machine learning technique: the dataset. Traditional tabular datasets, such as spreadsheets, represent data as rows and columns with each row representing a single data point. However, in many real-world scenarios, the relationships between data points are just as meaningful as the data points themselves. This is where graph datasets come in. Graph datasets represent data points as nodes in a graph and the relationships between those data points as edges.

Let's take the tabular dataset shown in *Figure 1.3* as an example.

**Tabular dataset**

| ID | Name | Age | Gender |
|----|------|-----|--------|
| 1 | Mary | 76 | Female |
| 2 | John | 75 | Male |
| 3 | Kate | 46 | Female |
| 4 | Robert | 47 | Male |
| 5 | Loise | 18 | Female |

**Graph dataset**

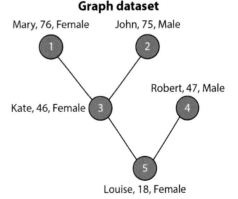

Figure 1.3 – Family tree as a tabular dataset versus a graph dataset

This dataset represents information about five members of a family. Each member has three features (or attributes): name, age, and gender. However, the tabular version of this dataset doesn't show the connections between these people. On the contrary, the graph version represents them with edges, which allows us to understand the relationships in this family. In many contexts, the connections between nodes are crucial in understanding the data, which is why representing data in graph form is becoming increasingly popular.

Now that we have a basic understanding of graph machine learning and the different types of tasks it involves, we can move on to exploring one of the most important approaches for solving these tasks: **graph neural networks**.

## Why graph neural networks?

In this book, we will focus on the deep learning family of graph learning techniques, often referred to as graph neural networks. GNNs are a new category of deep learning architecture and are specifically designed for graph-structured data. Unlike traditional deep learning algorithms, which have been primarily developed for text and images, GNNs are explicitly made to process and analyze graph datasets (see *Figure 1.4*).

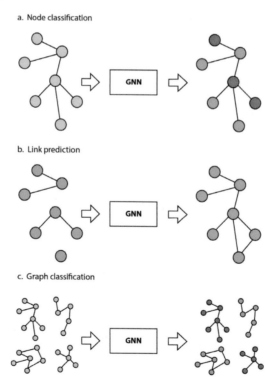

Figure 1.4 – High-level architecture of a GNN pipeline, with a graph as
input and an output that corresponds to a given task

GNNs have emerged as a powerful tool for graph learning and have shown excellent results in various tasks and industries. One of the most striking examples is how a GNN model identified a new antibiotic [2]. The model was trained on 2,500 molecules and was tested on a library of 6,000 compounds. It predicted that a molecule called halicin should be able to kill many antibiotic-resistant bacteria while having low toxicity to human cells. Based on this prediction, the researchers used halicin to treat mice infected with antibiotic-resistant bacteria. They demonstrated its effectiveness and believe the model could be used to design new drugs.

How do GNNs work? Let's take the example of a node classification task in a social network, like the previous family tree (*Figure 1.3*). In a node classification task, GNNs take advantage of information from different sources to create a vector representation of each node in the graph. This representation encompasses not only the original node features (such as name, age, and gender) but also information from edge features (such as the strength of relationships between nodes) and global features (such as network-wide statistics).

This is why GNNs are more efficient than traditional machine learning techniques on graphs. Instead of being limited to the original attributes, GNNs enrich the original node features with attributes from neighboring nodes, edges, and global features, making the representation much more comprehensive and meaningful. The new node representations are then used to perform a specific task, such as node classification, regression, or link prediction.

Specifically, GNNs define a graph convolution operation that aggregates information from the neighboring nodes and edges to update the node representation. This operation is performed iteratively, allowing the model to learn more complex relationships between nodes as the number of iterations increases. For example, *Figure 1.5* shows how a GNN would calculate the representation of node 5 using neighboring nodes.

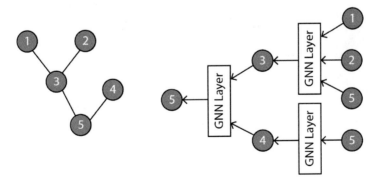

Figure 1.5 – Left: input graph; right: computation graph representing how a GNN computes the representation of node 5 based on its neighbors

It is worth noting that *Figure 1.5* provides a simplified illustration of a computation graph. In reality, there are various kinds of GNNs and GNN layers, each of which has a unique structure and way of aggregating information from neighboring nodes. These different variants of GNNs also have their own advantages and limitations and are well-suited for specific types of graph data and tasks. When selecting the appropriate GNN architecture for a particular problem, it is crucial to understand the characteristics of the graph data and the desired outcome.

More generally, GNNs, like other deep learning techniques, are most effective when applied to specific problems. These problems are characterized by high complexity, meaning that learning good representations is critical to solving the task at hand. For example, a highly complex task could be recommending the right products among billions of options to millions of customers. On the other hand, some problems, such as finding the youngest member of our family tree, can be solved without any machine learning technique.

Furthermore, GNNs require a substantial amount of data to perform effectively. Traditional machine learning techniques might be a better fit in cases where the dataset is small, as they are less reliant on large amounts of data. However, these techniques do not scale as well as GNNs. GNNs can process bigger datasets thanks to parallel and distributed training. They can also exploit the additional information more efficiently, which produces better results.

## Summary

In this chapter, we answered three main questions: why graphs, why graph learning, and why graph neural networks? First, we explored the versatility of graphs in representing various data types, such as social networks and transportation networks, but also text and images. We discussed the different applications of graph learning, including node classification and graph classification, and highlighted the four main families of graph learning techniques. Finally, we emphasized the significance of GNNs and their superiority over other techniques, especially regarding large, complex datasets. By answering these three main questions, we aimed to provide a comprehensive overview of the importance of GNNs and why they are becoming vital tools in machine learning.

In *Chapter 2*, *Graph Theory for Graph Neural Networks*, we will dive deeper into the basics of graph theory, which provides the foundation for understanding GNNs. This chapter will cover the fundamental concepts of graph theory, including concepts such as adjacency matrices and degrees. Additionally, we will delve into the different types of graphs and their applications, such as directed and undirected graphs, and weighted and unweighted graphs.

## Further reading

- [1] F. Xia et al., *Graph Learning: A Survey*, IEEE Transactions on Artificial Intelligence, vol. 2, no. 2, pp. 109–127, Apr. 2021, DOI: 10.1109/tai.2021.3076021. Available at https://arxiv.org/abs/2105.00696

- [2] A. Trafton, *Artificial intelligence yields new antibiotic*, MIT News, 20-Feb-2020. [Online]. Available at https://news.mit.edu/2020/artificial-intelligence-identifies-new-antibiotic-0220

# 2

# Graph Theory
# for Graph Neural Networks

**Graph theory** is a fundamental branch of mathematics that deals with the study of graphs and networks. A graph is a visual representation of complex data structures that helps us understand the relationships between different entities. Graph theory provides us with tools to model and analyze a vast array of real-world problems, such as transportation systems, social networks, and internet connectivity.

In this chapter, we will delve into the essentials of graph theory, covering three main topics: graph properties, graph concepts, and graph algorithms. We will begin by defining graphs and their components. We will then introduce the different types of graphs and explain their properties and applications. Next, we will cover fundamental graph concepts, objects, and measures, including the adjacency matrix. Finally, we will dive into graph algorithms, focusing on the two fundamental algorithms, **breadth-first search** (**BFS**) and **depth-first search** (**DFS**).

By the end of this chapter, you will have a solid foundation in graph theory, allowing you to tackle more advanced topics and design graph neural networks.

In this chapter, we will cover the following main topics:

- Introducing graph properties
- Discovering graph concepts
- Exploring graph algorithms

## Technical requirements

All the code examples from this chapter can be found on GitHub at `https://github.com/PacktPublishing/Hands-On-Graph-Neural-Networks-Using-Python/tree/main/Chapter02`.

The installation steps required to run the code on your local machine can be found in the *Preface* of this book.

## Introducing graph properties

In graph theory, a graph is a mathematical structure consisting of a set of objects, called **vertices** or **nodes**, and a set of connections, called **edges**, which link pairs of vertices. The notation $G = (V, E)$ is used to represent a graph, where $G$ is the graph, $V$ is the set of vertices, and $V$ is the set of edges.

The nodes of a graph can represent any objects, such as cities, people, web pages, or molecules, and the edges represent the relationships or connections between them, such as physical roads, social relationships, hyperlinks, or chemical bonds.

This section provides an overview of fundamental graph properties that will be used extensively in later chapters.

### Directed graphs

One of the most basic properties of a graph is whether it is directed or undirected. In a **directed graph**, also called a **digraph**, each edge has a direction or orientation. This means that the edge connects two nodes in a particular direction, where one node is the source and the other is the destination. In contrast, an undirected graph has undirected edges, where the edges have no direction. This means that the edge between two vertices can be traversed in either direction, and the order in which we visit the nodes does not matter.

In Python, we can use the `networkx` library to define an undirected graph as follows with `nx.Graph()`:

```
import networkx as nx
G = nx.Graph()
G.add_edges_from([('A', 'B'), ('A', 'C'), ('B', 'D'),
('B', 'E'), ('C', 'F'), ('C', 'G')])
```

The G graph corresponds to the following figure:

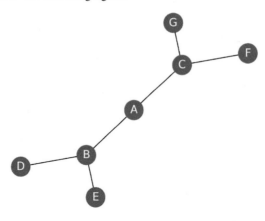

Figure 2.1 – Example of an undirected graph

The code to create a directed graph is similar; we simply replace nx.Graph() with nx.DiGraph():

```
DG = nx.DiGraph()
DG.add_edges_from([('A', 'B'), ('A', 'C'), ('B', 'D'),
('B', 'E'), ('C', 'F'), ('C', 'G')])
```

The DG graph corresponds to the following figure:

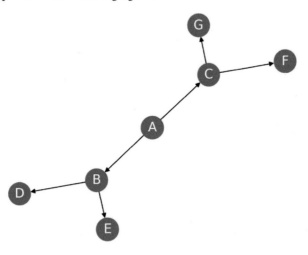

Figure 2.2 – Example of a directed graph

In directed graphs, edges are typically represented using arrows to denote their orientation, as in *Figure 2.2*.

## Weighted graphs

Another important property of graphs is whether the edges are weighted or unweighted. In a **weighted graph**, each edge has a weight or cost associated with it. These weights can represent various factors, such as distance, travel time, or cost.

For example, in a transportation network, the weights of edges might represent the distances between different cities or the time it takes to travel between them. In contrast, unweighted graphs have no weight associated with their edges. These types of graphs are commonly used in situations where the relationships between nodes are binary, and the edges simply indicate the presence or absence of a connection between them.

We can modify the previous undirected graph to add weights to our edges. In networkx, the edges of the graph are defined with a tuple containing the start and end nodes and a dictionary specifying the edge's weight:

```
WG = nx.Graph()
WG.add_edges_from([('A', 'B', {"weight": 10}), ('A', 'C',
{"weight": 20}), ('B', 'D', {"weight": 30}), ('B', 'E',
{"weight": 40}), ('C', 'F', {"weight": 50}), ('C', 'G',
{"weight": 60})])
labels = nx.get_edge_attributes(WG, "weight")
```

The WG graph corresponds to the following figure:

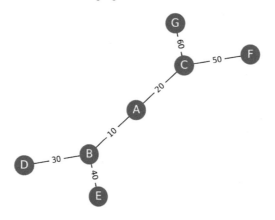

Figure 2.3 – Example of a weighted graph

## Connected graphs

Graph connectivity is a fundamental concept in graph theory that is closely related to the graph's structure and function.

In a **connected graph**, there is a path between any two vertices in the graph. Formally, a $G$ graph is connected if, and only if, for every pair of $u$ and $v$ vertices in $G$, there exists a path from $u$ to $v$. In contrast, a graph is disconnected if it is not connected, which means that at least two vertices are not connected by a path.

The networkx library provides a built-in function for verifying whether a graph is connected or not. In the following example, the first graph contains isolated nodes (4 and 5), unlike the second graph. This is visualized in *Figure 2.4*:

```
G1 = nx.Graph()
G1.add_edges_from([(1, 2), (2, 3), (3, 1), (4, 5)])
print(f"Is graph 1 connected? {nx.is_connected(G1)}")


G2 = nx.Graph()
G2.add_edges_from([(1, 2), (2, 3), (3, 1), (1, 4)])
print(f"Is graph 2 connected? {nx.is_connected(G2)}")
```

This code prints the following output:

```
Is graph 1 connected? False
Is graph 2 connected? True
```

The first graph is disconnected because of nodes 4 and 5. On the other hand, the second graph is connected. This property is easy to visualize with small graphs, as in the following figure:

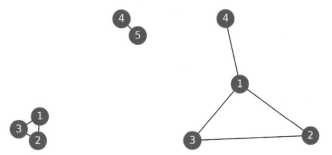

Figure 2.4 – Left: graph 1 with isolated nodes (disconnected graph); right: graph 2
where each node is connected to at least another one (connected graph)

Connected graphs have several interesting properties and applications. For example, in a communication network, a connected graph ensures that any two nodes can communicate with each other through a path. In contrast, disconnected graphs can have isolated nodes that cannot communicate with other nodes in the network, making it challenging to design efficient routing algorithms.

There are different ways to measure the connectivity of a graph. One of the most common measures is the minimum number of edges that need to be removed to disconnect the graph, which is known as the graph's minimum cut. The minimum cut problem has several applications in network flow optimization, clustering, and community detection.

## Types of graphs

In addition to the commonly used graph types, there are some special types of graphs that have unique properties and characteristics:

- A **tree** is a connected, undirected graph with no cycles (like the graph in *Figure 2.1*). Since there is only one path between any two nodes in a tree, a tree is a special case of a graph. Trees are often used to model hierarchical structures, such as family trees, organizational structures, or classification trees.

- A **rooted tree** is a tree in which one node is designated as the root, and all other vertices are connected to it by a unique path. Rooted trees are often used in computer science to represent hierarchical data structures, such as filesystems or the structure of XML documents.

- A **directed acyclic graph** (**DAG**) is a directed graph that has no cycles (like the graph in *Figure 2.2*). This means that the edges can only be traversed in a particular direction, and there are no loops or cycles. DAGs are often used to model dependencies between tasks or events – for example, in project management or in computing the critical path of a job.

- A **bipartite graph** is a graph in which the vertices can be divided into two disjoint sets, such that all edges connect vertices in different sets. Bipartite graphs are often used in mathematics and computer science to model relationships between two different types of objects, such as buyers and sellers, or employees and projects.

- A **complete graph** is a graph in which every pair of vertices is connected by an edge. Complete graphs are often used in combinatorics to model problems involving all possible pairwise connections, and in computer networks to model fully connected networks.

*Figure 2.5* illustrates these different types of graphs:

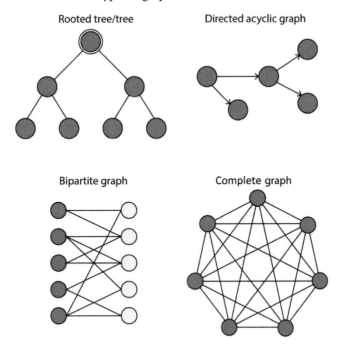

Figure 2.5 – Common types of graphs

Now that we have reviewed essential types of graphs, let's move on to exploring some of the most important graph objects. Understanding these concepts will help us analyze and manipulate graphs effectively.

# Discovering graph concepts

In this section, we will explore some of the essential concepts in graph theory, including graph objects (such as degree and neighbors), graph measures (such as centrality and density), and the adjacency matrix representation.

## Fundamental objects

One of the key concepts in graph theory is the **degree** of a node, which is the number of edges **incident** to this node. An edge is said to be incident on a node if that node is one of the edge's endpoints. The degree of a node $v$ is often denoted by $\deg(v)$. It can be defined for both directed and undirected graphs:

- In an undirected graph, the degree of a vertex is the number of edges that are connected to it. Note that if the node is connected to itself (called a **loop**, or **self-loop**), it adds two to the degree.

- In a directed graph, the degree is divided into two types: **indegree** and **outdegree**. The indegree (denoted by $deg^-(v)$) of a node represents the number of edges that point towards that node, while the outdegree (denoted by $deg^+(v)$) represents the number of edges that start from that node. In this case, a self-loop adds one to the indegree and to the outdegree.

Indegree and outdegree are essential for analyzing and understanding directed graphs, as they provide insight into how information or resources are distributed within the graph. For example, nodes with high indegree are likely to be important sources of information or resources. In contrast, nodes with high outdegree are likely to be important destinations or consumers of information or resources.

In `networkx`, we can simply calculate the node degree, indegree, or outdegree using built-in methods. Let's do it for the undirected graph from *Figure 2.1* and the directed graph from *Figure 2.2*:

```
G = nx.Graph()
G.add_edges_from([('A', 'B'), ('A', 'C'), ('B', 'D'), ('B',
'E'), ('C', 'F'), ('C', 'G')])
print(f"deg(A) = {G.degree['A']}")


DG = nx.DiGraph()
DG.add_edges_from([('A', 'B'), ('A', 'C'), ('B', 'D'), ('B',
'E'), ('C', 'F'), ('C', 'G')])
print(f"deg^-(A) = {DG.in_degree['A']}")
print(f"deg^+(A) = {DG.out_degree['A']}")
```

This code prints the following output:

```
deg(A) = 2
deg^-(A) = 0
deg^+(A) = 2
```

We can compare it to the graphs from *Figures 2.1* and *2.2*: node *A* is connected to two edges $(deg(A) = deg^+(A) = 2)$, but is not the destination of any of them $(deg^-(A) = 0)$.

The concept of node degree is related to that of **neighbors**. Neighbors refer to the nodes directly connected to a particular node through an edge. Moreover, two nodes are said to be **adjacent** if they share at least one common neighbor. The concepts of neighbors and adjacency are fundamental to many graph algorithms and applications, such as searching for a **path** between two nodes or identifying clusters in a network.

In graph theory, a path is a sequence of edges that connect two nodes (or more) in a graph. The length of a path is the number of edges that are traversed along the path. There are different types of paths, but two of them are particularly important:

- A **simple path** is a path that does not visit any node more than once, except for the start and end vertices

- A **cycle** is a path in which the first and last vertices are the same. A graph is said to be acyclic if it contains no cycles (such as trees and DAGs)

Degrees and paths can be used to determine the importance of a node in a network. This measure is referred to as **centrality**.

## Graph measures

Centrality quantifies the importance of a vertex or node in a network. It helps us to identify key nodes in a graph based on their connectivity and influence on the flow of information or interactions within the network. There are several measures of centrality, each providing a different perspective on the importance of a node:

- **Degree centrality** is one of the simplest and most commonly used measures of centrality. It is simply defined as the degree of the node. A high degree centrality indicates that a vertex is highly connected to other vertices in the graph, and thus significantly influences the network.

- **Closeness centrality** measures how close a node is to all other nodes in the graph. It corresponds to the average length of the shortest path between the target node and all other nodes in the graph. A node with high closeness centrality can quickly reach all other vertices in the network.

- **Betweenness centrality** measures the number of times a node lies on the shortest path between pairs of other nodes in the graph. A node with high betweenness centrality acts as a bottleneck or bridge between different parts of the graph.

Let's calculate these measures on our previous graphs using the built-in functions of networkx and analyze the result:

```
print(f"Degree centrality      = {nx.degree_centrality(G)}")
print(f"Closeness centrality   = {nx.closeness_centrality(G)}")
print(f"Betweenness centrality = {nx.betweenness_
centrality(G)}")
```

The previous code prints the dictionaries, containing a score for each node:

```
Degree centrality      = {'A': 0.333, 'B': 0.5, 'C': 0.5, 'D':
0.167, 'E': 0.167, 'F': 0.167, 'G': 0.167}
```

```
Closeness centrality   = {'A': 0.6, 'B': 0.545, 'C': 0.545,
'D': 0.375, 'E': 0.375, 'F': 0.375, 'G': 0.375}
Betweenness centrality = {'A': 0.6, 'B': 0.6, 'C': 0.6, 'D':
0.0, 'E': 0.0, 'F': 0.0, 'G': 0.0}
```

The importance of nodes $A$, $B$, and $C$ in a graph depends on the type of centrality used. Degree centrality considers nodes $B$ and $C$ to be more important because they have more neighbors than node $A$. However, in closeness centrality, node $A$ is the most important as it can reach any other node in the graph in the shortest possible path. On the other hand, nodes $A$, $B$, and $C$ have equal betweenness centrality, as they all lie on a large number of shortest paths between other nodes.

In addition to these measures, we will see how to calculate the importance of a node using machine learning techniques in the next chapters. However, it is not the only measure we will cover.

Indeed, **density** is another important measure, indicating how connected a graph is. It is a ratio between the actual number of edges and the maximum possible number of edges in the graph. A graph with high density is considered more connected and has more information flow compared to a graph with low density.

The formula to calculate density depends on whether the graph is directed or undirected. For an undirected graph with $n$ nodes, the maximum possible number of edges is $\frac{n(n-1)}{2}$. For a directed graph with $n$ nodes, the maximum number of edges is $n(n-1)$.

The density of a graph is calculated as the number of edges divided by the maximum number of edges. For example, the graph in *Figure 2.1* has 6 edges and the maximum possible number of $\frac{7(7-1)}{2} = 21$ edges. Therefore, it has a density of $\frac{6}{21} \approx 0.2857$.

A dense graph has a density closer to 1, while a sparse graph has a density closer to 0. There is no strict rule for what constitutes a dense or sparse graph, but generally, a graph is considered dense if its density is greater than 0.5 and sparse if its density is less than 0.1. This measure is directly connected to a fundamental problem with graphs: how to represent the **adjacency matrix**.

## Adjacency matrix representation

An adjacency matrix is a matrix that represents the edges in a graph, where each cell indicates whether there is an edge between two nodes. The matrix is a square matrix of size $n \times n$, where $n$ is the number of nodes in the graph. A value of 1 in the cell $(i, j)$ indicates that there is an edge between node $i$ and node $j$, while a value of 0 indicates that there is no edge. For an undirected graph, the matrix is symmetric, while for a directed graph, the matrix is not necessarily symmetric.

The following figure indicates the adjacency matrix associated with the graph:

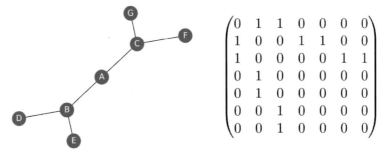

$$\begin{pmatrix} 0 & 1 & 1 & 0 & 0 & 0 & 0 \\ 1 & 0 & 0 & 1 & 1 & 0 & 0 \\ 1 & 0 & 0 & 0 & 0 & 1 & 1 \\ 0 & 1 & 0 & 0 & 0 & 0 & 0 \\ 0 & 1 & 0 & 0 & 0 & 0 & 0 \\ 0 & 0 & 1 & 0 & 0 & 0 & 0 \\ 0 & 0 & 1 & 0 & 0 & 0 & 0 \end{pmatrix}$$

Figure 2.6 – Example of the adjacency matrix

In Python, it can be implemented as a list of lists, as shown in this example:

```
adj = [[0,1,1,0,0,0,0],
       [1,0,0,1,1,0,0],
       [1,0,0,0,0,1,1],
       [0,1,0,0,0,0,0],
       [0,1,0,0,0,0,0],
       [0,0,1,0,0,0,0],
       [0,0,1,0,0,0,0]]
```

The adjacency matrix is a straightforward representation that can be easily visualized as a 2D array. One of the key advantages of using an adjacency matrix is that checking whether two nodes are connected is a constant time operation. This makes it an efficient way to test the existence of an edge in the graph. Moreover, it is used to perform matrix operations, which are useful for certain graph algorithms, such as calculating the shortest path between two nodes.

However, adding or removing nodes can be costly, as the matrix needs to be resized or shifted. One of the main drawbacks of using an adjacency matrix is its space complexity: as the number of nodes in the graph grows, the space required to store the adjacency matrix increases exponentially. Formally, we say that the adjacency matrix has a space complexity of $O(|V|^2)$, where $|V|$ represents the number of nodes in the graph.

Overall, while the adjacency matrix is a useful data structure for representing small graphs, it may not be practical for larger ones due to its space complexity. Additionally, the overhead of adding or removing nodes can make it inefficient for dynamically changing graphs.

This is why other representations can be helpful. For example, another popular way to store graphs is the **edge list**. An edge list is a list of all the edges in a graph. Each edge is represented by a tuple or a pair of vertices. The edge list can also include the weight or cost of each edge. This is the data structure we used to create our graphs with `networkx`:

```
edge_list = [(0, 1), (0, 2), (1, 3), (1, 4), (2, 5), (2, 6)]
```

When we compare both data structures applied to our graph, it is clear that the edge list is less verbose. This is the case because our graph is fairly sparse. On the other hand, if our graph was complete, we would require 21 tuples instead of 6. This is explained by a space complexity of $O(|E|)$, where $|E|$ is the number of edges. Edge lists are more efficient for storing sparse graphs, where the number of edges is much smaller than the number of nodes.

However, checking whether two vertices are connected in an edge list requires iterating through the entire list, which can be time-consuming for large graphs with many edges. Therefore, edge lists are more commonly used in applications where space is a concern.

A third and popular representation is the **adjacency list**. It consists of a list of pairs, where each pair represents a node in the graph and its adjacent nodes. The pairs can be stored in a linked list, dictionary, or other data structures, depending on the implementation. For example, an adjacency list for our graph might look like this:

```
adj_list = {
    0: [1, 2],
    1: [0, 3, 4],
    2: [0, 5, 6],
    3: [1],
    4: [1],
    5: [2],
    6: [2]
}
```

An adjacency list has several advantages over an adjacency matrix or an edge list. First, the space complexity is $O(|V| + |E|)$, where $|V|$ is the number of nodes and $E$ is the number of edges. This is more efficient than the $O(|V|^2)$ space complexity of an adjacency matrix for sparse graphs. Second, it allows for efficient iteration through the adjacent vertices of a node, which is useful in many graph algorithms. Finally, adding a node or an edge can be done in constant time.

However, checking whether two vertices are connected can be slower than with an adjacency matrix. This is because it requires iterating through the adjacency list of one of the vertices, which can be time-consuming for large graphs.

Each data structure has its own advantages and disadvantages that depend on the specific application and requirements. In the next section, we will process graphs and introduce the two most fundamental graph algorithms.

# Exploring graph algorithms

Graph algorithms are critical in solving problems related to graphs, such as finding the shortest path between two nodes or detecting cycles. This section will discuss two graph traversal algorithms: BFS and DFS.

## Breadth-first search

BFS is a graph traversal algorithm that starts at the root node and explores all the neighboring nodes at a particular level before moving to the next level of nodes. It works by maintaining a queue of nodes to visit and marking each visited node as it is added to the queue. The algorithm then dequeues the next node in the queue and explores all its neighbors, adding them to the queue if they haven't been visited yet.

The behavior of a BFS is illustrated in *Figure 2.7*:

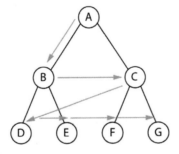

Figure 2.7 – Example of graph traversal made by a breadth-first search

Let's now see how we can implement it in Python:

1.  We create an empty graph and add edges with the add_edges_from() method:

    ```
    G = nx.Graph()
    G.add_edges_from([('A', 'B'), ('A', 'C'), ('B', 'D'),
    ('B', 'E'), ('C', 'F'), ('C', 'G')])
    ```

2.  We define a function called bfs() that implements the BFS algorithm on a graph. The function takes two arguments: the graph object and the starting node for the search:

    ```
    def bfs(graph, node):
    ```

3.  We initialize two lists (`visited` and `queue`) and add the starting node. The `visited` list keeps track of the nodes that have been visited during the search, while the `queue` list stores the nodes that need to be visited:

```
visited, queue = [node], [node]
```

4.  We enter a `while` loop that continues until the `queue` list is empty. Inside the loop, we remove the first node in the `queue` list using the `pop(0)` method and store the result in the node variable:

```
while queue:
    node = queue.pop(0)
```

5.  We iterate through the neighbors of the node using a `for` loop. For each neighbor that has not been visited yet, we add it to the `visited` list and to the end of the `queue` list using the `append()` method. When it's complete, we return the `visited` list:

```
for neighbor in graph[node]:
    if neighbor not in visited:
        visited.append(neighbor)
        queue.append(neighbor)
return visited
```

6.  We call the `bfs()` function with the G argument and the `'A'` starting node:

```
bfs(G, 'A')
```

7.  The function returns the list of visited nodes in the order in which they were visited:

```
['A', 'B', 'C', 'D', 'E', 'F', 'G']
```

The order we obtained is the one we anticipated in *Figure 2.7*.

BFS is particularly useful in finding the shortest path between two nodes in an unweighted graph. This is because the algorithm visits nodes in order of their distance from the starting node, so the first time the target node is visited, it must be along the shortest path from the starting node.

In addition to finding the shortest path, BFS can also be used to check whether a graph is connected or to find all connected components of a graph. It is also used in applications such as web crawlers, social network analysis, and shortest path routing in networks.

The time complexity of BFS is $O(|V| + |E|)$, where $|V|$ is the number of nodes and $|E|$ is the number of edges in the graph. This can be a significant issue for graphs with a high degree of connectivity or for graphs that are sparse. Several variants of BFS have been developed to mitigate this issue, such as **bidirectional BFS** and **A\*** search, which use heuristics to reduce the number of nodes that need to be explored.

## Depth-first search

DFS is a recursive algorithm that starts at the root node and explores as far as possible along each branch before backtracking.

It chooses a node and explores all of its unvisited neighbors, visiting the first neighbor that has not been explored and backtracking only when all the neighbors have been visited. By doing so, it explores the graph by following as deep a path from the starting node as possible before backtracking to explore other branches. This continues until all nodes have been explored.

The behavior of a DFS is illustrated in *Figure 2.8*:

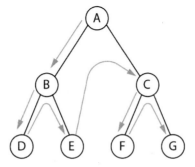

Figure 2.8 – Example of graph traversal made by a depth-first search

Let's implement DFS in Python:

1.  We first initialize an empty list called `visited`:

    ```
    visited = []
    ```

2.  We define a function called `dfs()` that takes in `visited`, `graph`, and `node` as arguments:

    ```
    def dfs(visited, graph, node):
    ```

3.  If the current `node` is not in the `visited` list, we append it to the list:

    ```
    if node not in visited:
        visited.append(node)
    ```

4.  We then iterate through each neighbor of the current node. For each neighbor, we recursively call the `dfs()` function passing in `visited`, `graph`, and the neighbor as arguments:

```
for neighbor in graph[node]:
    visited = dfs(visited, graph, neighbor)
```

5.  The `dfs()` function continues to explore the graph depth-first, visiting all the neighbors of each node until there are no more unvisited neighbors. Finally, the `visited` list is returned:

```
return visited
```

6.  We call the `dfs()` function with `visited` set to an empty list, G as the graph, and `'A'` as the starting node:

```
dfs(visited, G, 'A')
```

7.  The function returns the list of visited nodes in the order in which they were visited:

```
['A', 'B', 'D', 'E', 'C', 'F', 'G']
```

Once again, the order we obtained is the one we anticipated in *Figure 2.8*.

DFS is useful in solving various problems, such as finding connected components, topological sorting, and solving maze problems. It is particularly useful in finding cycles in a graph since it traverses the graph in a depth-first order, and a cycle exists if, and only if, a node is visited twice during the traversal.

Like BFS, it has a time complexity of $O(|V| + |E|)$, where $|V|$ is the number of nodes and $|E|$ is the number of edges in the graph. It requires less memory but doesn't guarantee the shallowest path solution. Finally, unlike BFS, you can be trapped in infinite loops using DFS.

Additionally, many other algorithms in graph theory build upon BFS and DFS, such as Dijkstra's shortest path algorithm, Kruskal's minimum spanning tree algorithm, and Tarjan's strongly connected components algorithm. Therefore, a solid understanding of BFS and DFS is essential for anyone who wants to work with graphs and develop more advanced graph algorithms.

## Summary

In this chapter, we covered the essentials of graph theory, a branch of mathematics that studies graphs and networks. We began by defining what a graph is and explained the different types of graphs, such as directed, weighted, and connected graphs. We then introduced fundamental graph objects (including neighbors) and measures (such as centrality and density), which are used to understand and analyze graph structures.

Additionally, we discussed the adjacency matrix and its different representations. Finally, we explored the two fundamental graph algorithms, BFS and DFS, which form the foundation for developing more complex graph algorithms.

In *Chapter 3, Creating Node Representations with DeepWalk*, we will explore the DeepWalk architecture and its two components: Word2Vec and random walks. We will start by understanding the Word2Vec architecture and then implement it using a specialized library. Then, we will delve into the DeepWalk algorithm and implement random walks on a graph.

# 3

# Creating Node Representations with DeepWalk

**DeepWalk** is one of the first major successful applications of **machine learning** (ML) techniques to graph data. It introduces important concepts such as embeddings that are at the core of GNNs. Unlike traditional neural networks, the goal of this architecture is to produce **representations** that are then fed to other models, which perform downstream tasks (for example, node classification).

In this chapter, we will learn about the DeepWalk architecture and its two major components: **Word2Vec** and **random walks**. We'll explain how the Word2Vec architecture works, with a particular focus on the skip-gram model. We will implement this model with the popular `gensim` library on a **natural language processing** (**NLP**) example to understand how it is supposed to be used.

Then, we will focus on the DeepWalk algorithm and see how performance can be improved using **hierarchical softmax** (**H-Softmax**). This powerful optimization of the softmax function can be found in many fields: it is incredibly useful when you have a lot of possible classes in your classification task. We will also implement random walks on a graph before wrapping things up with an end-to-end supervised classification exercise on Zachary's Karate Club.

By the end of this chapter, you will master Word2Vec in the context of NLP and beyond. You will be able to create node embeddings using the topological information of the graphs and solve classification tasks on graph data.

In this chapter, we will cover the following main topics:

- Introducing Word2Vec
- DeepWalk and random walks
- Implementing DeepWalk

## Technical requirements

All the code examples from this chapter can be found on GitHub at `https://github.com/PacktPublishing/Hands-On-Graph-Neural-Networks-Using-Python/tree/main/Chapter03`. Installation steps required to run the code on your local machine can be found in the *Preface* section of this book.

## Introducing Word2Vec

The first step to comprehending the DeepWalk algorithm is to understand its major component: Word2Vec.

Word2Vec has been one of the most influential deep-learning techniques in NLP. Published in 2013 by Tomas Mikolov et al. (Google) in two different papers, it proposed a new technique to translate words into vectors (also known as **embeddings**) using large datasets of text. These representations can then be used in downstream tasks, such as sentiment classification. It is also one of the rare examples of patented and popular ML architecture.

Here are a few examples of how Word2Vec can transform words into vectors:

$$vec(king) = [-2.1, 4.1, 0.6]$$

$$vec(queen) = [-1.9, 2.6, 1.5]$$

$$vec(man) = [3.0, -1.1, -2]$$

$$vec(woman) = [2.8, -2.6, -1.1]$$

We can see in this example that, in terms of the Euclidian distance, the word vectors for *king* and *queen* are closer than the ones for *king* and *woman* (4.37 versus 8.47). In general, other metrics, such as the popular **cosine similarity**, are used to measure the likeness of these words. Cosine similarity focuses on the angle between vectors and does not consider their magnitude (length), which is more helpful in comparing them. Here is how it is defined:

$$cosine\ similarity(\vec{A}, \vec{B}) = \cos(\theta) = \frac{\vec{A} \cdot \vec{B}}{\|\vec{A}\| \cdot \|\vec{B}\|}$$

One of the most surprising results of Word2Vec is its ability to solve analogies. A popular example is how it can answer the question *"man is to woman, what king is to ___?"* It can be calculated as follows:

$$vec(king) - vec(man) + vec(woman) \approx vec(queen)$$

This is not true with any analogy, but this property can bring interesting applications to perform arithmetic operations with embeddings.

## CBOW versus skip-gram

A model must be trained on a pretext task to produce these vectors. The task itself does not need to be meaningful: its only goal is to produce high-quality embeddings. In practice, this task is always related to predicting words given a certain context.

The authors proposed two architectures with similar tasks:

- **The continuous bag-of-words (CBOW) model**: This is trained to predict a word using its surrounding context (words coming before and after the target word). The order of context words does not matter since their embeddings are summed in the model. The authors claim to obtain better results using four words before and after the one that is predicted.

- **The continuous skip-gram model**: Here, we feed a single word to the model and try to predict the words around it. Increasing the range of context words leads to better embeddings but also increases the training time.

In summary, here are the inputs and outputs of both models:

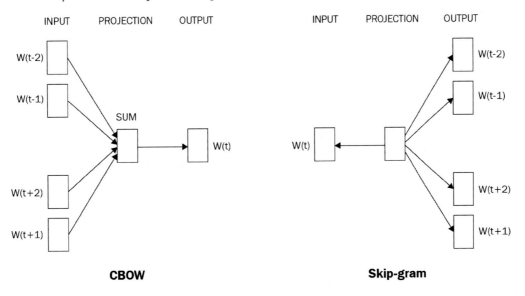

Figure 3.1 – CBOW and skip-gram architectures

In general, the CBOW model is considered faster to train, but the skip-gram model is more accurate thanks to its ability to learn infrequent words. This topic is still debated in the NLP community: a different implementation could fix issues related to CBOW in some contexts.

## Creating skip-grams

For now, we will focus on the skip-gram model since it is the architecture used by DeepWalk. Skip-grams are implemented as pairs of words with the following structure: (*target word*, *context word*), where *target word* is the input and *context word* is the word to predict. The number of skip grams for the same target word depends on a parameter called **context size**, as shown in *Figure 3.2*:

| Context Size | Text | Skip-grams |
|---|---|---|
| 1 | the **train** was late. | ('the', 'train') |
| | **the** train **was** late | ('train', 'the') <br> ('train', 'was') |
| | the **train** was **late** | ('was', 'train') <br> ('was', 'late') |
| | the train **was** **late** | ('late', 'was') |
| 2 | the **train** was late | ('the', 'train') <br> ('the', 'was') |
| | **the** train **was** **late** | ('train', 'the') <br> ('train', 'was') <br> ('train', 'late') |
| | **the** **train** was **late** | ('was', 'the') <br> ('was', 'train') <br> ('was', 'late') |
| | the **train** **was** late | ('late', 'train') <br> ('late', 'was') |

Figure 3.2 – Text to skip-grams

The same idea can be applied to a corpus of text instead of a single sentence.

In practice, we store all the context words for the same target word in a list to save memory. Let's see how it's done with an example on an entire paragraph.

In the following example, we create skip-grams for an entire paragraph stored in the text variable. We set the CONTEXT_SIZE variable to 2, which means we will look at the two words before and after our target word:

1.  Let's start by importing the necessary libraries:

    ```
    import numpy as np
    ```

2.  Then, we need to set the CONTEXT_SIZE variable to 2 and bring in the text we want to analyze:

    ```
    CONTEXT_SIZE = 2
    ```

```
text = """Lorem ipsum dolor sit amet, consectetur
adipiscing elit. Nunc eu sem scelerisque, dictum eros
aliquam, accumsan quam. Pellentesque tempus, lorem ut
semper fermentum, ante turpis accumsan ex, sit amet
ultricies tortor erat quis nulla. Nunc consectetur ligula
sit amet purus porttitor, vel tempus tortor scelerisque.
Vestibulum ante ipsum primis in faucibus orci luctus
et ultrices posuere cubilia curae; Quisque suscipit
ligula nec faucibus accumsan. Duis vulputate massa sit
amet viverra hendrerit. Integer maximus quis sapien id
convallis. Donec elementum placerat ex laoreet gravida.
Praesent quis enim facilisis, bibendum est nec, pharetra
ex. Etiam pharetra congue justo, eget imperdiet diam
varius non. Mauris dolor lectus, interdum in laoreet
quis, faucibus vitae velit. Donec lacinia dui eget
maximus cursus. Class aptent taciti sociosqu ad litora
torquent per conubia nostra, per inceptos himenaeos.
Vivamus tincidunt velit eget nisi ornare convallis.
Pellentesque habitant morbi tristique senectus et netus
et malesuada fames ac turpis egestas. Donec tristique
ultrices tortor at accumsan.
""".split()
```

3. Next, we create the skip-grams thanks to a simple `for` loop to consider every word in `text`. A list comprehension generates the context words, stored in the `skipgrams` list:

```
skipgrams = []
for i in range(CONTEXT_SIZE, len(text) - CONTEXT_SIZE):
    array = [text[j] for j in np.arange(i - CONTEXT_SIZE,
i + CONTEXT_SIZE + 1) if j != i]
    skipgrams.append((text[i], array))
```

4. Finally, use the `print()` function to see the skip-grams we generated:

```
print(skipgrams[0:2])
```

5. This produces the following output:

```
[('dolor', ['Lorem', 'ipsum', 'sit', 'amet,']), ('sit',
['ipsum', 'dolor', 'amet,', 'consectetur'])]
```

These two target words, with their corresponding context, work to show what the inputs to Word2Vec look like.

## The skip-gram model

The goal of Word2Vec is to produce high-quality word embeddings. To learn these embeddings, the training task of the skip-gram model consists of predicting the correct context words given a target word.

Imagine that we have a sequence of $N$ words $w_1, w_2, \ldots, w_N$. The probability of seeing the word $w_2$ given the word $w_2$ is written $p(w_2|w_1)$. Our goal is to maximize the sum of every probability of seeing a context word given a target word in an entire text:

$$\frac{1}{N} \sum_{n=1}^{N} \sum_{-c \leq j \leq c, j \neq 0} \log p(w_{n+j}|w_n)$$

Where $C$ is the size of the context vector.

> **Note**
>
> Why do we use a log probability in the previous equation? Transforming probabilities into log probabilities is a common technique in ML (and computer science in general) for two main reasons.
>
> Products become additions (and divisions become subtractions). Multiplications are more computationally expensive than additions, so it's faster to compute the log probability:
>
> $$\log(A \times B) = \log(A) + \log(B)$$
>
> The way computers store very small numbers (such as 3.14e-128) is not perfectly accurate, unlike the log of the same numbers (-127.5 in this case). These small errors can add up and bias the final results when events are extremely unlikely.
>
> On the whole, this simple transformation allows us to gain speed and accuracy without changing our initial objective.

The basic skip-gram model uses the softmax function to calculate the probability of a context word embedding $h_c$ given a target word embedding $h_t$:

$$p(w_c|w_t) = \frac{\exp\left(h_c\, h_t^T\right)}{\sum_{i=1}^{|V|} \exp\left(h_i\, h_t^T\right)}$$

Where $V$ is the vocabulary of size $|V|$. This vocabulary corresponds to the list of unique words the model tries to predict. We can obtain this list using the `set` data structure to remove duplicate words:

```
vocab = set(text)
VOCAB_SIZE = len(vocab)
print(f"Length of vocabulary = {VOCAB_SIZE}")
```

This gives us the following output:

```
Length of vocabulary = 121
```

Now that we have the size of our vocabulary, there is one more parameter we need to define: $N$, the dimensionality of the word vectors. Typically, this value is set between 100 and 1,000. In this example, we will set it to 10 because of the limited size of our dataset.

The skip-gram model is composed of only two layers:

- A **projection layer** with a weight matrix $W_{embed}$, which takes a one-hot encoded-word vector as an input and returns the corresponding $N$-dim word embedding. It acts as a simple lookup table that stores embeddings of a predefined dimensionality.

- A **fully connected layer** with a weight matrix $W_{output}$, which takes a word embedding as input and outputs $|V|$-dim logits. A softmax function is applied to these predictions to transform logits into probabilities.

> **Note**
>
> There is no activation function: Word2Vec is a linear classifier that models a linear relationship between words.

Let's call $x$ the one-hot encoded-word vector the *input*. The corresponding word embedding can be calculated as a simple projection:

$$h = W_{embed}^T \cdot x$$

Using the skip-gram model, we can rewrite the previous probability as follows:

$$p(w_c|w_t) = \frac{\exp(W_{output} \cdot h)}{\sum_{i=1}^{|V|} \exp(W_{output_{(i)}} \cdot h)}$$

The skip-gram model outputs a $|V|$-dim vector, which is the conditional probability of every word in the vocabulary:

$$word2vec(w_t) = \begin{bmatrix} p(w_1|w_t) \\ p(w_2|w_t) \\ \vdots \\ p(w_{|V|}|w_t) \end{bmatrix}$$

During training, these probabilities are compared to the correct one-hot encoded-target word vectors. The difference between these values (calculated by a loss function such as the cross-entropy loss) is backpropagated through the network to update the weights and obtain better predictions.

The entire Word2Vec architecture is summarized in the following diagram, with both matrices and the final softmax layer:

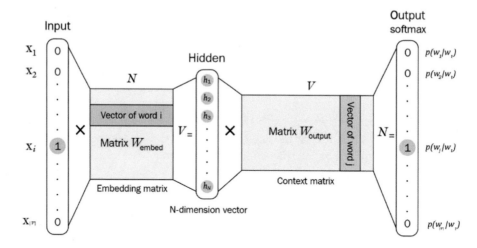

Figure 3.3 – The Word2Vec architecture

We can implement this model using the gensim library, which is also used in the official implementation of DeepWalk. We can then build the vocabulary and train our model based on the previous text:

1.  Let's begin by installing gensim and importing the Word2Vec class:

    ```
    !pip install -qU gensim
    from gensim.models.word2vec import Word2Vec
    ```

2.  We initialize a skip-gram model with a Word2Vec object and an sg=1 parameter (skip-gram = 1):

    ```
    model = Word2Vec([text],
                    sg=1,     # Skip-gram
                    vector_size=10,
                    min_count=0,
                    window=2,
                    workers=2,
                    seed=0)
    ```

3.  It's a good idea to check the shape of our first weight matrix. It should correspond to the vocabulary size and the word embeddings' dimensionality:

    ```
    print(f'Shape of W_embed: {model.wv.vectors.shape}')
    ```

4. This produces the following output:

```
Shape of W_embed = (121, 10)
```

5. Next, we train the model for 10 epochs:

```
model.train([text], total_examples=model.corpus_count,
epochs=10)
```

6. Finally, we can print a word embedding to see what the result of this training looks like:

```
print('Word embedding =')
print(model.wv[0])
```

7. This gives us the following output:

```
Word embedding =
[ 0.06947816 -0.06254371 -0.08287395  0.07274164
-0.09449387  0.01215031  -0.08728203 -0.04045384
-0.00368091 -0.0141237 ]
```

While this approach works well with small vocabularies, the computational cost of applying a full softmax function to millions of words (the vocabulary size ) is too costly in most cases. This has been a limiting factor in developing accurate language models for a long time. Fortunately for us, other approaches have been designed to solve this issue.

Word2Vec (and DeepWalk) implements one of these techniques, called H-Softmax. Instead of a flat softmax that directly calculates the probability of every word, this technique uses a binary tree structure where leaves are words. Even more interestingly, a Huffman tree can be used, where infrequent words are stored at deeper levels than common words. In most cases, this dramatically speeds up the word prediction by a factor of at least 50.

H-Softmax can be activated in gensim using hs=1.

This was the most difficult part of the DeepWalk architecture. But before we can implement it, we need one more component: how to create our training data.

# DeepWalk and random walks

Proposed in 2014 by Perozzi et al., DeepWalk quickly became extremely popular among graph researchers. Inspired by recent advances in NLP, it consistently outperformed other methods on several datasets. While more performant architectures have been proposed since then, DeepWalk is a simple and reliable baseline that can be quickly implemented to solve a lot of problems.

The goal of DeepWalk is to produce high-quality feature representations of nodes in an unsupervised way. This architecture is heavily inspired by Word2Vec in NLP. However, instead of words, our dataset is composed of nodes. This is why we use random walks to generate meaningful sequences of nodes that act like sentences. The following diagram illustrates the connection between sentences and graphs:

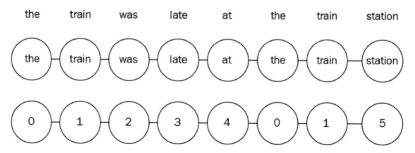

Figure 3.4 – Sentences can be represented as graphs

Random walks are sequences of nodes produced by randomly choosing a neighboring node at every step. Thus, nodes can appear several times in the same sequence.

Why are random walks important? Even if nodes are randomly selected, the fact that they often appear together in a sequence means that they are close to each other. Under the **network homophily** hypothesis, nodes that are close to each other are similar. This is particularly the case in social networks, where people are connected to friends and family.

This idea is at the core of the DeepWalk algorithm: when nodes are close to each other, we want to obtain high similarity scores. On the contrary, we want low scores when they are farther apart.

Let's implement a random walk function using a `networkx` graph:

1.  Let's import the required libraries and initialize the random number generator for reproducibility:

```
import networkx as nx
import matplotlib.pyplot as plt
import numpy as np
import random
random.seed(0)
```

2.  We generate a random graph thanks to the `erdos_renyi_graph` function with a fixed number of nodes (`10`) and a predefined probability of creating an edge between two nodes (`0.3`):

```
G = nx.erdos_renyi_graph(10, 0.3, seed=1, directed=False)
```

3.  We plot this random graph to see what it looks like:

```
plt.figure(dpi=300)
plt.axis('off')
nx.draw_networkx(G,
                 pos=nx.spring_layout(G, seed=0),
                 node_size=600,
                 cmap='coolwarm',
                 font_size=14,
                 font_color='white'
                 )
```

This produces the following graph:

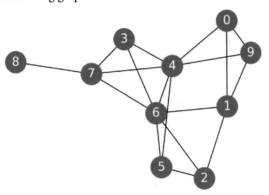

Figure 3.5 – Random graph

4.  Let's implement random walks with a simple function. This function takes two parameters: the starting node (`start`) and the length of the walk (`length`). At every step, we randomly select a neighboring node (using `np.random.choice`) until the walk is complete:

```
def random_walk(start, length):
    walk = [str(start)]  # starting node

    for i in range(length):
        neighbors = [node for node in G.neighbors(start)]
        next_node = np.random.choice(neighbors, 1)[0]
        walk.append(str(next_node))
        start = next_node

    return walk
```

5. Next, we print the result of this function with the starting node as 0 and a length of 10:

```
print(random_walk(0, 10))
```

6. This produces the following list:

```
['0', '4', '3', '6', '3', '4', '7', '8', '7', '4', '9']
```

We can see that certain nodes, such as 0 and 9, are often found together. Considering that it is a homophilic graph, it means that they are similar. It is precisely the type of relationship we're trying to capture with DeepWalk.

Now that we have implemented Word2Vec and random walks separately, let's combine them to create DeepWalk.

## Implementing DeepWalk

Now that we have a good understanding of every component in this architecture, let's use it to solve an ML problem.

The dataset we will use is Zachary's Karate Club. It simply represents the relationships within a karate club studied by Wayne W. Zachary in the 1970s. It is a kind of social network where every node is a member, and members who interact outside the club are connected.

In this example, the club is divided into two groups: we would like to assign the right group to every member (node classification) just by looking at their connections:

1. Let's import the dataset using nx.karate_club_graph():

```
G = nx.karate_club_graph()
```

2. Next, we need to convert string class labels into numerical values (Mr. Hi = 0, Officer = 1):

```
labels = []
for node in G.nodes:
    label = G.nodes[node]['club']
    labels.append(1 if label == 'Officer' else 0)
```

3. Let's plot this graph using our new labels:

```
plt.figure(figsize=(12,12), dpi=300)
plt.axis('off')
nx.draw_networkx(G,
                 pos=nx.spring_layout(G, seed=0),
                 node_color=labels,
```

```
        node_size=800,
        cmap='coolwarm',
        font_size=14,
        font_color='white'
    )
```

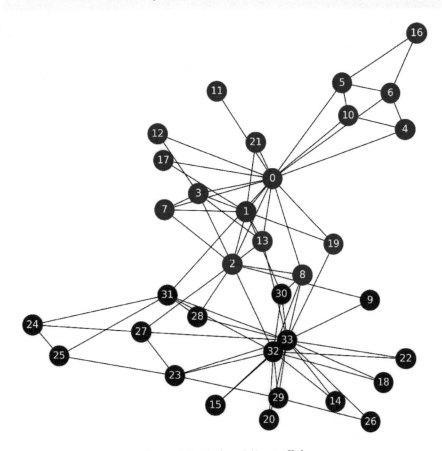

Figure 3.6 – Zachary's Karate Club

4.   The next step is to generate our dataset, the random walks. We want to be as exhaustive as possible, which is why we will create 80 random walks of a length of 10 for every node in the graph:

```
walks = []
for node in G.nodes:
    for _ in range(80):
        walks.append(random_walk(node, 10))
```

5. Let's print a walk to verify that it is correct:

```
print(walks[0])
```

6. This is the first walk that was generated:

```
['0', '19', '1', '2', '0', '3', '2', '8', '33', '14',
'33']
```

7. The final step consists of implementing Word2Vec. Here, we use the skip-gram model previously seen with H-Softmax. You can play with the other parameters to improve the quality of the embeddings:

```
model = Word2Vec(walks,
                 hs=1,    # Hierarchical softmax
                 sg=1,    # Skip-gram
                 vector_size=100,
                 window=10,
                 workers=2,
                 seed=0)
```

8. The model is then simply trained on the random walks we generated.

```
model.train(walks, total_examples=model.corpus_count,
epochs=30, report_delay=1)
```

9. Now that our model is trained, let's see its different applications. The first one allows us to find the most similar nodes to a given one (in terms of cosine similarity):

```
print('Nodes that are the most similar to node 0:')
for similarity in model.wv.most_similar(positive=['0']):
    print(f'   {similarity}')
```

This produces the following output for Nodes that are the most similar to node 0:

```
('4', 0.6825815439224243)
('11', 0.6330500245094299)
('5', 0.6324777603149414)
('10', 0.6097837090492249)
('6', 0.6096848249435425)
('21', 0.5936519503593445)
```

```
('12', 0.5906376242637634)
('3', 0.5797219276428223)
('16', 0.5388344526290894)
('13', 0.534131646156311)
```

Another important application is calculating the similarity score between two nodes. It can be performed as follows:

```
# Similarity between two nodes
print(f"Similarity between node 0 and 4: {model.
wv.similarity('0', '4')}")
```

This code directly gives us the cosine similarity between two nodes:

```
Similarity between node 0 and 4: 0.6825816631317139
```

We can plot the resulting embeddings using **t-distributed stochastic neighbor embedding** (t-SNE) to visualize these high-dimensional vectors in 2D:

1.  We import the TSNE class from sklearn:

    ```
    from sklearn.manifold import TSNE
    ```

2.  We create two arrays: one to store the word embeddings and the other one to store the labels:

    ```
    nodes_wv = np.array([model.wv.get_vector(str(i)) for i in
    range(len(model.wv))])
    labels = np.array(labels)
    ```

3.  Next, we train the t-SNE model with two dimensions (n_components=2) on the embeddings:

    ```
    tsne = TSNE(n_components=2,
                learning_rate='auto',
                init='pca',
                random_state=0).fit_transform(nodes_wv)
    ```

4.  Finally, let's plot the 2D vectors produced by the trained t-SNE model with the corresponding labels:

    ```
    plt.figure(figsize=(6, 6), dpi=300)
    plt.scatter(tsne[:, 0], tsne[:, 1], s=100, c=labels,
    cmap="coolwarm")
    plt.show()
    ```

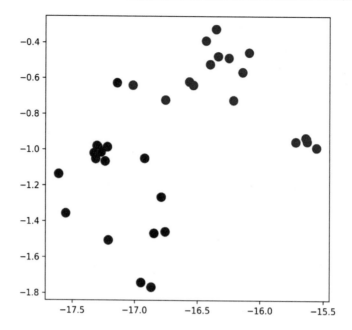

Figure 3.7 – A t-SNE plot of the nodes

This plot is quite encouraging since we can see a clear line that separates the two classes. It should be possible for a simple ML algorithm to classify these nodes with enough examples (training data). Let's implement a classifier and train it on our node embeddings:

1.  We import a Random Forest model from sklearn, which is a popular choice when it comes to classification. The accuracy score is the metric we'll use to evaluate this model:

    ```
    from sklearn.ensemble import RandomForestClassifier
    from sklearn.metrics import accuracy_score
    ```

2.  We need to split the embeddings into two groups: training and test data. A simple way of doing it is to create masks as follows:

    ```
    train_mask = [0, 2, 4, 6, 8, 10, 12, 14, 16, 18, 20, 22,
    24, 26, 28]
    test_mask = [1, 3, 5, 7, 9, 11, 13, 15, 17, 19, 21, 23,
    25, 27, 29, 30, 31, 32, 33]
    ```

3.  Next, we train the Random Forest classifier on the training data with the appropriate labels:

    ```
    clf = RandomForestClassifier(random_state=0)
    clf.fit(nodes_wv[train_mask], labels[train_mask])
    ```

4.  Finally, we evaluate the trained model on the test data based on its accuracy score:

```
y_pred = clf.predict(nodes_wv[test_mask])
accuracy_score(y_pred, labels[test_mask])
```

5.  This is the final result of our classifier:

```
0.9545454545454546
```

Our model obtains an accuracy score of 95.45%, which is pretty good considering the unfavorable train/test split we gave it. There is still room for improvement, but this example showed two useful applications of DeepWalk:

- *Discovering similarities between nodes* using embeddings and cosine similarity (unsupervised learning)
- *Using these embeddings as a dataset* for a supervised task such as node classification

As we are going to see in the following chapters, the ability to learn node representations offers a lot of flexibility to design deeper and more complex architectures.

## Summary

In this chapter, we learned about DeepWalk architecture and its major components. Then, we transformed graph data into sequences using random walks to apply the powerful Word2Vec algorithm. The resulting embeddings can be used to find similarities between nodes or as input to other algorithms. In particular, we solved a node classification problem using a supervised approach.

In *Chapter 4, Improving Embeddings with Biased Random Walks in Node2Vec*, we will introduce a second algorithm based on Word2Vec. The difference with DeepWalk is that the random walks can be biased towards more or less exploration, which directly impacts the embeddings that are produced. We will implement this algorithm on a new example and compare its representations with those obtained using DeepWalk.

## Further reading

- [1] B. Perozzi, R. Al-Rfou, and S. Skiena, *DeepWalk*, Aug. 2014. DOI: 10.1145/2623330.2623732. Available at https://arxiv.org/abs/1403.6652.

# Part 2:
# Fundamentals

In this second part of the book, we will delve into the process of constructing node representations using graph learning. We will start by exploring traditional graph learning techniques, drawing on the advancements made in natural language processing. Our aim is to understand how these techniques can be applied to graphs and how they can be used to build node representations.

We will then move on to incorporating node features into our models and explore how they can be used to build even more accurate representations. Finally, we will introduce two of the most fundamental GNN architectures, the **Graph Convolutional Network (GCN)** and the **Graph Attention Network (GAT)**. These two architectures are the building blocks of many state-of-the-art graph learning methods and will provide a solid foundation for the next part.

By the end of this part, you will have a deeper understanding of how traditional graph learning techniques, such as random walks, can be used to create node representations and develop graph applications. Additionally, you will learn how to build even more powerful representations using GNNs. You will be introduced to two key GNN architectures and learn how they can be used to tackle various graph-based tasks.

This part comprises the following chapters:

- *Chapter 3, Creating Node Representations with DeepWalk*

- *Chapter 4, Improving Embeddings with Biased Random Walks in Node2Vec*

- *Chapter 5, Including Node Features with Vanilla Neural Networks*

- *Chapter 6, Introducing Graph Convolutional Networks*

- *Chapter 7, Graph Attention Networks*

# 4

# Improving Embeddings with Biased Random Walks in Node2Vec

**Node2Vec** is an architecture largely based on DeepWalk. In the previous chapter, we saw the two main components of this architecture: random walks and Word2Vec. How can we improve the quality of our embeddings? Interestingly enough, not with more machine learning. Instead, Node2Vec brings critical modifications to the way random walks themselves are generated.

In this chapter, we will talk about these modifications and how to find the best parameters for a given graph. We will implement the Node2Vec architecture and compare it to using DeepWalk on Zachary's Karate Club. This will give you a good understanding of the differences between the two architectures. Finally, we will use this technology to build a real application: a movie **recommender system (RecSys)** powered by Node2Vec.

By the end of this chapter, you will know how to implement Node2Vec on any graph dataset and how to select good parameters. You will understand why this architecture works better than DeepWalk in general, and how to apply it to build creative applications.

In this chapter, we'll cover the following topics:

- Introducing Node2Vec
- Implementing Node2Vec
- Building a movie RecSys

## Technical requirements

All the code examples from this chapter can be found on GitHub at `https://github.com/PacktPublishing/Hands-On-Graph-Neural-Networks-Using-Python/tree/main/Chapter04`.

Installation steps required to run the code on your local machine can be found in the *Preface* of this book.

## Introducing Node2Vec

Node2Vec was introduced in 2016 by Grover and Leskovec from Stanford University [1]. It keeps the same two main components from DeepWalk: random walks and Word2Vec. The difference is that instead of obtaining sequences of nodes with a uniform distribution, the random walks are carefully biased in Node2Vec. We will see why these **biased random walks** perform better and how to implement them in the two following sections:

- Defining a **neighborhood**
- Introducing biases in random walks

Let's start by questioning our intuitive concept of neighborhoods.

## Defining a neighborhood

How do you define the neighborhood of a node? The key concept introduced in Node2Vec is the flexible notion of a neighborhood. Intuitively, we think of it as something close to the initial node, but what does "close" mean in the context of a graph? Let's take the following graph as an example:

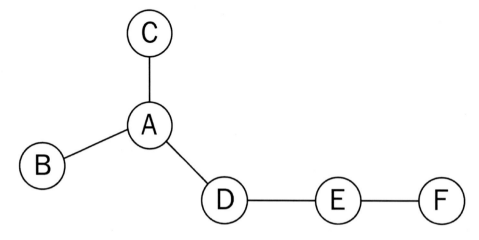

Figure 4.1 – Example of a random graph

We want to explore three nodes in the neighborhood of node **A**. This exploration process is also called a **sampling strategy**:

- A possible solution would be to consider the three closest nodes in terms of connections. In this case, the neighborhood of $A$, noted $N(A)$, would be $N(A) = \{B, C, D\}$:

- Another possible sampling strategy consists of selecting nodes that are not adjacent to previous nodes first. In our example, the neighborhood of $A$ would be $N(A) = \{D, E, F\}$:

In other words, we want to implement a **Breadth-First Search** (**BFS**) in the first case and a **Depth-First Search** (**DFS**) in the second one. You can find more information about these algorithms and implementations in *Chapter 2, Graph Theory for Graph Neural Networks*.

What is important to notice here is that these sampling strategies have opposite behaviors: BFS focuses on the local network around a node while DFS establishes a more macro view of the graph. Considering our intuitive definition of a neighborhood, it is tempting to simply discard DFS. However, Node2Vec's authors argue that this would be a mistake: each approach captures a different but valuable representation of the network.

They make a connection between these algorithms and two network properties:

- **Structural equivalence**, which means that nodes are structurally equivalent if they share many of the same neighbors. So, if they share many neighbors, their structural equivalence is higher.

- **Homophily**, as seen previously, states that similar nodes are more likely to be connected.

They argue that BFS is ideal to emphasize structural equivalence since this strategy only looks at neighboring nodes. In these random walks, nodes are often repeated and stay close to each other. DFS, on the other hand, emphasizes the opposite of homophily by creating sequences of distant nodes. These random walks can sample nodes that are far from the source and thus become less representative. This is why we're looking for a trade-off between these two properties: homophily may be more helpful for understanding certain graphs and vice versa.

If you're confused about this connection, you're not alone: several papers and blogs wrongly assume that BFS emphasizes homophily and DFS is connected to structural equivalence. In any case, we consider graphs that combine homophily and structural equivalence to be the desired solution. This is why, regardless of these connections, we want to use both sampling strategies to create our dataset.

Let's see how we can implement them to generate random walks.

## Introducing biases in random walks

As a reminder, random walks are sequences of nodes that are randomly selected in a graph. They have a starting point, which can also be random, and a predefined length. Nodes that often appear together in these walks are like words that appear together in sentences: under the homophily hypothesis, they share a similar meaning, hence a similar representation.

In Node2Vec, our goal is to bias the randomness of these walks to either one of the following:

- Promoting nodes that are not connected to the previous one (similar to DFS)
- Promoting nodes that are close to the previous one (similar to BFS)

Let's take *Figure 4.2* as an example. The current node is called $j$, the previous node is $i$, and the future node is $k$. We note $\pi_{jk}$, the unnormalized transition probability from node $j$ to node $k$. This probability can be decomposed as $\pi_{jk} = \alpha(i, k) \cdot \omega_{jk}$ , where $\alpha(i, k)$ is the **search bias** between nodes $i$ and $k$ and $\omega_{jk}$ is the weight of the edge from $j$ to $k$.

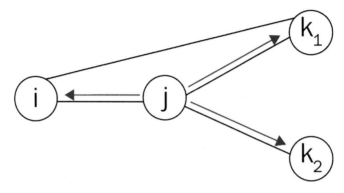

Figure 4.2 – Example of a random graph

In DeepWalk, we have $\alpha(a, b) = 1$ for any pair of nodes $a$ and $b$. In Node2Vec, the value of $\alpha(a, b)$ is defined based on the distance between the nodes and two additional parameters: $p$, the return parameter, and $q$, the in-out parameter. Their role is to approximate DFS and BFS, respectively.

Here is how the value of $\alpha(a, b)$ is defined:

$$\alpha(a, b) = \begin{cases} \dfrac{1}{p} \; if \; d_{ab} = 0 \\ 1 \; if \; d_{ab} = 1 \\ \dfrac{1}{q} \; if \; d_{ab} = 2 \end{cases}$$

Here, $d_{ab}$ is the shortest path distance between nodes $a$ and $b$. We can update the unnormalized transition probability from the previous graph as follows:

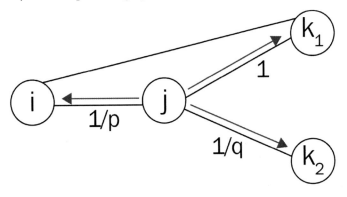

Figure 4.3 – Graph with transition probabilities

Let's decrypt these probabilities:

- The walk starts from node $i$ and now arrives at node $j$. The probability of going back to the previous node $i$ is controlled by the parameter $p$. The higher it is, the more the random walk will explore new nodes instead of repeating the same ones and looking like DFS.

- The unnormalized probability of going to $k_1$ is 1 because this node is in the immediate neighborhood of our previous node, $i$.

- Finally, the probability of going to node $k_2$ is controlled by the parameter $q$. The higher it is, the more the random walk will focus on nodes that are close to the previous one and look like BFS.

The best way to understand this is to actually implement this architecture and play with the parameters. Let's do it step by step on Zachary's Karate Club (a graph from the previous chapter), as shown in *Figure 4.4*:

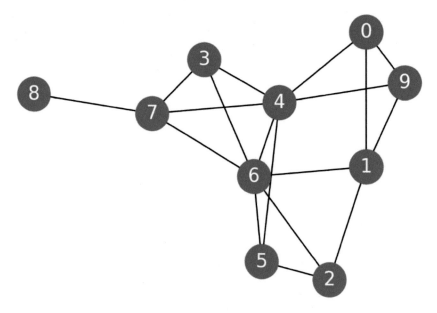

Figure 4.4 – Zachary's Karate Club

Note that it is an unweighted network, which is why the transition probability is only determined by the search bias.

First, we want to create a function that will randomly select the next node in a graph based on the previous node, the current node, and the two parameters $p$ and $q$.

1.  We start by importing the required libraries: `networkx`, `random`, and `numpy`:

    ```
    import networkx as nx
    import random
    random.seed(0)
    import numpy as np
    np.random.seed(0)


    G = nx.erdos_renyi_graph(10, 0.3, seed=1, directed=False)
    ```

2.  We defined the `next_node` function with the list of our parameters:

    ```
    def next_node(previous, current, p, q):
    ```

3.  We retrieve the list of neighboring nodes from the current node and initialize a list of alpha values:

```
neighbors = list(G.neighbors(current))
alphas = []
```

4.  For each neighbor, we want to calculate the appropriate alpha value: $1/p$ if this neighbor is the previous node, 1 if this neighbor is connected to the previous node, and $1/q$ otherwise:

```
for neighbor in neighbors:
    if neighbor == previous:
        alpha = 1/p
    elif G.has_edge(neighbor, previous):
        alpha = 1
    else:
        alpha = 1/q
    alphas.append(alpha)
```

5.  We normalize these values to create probabilities:

```
probs = [alpha / sum(alphas) for alpha in alphas]
```

6.  We randomly select the next node based on the transition probabilities calculated in the previous step using np.random.choice() and return it:

```
next = np.random.choice(neighbors, size=1, p=probs)
[0]
return next
```

Before this function can be tested, we need the code to generate the entire random walk.

The way we generate these random walks is similar to what we saw in the previous chapter. The difference is that the next node is chosen by the next_node() function, which requires additional parameters: $p$ and $q$, but also the previous and current nodes. These nodes can easily be obtained by looking at the two last elements added to the walk variable. We also return strings instead of integers for compatibility reasons.

Here is the new version of the random_walk() function:

```
def random_walk(start, length, p, q):
    walk = [start]

    for i in range(length):
        current = walk[-1]
```

```
        previous = walk[-2] if len(walk) > 1 else None
        next = next_node(previous, current, p, q)
        walk.append(next)


    return [str(x) for x in walk]
```

We now have every element to generate our random walks. Let's try one with a length of 5, $p = 1$, and $q = 1$:

```
random_walk(0, 8, p=1, q=1)
```

This function returns the following sequence:

```
[0, 4, 7, 6, 4, 5, 4, 5, 6]
```

This should be random since every neighboring node has the same transition probability. With these parameters, we reproduce the exact DeepWalk algorithm.

Now, let's bias them toward going back to the previous node with $q = 10$:

```
random_walk(0, 8, p=1, q=10)
```

This function returns the following sequence:

```
[0, 9, 1, 9, 1, 9, 1, 0, 1]
```

This time, the random walk explores more nodes in the graph. You can see that it never goes back to the previous node because the probability is low with $p = 10$:

```
random_walk(0, 8, p=10, q=1)
```

This function returns the following sequence:

```
[0, 1, 9, 4, 7, 8, 7, 4, 6]
```

Let's see how to use these properties in a real example and compare it to DeepWalk.

# Implementing Node2Vec

Now that we have the functions to generate biased random walks, the implementation of Node2Vec is very similar to implementing DeepWalk. It is so similar that we can reuse the same code and create sequences with $p = 1$ and $q = 1$ to implement DeepWalk as a special case of Node2Vec. Let's reuse Zachary's Karate Club for this task:

As in the previous chapter, our goal is to correctly classify each member of the club as part of one of the two groups ("Mr. Hi" and "Officer"). We will use the node embeddings provided by Node2Vec as input to a machine learning classifier (Random Forest in this case).

Let's see how to implement it step by step:

1.  First, we want to install the `gensim` library to use Word2Vec. This time, we will use version 3.8.0 for compatibility reasons:

    ```
    !pip install -qI gensim==3.8.0
    ```

2.  We import the required libraries:

    ```
    from gensim.models.word2vec import Word2Vec
    from sklearn.ensemble import RandomForestClassifier
    from sklearn.metrics import accuracy_score
    ```

3.  We load the dataset (Zachary's Karate Club):

    ```
    G = nx.karate_club_graph()
    ```

4.  We transform the nodes' labels into numerical values (0 and 1):

    ```
    labels = []
    for node in G.nodes:
        label = G.nodes[node]['club']
        labels.append(1 if label == 'Officer' else 0)
    ```

5.  We generate a list of random walks as seen previously using our `random_walk()` function 80 times for each node in the graph. The parameters $p$ and $q$ as specified here (2 and 1, respectively):

    ```
    walks = []
    for node in G.nodes:
        for _ in range(80):
            walks.append(random_walk(node, 10, 3, 2))
    ```

6.  We create an instance of Word2Vec (a skip-gram model) with a hierarchical `softmax` function:

```
node2vec = Word2Vec(walks,
                    hs=1,    # Hierarchical softmax
                    sg=1,    # Skip-gram
                    vector_size=100,
                    window=10,
                    workers=2,
                    min_count=1,
                    seed=0)
```

7.  The skip-gram model is trained on the sequences we generated for 30 epochs:

```
node2vec.train(walks, total_examples=node2vec.corpus_
count, epochs=30, report_delay=1)
```

8.  We create masks to train and test the classifier:

```
train_mask = [2, 4, 6, 8, 10, 12, 14, 16, 18, 20, 22, 24]
train_mask_str = [str(x) for x in train_mask]
test_mask = [0, 1, 3, 5, 7, 9, 11, 13, 15, 17, 19, 21,
23, 25, 26, 27, 28, 29, 30, 31, 32, 33]
test_mask_str = [str(x) for x in test_mask]
labels = np.array(labels)
```

9.  The Random Forest classifier is trained on the training data:

```
clf = RandomForestClassifier(random_state=0)
clf.fit(node2vec.wv[train_mask_str], labels[train_mask])
```

10.  We evaluate it in terms of accuracy for the test data:

```
y_pred = clf.predict(node2vec.wv[test_mask_str])
acc = accuracy_score(y_pred, labels[test_mask])
print(f'Node2Vec accuracy = {acc*100:.2f}%')
```

To implement DeepWalk, we can repeat the exact same process with $p = 1$ and $q = 1$. However, to make a fair comparison, we cannot use a single accuracy score. Indeed, there are a lot of stochastic processes involved – we could be unlucky and get a better result from the worst model.

To limit the randomness of our results, we can repeat this process 100 times and take the mean value. This result is a lot more stable and can even include the standard deviation (using `np.std()`) to measure the variability in the accuracy scores.

But just before we do that, let's play a game. In the previous chapter, we talked about Zachary's Karate Club as a homophilic network. This property is emphasized by DFS, which is encouraged by increasing the parameter $p$. If this statement and the connection between DFS and homophily are true, we should get better results with higher values of $p$.

I repeated the same experiment for values of $p$ and $q$ between 1 and 7. In a real machine learning project, we would use validation data to perform this parameter search. In this example, we use the test data because this study is already our final application.

The following table summarizes the results:

|  | p=1 | p=2 | p=3 | p=4 | p=5 | p=6 | p=7 |
|---|---|---|---|---|---|---|---|
| q=1 | 92.95% (± 4.61%) | 94.45% (± 4.19%) | 96.36% (± 4.69%) | 95.41% (± 4.14%) | 95.59% (± 4.30%) | 95.82% (± 4.67%) | 95.41% (± 3.94%) |
| q=2 | 93.64% (± 4.36%) | 93.95% (± 3.97%) | 95.09% (± 4.34%) | 95.55% (± 3.80%) | 96.27% (± 3.82%) | 96.18% (± 3.90%) | 97.45% (± 3.60%) |
| q=3 | 93.45% (± 3.82%) | 94.41% (± 4.11%) | 95.77% (± 3.59%) | 95.27% (± 3.63%) | 96.68% (± 3.90%) | 95.64% (± 3.69%) | 96.00% (± 3.82%) |
| q=4 | 94.14% (± 3.93%) | 94.14% (± 3.93%) | 95.45% (± 3.40%) | 95.05% (± 3.58%) | 95.95% (± 3.46%) | 96.41% (± 3.71%) | 95.59% (± 3.31%) |
| q=5 | 94.41% (± 3.68%) | 94.18% (± 3.64%) | 94.68% (± 3.58%) | 95.36% (± 3.75%) | 95.64% (± 3.34%) | 95.55% (± 3.58%) | 95.27% (± 4.01%) |
| q=6 | 94.91% (± 3.71%) | 94.55% (± 3.08%) | 94.59% (± 3.13%) | 95.05% (± 3.86%) | 95.77% (± 3.23%) | 94.55% (± 4.17%) | 95.05% (± 3.75%) |
| q=7 | 94.64% (± 4.03%) | 95.00% (± 3.78%) | 93.59% (± 3.97%) | 94.86% (± 3.67%) | 94.14% (± 3.87%) | 95.27% (± 3.74%) | 95.82% (± 3.38%) |

Figure 4.5 – Average accuracy score and standard deviation for different values of p and q

There are several noticeable results:

- DeepWalk ($p = 1$ and $q = 1$) performs worse than any other combination of $p$ and $q$ that is covered here. This is true for this dataset and shows how useful biased random walks can be. However, it is not always the case: non-biased random walks can also perform better on other datasets.

- High values of $p$ lead to better performance, which validates our hypothesis. Knowing that this is a social network strongly suggests that biasing our random walks toward homophily is a good strategy. This is something to keep in mind when dealing with this kind of graph.

Feel free to play with the parameters and try to find other interesting results. We could explore results with very high values of $p$ ($> 7$) or, on the contrary, values of $p$ and $q$ between 0 and 1.

Zachary's Karate Club is a basic dataset, but we'll see in the next section how we can use this technology to build much more interesting applications.

## Building a movie RecSys

One of the most popular applications of GNNs is RecSys. If you think about the foundation of Word2Vec (and, thus, DeepWalk and Node2Vec), the goal is to produce vectors with the ability to measure their similarity. Encode movies instead of words, and you can suddenly ask for movies that are the most similar to a given input title. It sounds a lot like a RecSys, right?

But how to encode movies? We want to create (biased) random walks of movies, but this requires a graph dataset where similar movies are connected to each other. This is not easy to find.

Another approach is to look at user ratings. There are different techniques to build a graph based on ratings: bipartite graphs, edges based on pointwise mutual information, and so on. In this section, we'll implement a simple and intuitive approach: movies that are liked by the same users are connected. We'll then use this graph to learn movie embeddings using Node2Vec:

1.  First, let's download a dataset. `MovieLens` [2] is a popular choice, with a small version of the latest dataset (09/2018) comprising 100,836 ratings, 9,742 movies, and 610 users. We can download it with the following Python code:

    ```python
    from io import BytesIO
    from urllib.request import urlopen
    from zipfile import ZipFile


    url = 'https://files.grouplens.org/datasets/movielens/
    ml-100k.zip'
    with urlopen(url) as zurl:
        with ZipFile(BytesIO(zurl.read())) as zfile:
            zfile.extractall('.')
    ```

2.  We are interested in two files: `ratings.csv` and `movies.csv`. The first one stores all the ratings made by users, and the second one allows us to translate movie identifiers into titles.

3.  Let's see what they look like by importing them with `pandas` using `pd.read_csv()`:

    ```python
    import pandas as pd
    ```

```
ratings = pd.read_csv('ml-100k/u.data', sep='\t',
names=['user_id', 'movie_id', 'rating', 'unix_
timestamp'])
ratings
```

4.  This gives us the following output:

|  | user_id | movie_id | rating | unix_timestamp |
|---|---|---|---|---|
| 0 | 196 | 242 | 3 | 881250949 |
| 1 | 186 | 302 | 3 | 891717742 |
| 2 | 22 | 377 | 1 | 878887116 |
| ... | ... | ... | ... | ... |
| 99998 | 13 | 225 | 2 | 882399156 |
| 99999 | 12 | 203 | 3 | 879959583 |
| 100000 rows × 4 columns | | | | |

5.  Let's import `movies.csv` now:

```
movies = pd.read_csv('ml-100k/u.item', sep='|',
usecols=range(2), names=['movie_id', 'title'],
encoding='latin-1')
```

6.  This dataset gives us this output:

```
movies
```

| | movie_id | title |
|---|---|---|
| 0 | 1 | Toy Story (1995) |
| 1 | 2 | GoldenEye (1995) |
| 2 | 3 | Four Rooms (1995) |
| ... | ... | ... |
| 1680 | 1681 | You So Crazy (1994) |
| 1681 | 1682 | Scream of Stone (Schrei aus Stein) (1991) |
| 1682 rows × 2 columns | | |

7.  Here, we want to see movies that have been liked by the same users. This means that ratings such as 1, 2, and 3 are not very relevant. We can discard those and only keep scores of 4 and 5:

```
ratings = ratings[ratings.rating >= 4]
ratings
```

8.  This gives us the following output:

| | user_id | movie_id | rating | unix_timestamp |
|---|---|---|---|---|
| 5 | 298 | 474 | 4 | 884182806 |
| 7 | 253 | 465 | 5 | 891628467 |
| 11 | 286 | 1014 | 5 | 879781125 |
| ... | ... | ... | ... | ... |
| 99991 | 676 | 538 | 4 | 892685437 |
| 99996 | 716 | 204 | 5 | 879795543 |

55375 rows × 4 columns

9.  We now have 48,580 ratings made by 610 users. The next step is to count every time that two movies are liked by the same user. We will repeat this process for every user in the dataset.

10. To simplify things, we will use a `defaultdict` data structure, which automatically creates missing entries instead of raising an error. We'll use this structure to count movies that are liked together:

```
from collections import defaultdict

pairs = defaultdict(int)
```

11. We loop through the entire list of users in our dataset:

```
for group in ratings.groupby("userId"):
```

12. We retrieve the list of movies that have been liked by the current user:

```
user_movies = list(group[1]["movieId"])
```

13. We increment a counter specific to a pair of movies every time they are seen together in the same list:

```
for i in range(len(user_movies)):
        for j in range(i+1, len(user_movies)):
            pairs[(user_movies[i], user_movies[j])]
+= 1
```

14. The `pairs` object now stores the number of times two movies have been liked by the same user. We can use this information to build the edges of our graph as follows.

15. We create a graph using the `networkx` library:

```
G = nx.Graph()
```

16. For each pair of movies in our `pairs` structure, we unpack the two movies and their corresponding score:

```
for pair in pairs:
    movie1, movie2 = pair
    score = pairs[pair]
```

17. If this score is higher than 10, we add a weighted link to the graph to connect both movies based on this score. We don't consider scores lower than 10 because that would create a large graph in which connections were less meaningful:

```
if score >= 20:
    G.add_edge(movie1, movie2, weight=score)
```

18. The graph we created has 410 nodes (movies) and 14,936 edges. We can now train Node2Vec on it to learn the node embeddings!

We could reuse our implementation from the previous section, but there is actually an entire Python library dedicated to Node2Vec (also called `node2vec`). Let's try it in this example:

1. We install the `node2vec` library and import the `Node2Vec` class:

```
!pip install node2vec
from node2vec import Node2Vec
```

2. We create an instance of `Node2Vec` that will automatically generate biased random walks based on *p* and *q* parameters:

```
node2vec = Node2Vec(G, dimensions=64, walk_length=20,
num_walks=200, p=2, q=1, workers=1)
```

3. We train a model on these biased random walks with a window of 10 (5 nodes before, 5 nodes after):

```
model = node2vec.fit(window=10, min_count=1,
batch_words=4)
```

The Node2Vec model is trained and we can now use it the same way we use the Word2Vec object from the `gensim` library. Let's create a function to recommend movies based on a given title:

4. We create the `recommend()` function, which takes a movie title as input. It starts by converting the title into a movie ID we can use to query our model:

```
def recommend(movie):
    movie_id = str
        movies.title == movie].movie_id.values[0])
```

5.  We loop through the five most similar word vectors. We convert these IDs into movie titles that we print with their corresponding similarity scores:

```
for id in model.wv.most_similar(movie_id)[:5]:
        title = movies[movies.movie_id == int(id[0])].
    title.values[0]
        print(f'{title}: {id[1]:.2f}')
```

6.  We call this function to obtain the five movies that are the most similar to Star Wars in terms of cosine similarity:

```
recommend('Star Wars (1977)')
```

7.  We receive the following output:

```
Return of the Jedi (1983): 0.61
Raiders of the Lost Ark (1981): 0.55
Godfather, The (1972): 0.49
Indiana Jones and the Last Crusade (1989): 0.46
White Squall (1996): 0.44
```

The model tells us that `Return of the Jedi` and `Raiders of the Lost Ark` are the most similar to `Star Wars`, although with a relatively low score (< 0.7). Nonetheless, this is a good result for our first step into the RecSys world! In later chapters, we'll see more powerful models and approaches to building state-of-the-art RecSys.

## Summary

In this chapter, we learned about Node2Vec, a second architecture based on the popular Word2Vec. We implemented functions to generate biased random walks and explained the connection between their parameters and two network properties: homophily and structural equivalence. We showed their usefulness by comparing Node2Vec's results to DeepWalk's for Zachary's Karate Club. Finally, we built our first RecSys using a custom graph dataset and another implementation of Node2Vec. It gave us correct recommendations that we will improve even more in later chapters.

In *Chapter 5, Including Node Features with Vanilla Neural Networks*, we will talk about one overlooked issue concerning DeepWalk and Node2Vec: the lack of proper node features. We will try to address this problem using traditional neural networks, which cannot understand the network topology. This dilemma is important to understand before we finally introduce the answer: graph neural networks.

# Further reading

- [1] A. Grover and J. Leskovec, *node2vec: Scalable Feature Learning for Networks.* arXiv, 2016. DOI: 10.48550/ARXIV.1607.00653. Available: `https://arxiv.org/abs/1607.00653`.

- [2] F. Maxwell Harper and Joseph A. Konstan. 2015. *The MovieLens Datasets: History and Context. ACM Transactions on Interactive Intelligent Systems (TiiS)* 5, 4: 19:1–19:19. `https://doi.org/10.1145/2827872`. Available: `https://dl.acm.org/doi/10.1145/2827872`.

# 5
# Including Node Features with Vanilla Neural Networks

So far, the only type of information we've considered is the graph topology. However, graph datasets tend to be richer than a mere set of connections: nodes and edges can also have features to represent scores, colors, words, and so on. Including this additional information in our input data is essential to produce the best embeddings possible. In fact, this is something natural in machine learning: node and edge features have the same structure as a tabular (non-graph) dataset. This means that traditional techniques can be applied to this data, such as neural networks.

In this chapter, we will introduce two new graph datasets: `Cora` and `Facebook Page-Page`. We will see how **Vanilla Neural Networks** perform on node features only by considering them as tabular datasets. We will then experiment to include topological information in our neural networks. This will give us our first GNN architecture: a simple model that considers both node features and edges. Finally, we'll compare the performance of the two architectures and obtain one of the most important results of this book.

By the end of this chapter, you will master the implementation of vanilla neural networks and vanilla GNNs in PyTorch. You will be able to embed topological features into the node representations, which is the basis of every GNN architecture. This will allow you to greatly improve the performance of your models by transforming tabular datasets into graph problems.

In this chapter, we'll cover the following topics:

- Introducing graph datasets
- Classifying nodes with vanilla neural networks
- Classifying nodes with vanilla graph neural networks

# Technical requirements

All the code examples from this chapter can be found on GitHub at `https://github.com/PacktPublishing/Hands-On-Graph-Neural-Networks-Using-Python/tree/main/Chapter05`.

Installation steps required to run the code on your local machine can be found in the *Preface* of this book.

# Introducing graph datasets

The graph datasets we're going to use in this chapter are richer than Zachary's Karate Club: they have more nodes, more edges, and include node features. In this section, we will introduce them to give us a good understanding of these graphs and how to process them with PyTorch Geometric. Here are the two datasets we will use:

- The `Cora` dataset
- The `Facebook Page-Page` dataset

Let's start with the smaller one: the popular `Cora` dataset.

## The Cora dataset

Introduced by Sen et al. in 2008 [1], `Cora` (no license) is the most popular dataset for node classification in the scientific literature. It represents a network of 2,708 publications, where each connection is a reference. Each publication is described as a binary vector of 1,433 unique words, where 0 and 1 indicate the absence or presence of the corresponding word, respectively. This representation is also called a binary **bag of words** in natural language processing. Our goal is to classify each node into one of seven categories.

Regardless of the type of data, visualization is always an important step to getting a good grasp of the problem we face. However, graphs can quickly become too big to visualize using Python libraries such as `networkx`. This is why dedicated tools have been developed specifically for graph data visualization. In this book, we utilize two of the most popular ones: **yEd Live** (`https://www.yworks.com/yed-live/`) and **Gephi** (`https://gephi.org/`).

The following figure is a plot of the `Cora` dataset made with yEd Live. You can see nodes corresponding to papers in orange and connections between them in green. Some papers are so interconnected that they form clusters. These clusters should be easier to classify than poorly connected nodes.

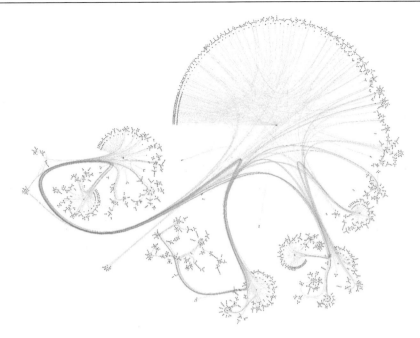

Figure 5.1 – The Cora dataset visualized with yEd Live

Let's import it and analyze its main characteristics with PyTorch Geometric. This library has a dedicated class to download the dataset and return a relevant data structure. We assume here that PyTorch Geometric has already been installed:

1.  We import the `Planetoid` class from PyTorch Geometric:

    ```
    from torch_geometric.datasets import Planetoid
    ```

2.  We download it using this class:

    ```
    dataset = Planetoid(root=".", name="Cora")
    ```

3.  `Cora` only has one graph we can store in a dedicated `data` variable:

    ```
    data = dataset[0]
    ```

4.  Let's print information about the dataset in general:

    ```
    print(f'Dataset: {dataset}')
    print('---------------')
    print(f'Number of graphs: {len(dataset)}')
    print(f'Number of nodes: {data.x.shape[0]}')
    ```

```
print(f'Number of features: {dataset.num_features}')
print(f'Number of classes: {dataset.num_classes}')
```

5.  This gives us the following output:

```
Dataset: Cora()
---------------
Number of graphs: 1
Number of nodes: 2708
Number of features: 1433
Number of classes: 7
```

6.  We can also get detailed information thanks to dedicated functions from PyTorch Geometric:

```
print(f'Graph:')
print('------')
print(f'Edges are directed: {data.is_directed()}')
print(f'Graph has isolated nodes: {data.has_isolated_
nodes()}')
print(f'Graph has loops: {data.has_self_loops()}')
```

7.  This is the result of the previous block:

```
Graph:
------
Edges are directed: False
Graph has isolated nodes: False
Graph has loops: False
```

The first output confirms the information about the number of nodes, features, and classes. The second one gives more insights into the graph itself: edges are undirected, every node has neighbors, and the graph doesn't have any self-loop. We could test other properties using PyTorch Geometric's utils functions, but we wouldn't learn anything new in this example.

Now that we know more about Cora, let's see one that is more representative of the size of real-world social networks: the Facebook Page-Page dataset.

## The Facebook Page-Page dataset

This dataset was introduced by Rozemberczki et al. in 2019 [2]. It was created using the Facebook Graph API in November 2017. In this dataset, each of the 22,470 nodes represents an official Facebook page. Pages are connected when there are mutual likes between them. Node features (128-dim vectors) are created from textual descriptions written by the owners of these pages. Our goal is to classify each node into one of four categories: politicians, companies, television shows, and governmental organizations.

The Facebook Page-Page dataset is similar to the previous one: it's a social network with a node classification task. However, there are three major differences with Cora:

- The number of nodes is much higher (2,708 versus 22,470)

- The dimensionality of the node features decreased dramatically (from 1,433 to 128)

- The goal is to classify each node into four categories instead of seven (which is easier since there are fewer options)

The following figure is a visualization of the dataset using Gephi. First, nodes with few connections have been filtered out to improve performance. The size of the remaining nodes depends on their number of connections, and their color indicates the category they belong to. Finally, two layouts have been applied: Fruchterman-Reingold and ForceAtlas2.

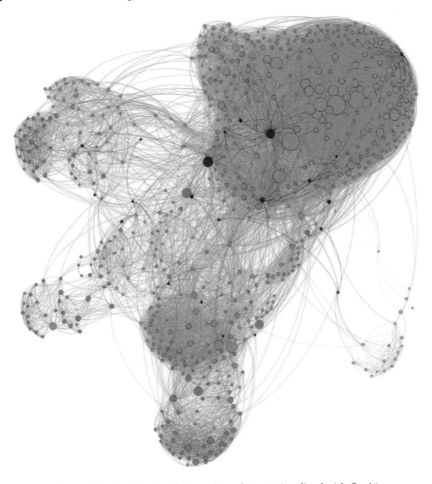

Figure 5.2 – The Facebook Page-Page dataset visualized with Gephi

We can import the Facebook Page-Page dataset the same way we did it for Cora:

1.  We import the FacebookPagePage class from PyTorch Geometric:

    ```
    from torch_geometric.datasets import FacebookPagePage
    ```

2.  We download it using this class:

    ```
    dataset = FacebookPagePage(root=".")
    ```

3.  We store the graph in a dedicated data variable:

    ```
    data = dataset[0]
    ```

4.  Let's print information about the dataset in general:

    ```
    print(f'Dataset: {dataset}')
    print('-----------------------')
    print(f'Number of graphs: {len(dataset)}')
    print(f'Number of nodes: {data.x.shape[0]}')
    print(f'Number of features: {dataset.num_features}')
    print(f'Number of classes: {dataset.num_classes}')
    ```

5.  This gives us the following output:

    ```
    Dataset: FacebookPagePage()
    -----------------------
    Number of graphs: 1
    Number of nodes: 22470
    Number of features: 128
    Number of classes: 4
    ```

6.  The same dedicated functions can be applied here:

    ```
    print(f'\nGraph:')
    print('------')
    print(f'Edges are directed: {data.is_directed()}')
    print(f'Graph has isolated nodes: {data.has_isolated_
    nodes()}')
    print(f'Graph has loops: {data.has_self_loops()}')
    ```

This is the result of the previous block:

```
Graph:
------
Edges are directed: False
Graph has isolated nodes: False
Graph has loops: True
```

7.  Unlike Cora, Facebook Page-Page doesn't have training, evaluation, and test masks by default. We can arbitrarily create masks with the range() function:

```
data.train_mask = range(18000)
data.val_mask = range(18001, 20000)
data.test_mask = range(20001, 22470)
```

Alternatively, PyTorch Geometric offers a transform function to calculate random masks when the dataset is loaded:

```
import torch_geometric.transforms as T
dataset = Planetoid(root=".", name="Cora")
data = dataset[0]
```

The first output confirms the number of nodes and classes we saw in the description of the dataset. The second output tells us that this graph has self loops: some pages are connected to themselves. This is surprising but, in practice, it will not matter, as we're going to see soon.

These are the two graph datasets we will use in the next section, to compare the performance of a Vanilla Neural Network to the performance of our first GNN. Let's implement them step by step.

## Classifying nodes with vanilla neural networks

Compared to Zachary's Karate Club, these two datasets include a new type of information: node features. They provide additional information about the nodes in a graph, such as a user's age, gender, or interests in a social network. In a vanilla neural network (also called **multilayer perceptron**), these embeddings are directly used in the model to perform downstream tasks such as node classification.

In this section, we will consider node features as a regular tabular dataset. We will train a simple neural network on this dataset to classify our nodes. Note that this architecture does not take into account the topology of the network. We will try to fix this issue in the next section and compare our results.

The tabular dataset of node features can be easily accessed through the data object we created. First, I would like to convert this object into a regular pandas DataFrame by merging data.x (containing the node features) and data.y (containing the class label of each node among seven classes). In the following, we will use the Cora dataset:

```
import pandas as pd

df_x = pd.DataFrame(data.x.numpy())
df_x['label'] = pd.DataFrame(data.y)
```

This gives us the following dataset:

| | 0 | 1 | ... | 1432 | label |
|---|---|---|---|---|---|
| **0** | 0 | 0 | ... | 0 | 3 |
| **1** | 0 | 0 | ... | 0 | 4 |
| **...** | ... | ... | ... | ... | ... |
| **2707** | 0 | 0 | ... | 0 | 3 |

Figure 5.3 – Tabular representation of the Cora dataset (without topological information)

If you're familiar with machine learning, you probably recognize a typical dataset with data and labels. We can develop a simple **Multilayer Perceptron (MLP)** and train it on data.x with the labels provided by data.y.

Let's create our own MLP class with four methods:

- __init__() to initialize an instance
- forward() to perform the forward pass
- fit() to train the model
- test() to evaluate it

Before we can train our model, we must define the main metric. There are several metrics for multiclass classification problems: accuracy, F1 score, **Area Under the Receiver Operating Characteristic Curve (ROC AUC)** score, and so on. For this work, let's implement a simple accuracy, which is defined as the fraction of correct predictions. It is not the best metric for multiclass classification, but it is simpler to understand. Feel free to replace it with your metric of choice:

```
def accuracy(y_pred, y_true):
    return torch.sum(y_pred == y_true) / len(y_true)
```

Now, we can start the actual implementation. We don't need PyTorch Geometric to implement the MLP in this section. Everything can be done in regular PyTorch with the following steps:

1.  We import the required classes from PyTorch:

```
import torch
from torch.nn import Linear
import torch.nn.functional as F
```

2.  We create a new class called MLP, which will inherit all the methods and properties from `torch.nn.Module`:

```
class MLP(torch.nn.Module):
```

3.  The `__init__()` method has three arguments (`dim_in`, `dim_h`, and `dim_out`) for the number of neurons in the input, hidden, and output layers, respectively. We also define two linear layers:

```
def __init__(self, dim_in, dim_h, dim_out):
    super().__init__()
    self.linear1 = Linear(dim_in, dim_h)
    self.linear2 = Linear(dim_h, dim_out)
```

4.  The `forward()` method performs the forward pass. The input is fed to the first linear layer with a **Rectified Linear Unit (ReLU)** activation function, and the result is passed to the second linear layer. We return the log softmax of this final result for classification:

```
def forward(self, x):
    x = self.linear1(x)
    x = torch.relu(x)
    x = self.linear2(x)
    return F.log_softmax(x, dim=1)
```

5.  The `fit()` method is in charge of the training loop. First, we initialize a loss function and an optimizer that will be used during the training process:

```
def fit(self, data, epochs):
    criterion = torch.nn.CrossEntropyLoss()
    optimizer = torch.optim.Adam(self.parameters(),
lr=0.01, weight_decay=5e-4)
```

6. A regular PyTorch training loop is then implemented. We use our `accuracy()` function on top of the loss function:

```
self.train()
for epoch in range(epochs+1):
    optimizer.zero_grad()
    out = self(data.x)
    loss = criterion(out[data.train_mask],
data.y[data.train_mask])
    acc = accuracy(out[data.train_mask].
argmax(dim=1), data.y[data.train_mask])
    loss.backward()
    optimizer.step()
```

7. In the same loop, we plot the loss and accuracy for training and evaluation data every 20 epochs:

```
if epoch % 20 == 0:
    val_loss = criterion(out[data.val_mask],
data.y[data.val_mask])
    val_acc = accuracy(out[data.val_mask].
argmax(dim=1), data.y[data.val_mask])
    print(f'Epoch {epoch:>3} | Train Loss:
{loss:.3f} | Train Acc: {acc*100:>5.2f}% | Val Loss:
{val_loss:.2f} | Val Acc: {val_acc*100:.2f}%')
```

8. The `test()` method evaluates the model on the test set and returns the accuracy score:

```
def test(self, data):
    self.eval()
    out = self(data.x)
    acc = accuracy(out.argmax(dim=1)[data.test_mask],
data.y[data.test_mask])
    return acc
```

Now that our class is complete, we can create, train, and test an instance of MLP.

We have two datasets, so we need a model dedicated to `Cora` and another one for `Facebook Page-Page`. First, let's train an MLP on `Cora`:

1. We create an MLP model and print it to check that our layers are correct:

```
mlp = MLP(dataset.num_features, 16, dataset.num_classes)
print(mlp)
```

2.  This gives us the following output:

```
MLP(
    (linear1): Linear(in_features=1433, out_features=16,
bias=True)
    (linear2): Linear(in_features=16, out_features=7,
bias=True)
)
```

3.  Good, we get the right number of features. Let's train this model for 100 epochs:

```
mlp.fit(data, epochs=100)
```

4.  Here are the metrics that are printed in the training loop:

```
Epoch   0 | Train Loss: 1.954 | Train Acc: 14.29% | Val
Loss: 1.93 | Val Acc: 30.80%
Epoch  20 | Train Loss: 0.120 | Train Acc: 100.00% | Val
Loss: 1.42 | Val Acc: 49.40%
Epoch  40 | Train Loss: 0.015 | Train Acc: 100.00% | Val
Loss: 1.46 | Val Acc: 50.40%
Epoch  60 | Train Loss: 0.008 | Train Acc: 100.00% | Val
Loss: 1.44 | Val Acc: 53.40%
Epoch  80 | Train Loss: 0.008 | Train Acc: 100.00% | Val
Loss: 1.40 | Val Acc: 54.60%
Epoch 100 | Train Loss: 0.009 | Train Acc: 100.00% | Val
Loss: 1.39 | Val Acc: 54.20%
```

5.  Finally, we can evaluate its performance in terms of accuracy with the following lines:

```
acc = mlp.test(data)
print(f'MLP test accuracy: {acc*100:.2f}%')
```

6.  We obtain the following accuracy score on test data:

```
MLP test accuracy: 52.50%
```

7.  We repeat the same process for the Facebook Page-Page dataset, and here is the output we obtain:

```
Epoch   0 | Train Loss: 1.398 | Train Acc: 23.94% | Val
Loss: 1.40 | Val Acc: 24.21%
Epoch  20 | Train Loss: 0.652 | Train Acc: 74.52% | Val
Loss: 0.67 | Val Acc: 72.64%
```

```
Epoch  40 | Train Loss: 0.577 | Train Acc: 77.07% | Val
Loss: 0.61 | Val Acc: 73.84%
Epoch  60 | Train Loss: 0.550 | Train Acc: 78.30% | Val
Loss: 0.60 | Val Acc: 75.09%
Epoch  80 | Train Loss: 0.533 | Train Acc: 78.89% | Val
Loss: 0.60 | Val Acc: 74.79%
Epoch 100 | Train Loss: 0.520 | Train Acc: 79.49% | Val
Loss: 0.61 | Val Acc: 74.94%
MLP test accuracy: 74.52%
```

Even though these datasets are similar in some aspects, we can see that the accuracy scores we obtain are vastly different. This will make an interesting comparison when we combine node features and network topology in the same model.

## Classifying nodes with vanilla graph neural networks

Instead of directly introducing well-known GNN architectures, let's try to build our own model to understand the thought process behind GNNs. First, we need to go back to the definition of a simple linear layer.

A basic neural network layer corresponds to a linear transformation $h_A = x_A W^T$, where $x_A$ is the input vector of node $A$ and $W$ is the weight matrix. In PyTorch, this equation can be implemented with the `torch.mm()` function, or with the `nn.Linear` class that adds other parameters such as biases.

With our graph datasets, the input vectors are node features. It means that nodes are completely separate from each other. This is not enough to capture a good understanding of the graph: like a pixel in an image, the context of a node is essential to understand it. If you look at a group of pixels instead of a single one, you can recognize edges, patterns, and so on. Likewise, to understand a node, you need to look at its neighborhood.

Let's call $N_A$ the set of neighbors of node $A$. Our **graph linear layer** can be written as follows:

$$h_A = \sum_{i \in \mathcal{N}_A} x_i W^T$$

You can imagine several variants of this equation. For instance, we could have a weight matrix $W_1$ dedicated to the central node, and another one $W_2$ for the neighbors. Note that we cannot have a weight matrix per neighbor, as this number can change from node to node.

We're talking about neural networks, so we can't apply the previous equation to each node. Instead, we perform matrix multiplications that are much more efficient. For instance, the equation of the linear layer can be rewritten as $H = XW^T$, where $X$ is the input matrix.

In our case, the adjacency matrix $A$ contains the connections between every node in the graph. Multiplying the input matrix by this adjacency matrix will directly sum up the neighboring node features. We can add self loops to the adjacency matrix so that the central node is also considered in this operation. We call this updated adjacency matrix $\tilde{A} = A + I$. Our graph linear layer can be rewritten as follows:

$$H = \tilde{A}^T X W^T$$

Let's test this layer by implementing it in PyTorch Geometric. We'll then be able to use it as a regular layer to build a GNN:

1.  First, we create a new class, which is a subclass of torch.nn.Module:

    ```
    class VanillaGNNLayer(torch.nn.Module):
    ```

2.  This class takes two parameters, dim_in and dim_out, for the number of features of the input and the output, respectively. We add a basic linear transformation without bias:

    ```
    def __init__(self, dim_in, dim_out):
        super().__init__()
        self.linear = Linear(dim_in, dim_out, bias=False)
    ```

3.  We perform two operations – the linear transformation, and then the multiplication with the adjacency matrix $\tilde{A}$:

    ```
    def forward(self, x, adjacency):
        x = self.linear(x)
        x = torch.sparse.mm(adjacency, x)
        return x
    ```

    Before we can create our vanilla GNN, we need to convert the edge index from our dataset (data.edge_index) in coordinate format to a dense adjacency matrix. We also need to include self loops; otherwise, the central nodes won't be taken into account in their own embeddings.

4.  This is easily implemented with the to_den_adj() and torch.eye() functions:

    ```
    from torch_geometric.utils import to_dense_adj

    adjacency = to_dense_adj(data.edge_index)[0]
    adjacency += torch.eye(len(adjacency))
    adjacency
    ```

Here is what the adjacency matrix looks like:

```
tensor([[0., 0., 0.,   ..., 0., 0., 0.],
        [0., 0., 0.,   ..., 0., 0., 0.],
        [0., 0., 0.,   ..., 0., 0., 0.],
        ...,
        [0., 0., 0.,   ..., 0., 0., 0.],
        [0., 0., 0.,   ..., 0., 0., 0.],
        [0., 0., 0.,   ..., 0., 0., 0.]])
```

Unfortunately, we only see zeros in this tensor because it's a sparse matrix. A more detailed print would show a few connections between nodes (represented by ones). Now that we have our dedicated layer and the adjacency matrix, the implementation of the vanilla GNN is very similar to that of the MLP.

5.  We create a new class with two vanilla graph linear layers:

```
class VanillaGNN(torch.nn.Module):
    def __init__(self, dim_in, dim_h, dim_out):
        super().__init__()
        self.gnn1 = VanillaGNNLayer(dim_in, dim_h)
        self.gnn2 = VanillaGNNLayer(dim_h, dim_out)
```

6.  We perform the same operations with our new layers, which take the adjacency matrix we previously calculated as an additional input:

```
def forward(self, x, adjacency):
    h = self.gnn1(x, adjacency)
    h = torch.relu(h)
    h = self.gnn2(h, adjacency)
    return F.log_softmax(h, dim=1)
```

7.  The fit() and test() methods work in the exact same way:

```
def fit(self, data, epochs):
    criterion = torch.nn.CrossEntropyLoss()
    optimizer = torch.optim.Adam(self.parameters(),
lr=0.01, weight_decay=5e-4)
    self.train()
    for epoch in range(epochs+1):
        optimizer.zero_grad()
        out = self(data.x, adjacency)
```

```
            loss = criterion(out[data.train_mask],
data.y[data.train_mask])
            acc = accuracy(out[data.train_mask].
argmax(dim=1), data.y[data.train_mask])
            loss.backward()
            optimizer.step()
            if epoch % 20 == 0:
                val_loss = criterion(out[data.val_mask],
data.y[data.val_mask])
                val_acc = accuracy(out[data.val_mask].
argmax(dim=1), data.y[data.val_mask])
                print(f'Epoch {epoch:>3} | Train Loss:
{loss:.3f} | Train Acc: {acc*100:>5.2f}% | Val Loss:
{val_loss:.2f} | Val Acc: {val_acc*100:.2f}%')

    def test(self, data):
        self.eval()
        out = self(data.x, adjacency)
        acc = accuracy(out.argmax(dim=1)[data.test_mask],
data.y[data.test_mask])
        return acc
```

8. We can create, train, and evaluate our model with the following lines:

```
gnn = VanillaGNN(dataset.num_features, 16, dataset.num_
classes)
print(gnn)
gnn.fit(data, epochs=100)
acc = gnn.test(data)
print(f'\nGNN test accuracy: {acc*100:.2f}%')
```

9. This gives us the following output:

```
VanillaGNN(
  (gnn1): VanillaGNNLayer(
    (linear): Linear(in_features=1433, out_features=16,
bias=False)
  )
  (gnn2): VanillaGNNLayer(
    (linear): Linear(in_features=16, out_features=7,
```

```
bias=False)
  )
)
Epoch    0 | Train Loss: 2.008 | Train Acc: 20.00% | Val
Loss: 1.96 | Val Acc: 23.40%
Epoch   20 | Train Loss: 0.047 | Train Acc: 100.00% | Val
Loss: 2.04 | Val Acc: 74.60%
Epoch   40 | Train Loss: 0.004 | Train Acc: 100.00% | Val
Loss: 2.49 | Val Acc: 75.20%
Epoch   60 | Train Loss: 0.002 | Train Acc: 100.00% | Val
Loss: 2.61 | Val Acc: 74.60%
Epoch   80 | Train Loss: 0.001 | Train Acc: 100.00% | Val
Loss: 2.61 | Val Acc: 75.20%
Epoch  100 | Train Loss: 0.001 | Train Acc: 100.00% | Val
Loss: 2.56 | Val Acc: 75.00%

GNN test accuracy: 76.80%
```

We replicate the same training process with the Facebook Page-Page dataset. In order to obtain comparable results, the same experiment is repeated 100 times for each model on each dataset. The following table summarizes the results:

|  | MLP | GNN |
| --- | --- | --- |
| **Cora** | 53.47% | 74.98% |
|  | (±1.81%) | (±1.50%) |
| **Facebook** | 75.21% | 84.85% |
|  | (±0.40%) | (±1.68%) |

Figure 5.4 – Summary of accuracy scores with a standard deviation

As we can see, the MLP has poor accuracy on Cora. It performs better on the Facebook Page-Page dataset but is still surpassed by our vanilla GNN in both cases. These results show the importance of including topological information in node features. Instead of a tabular dataset, our GNN considers the entire neighborhood of each node, which leads to a 10-20% boost in terms of accuracy in these examples. This architecture is still crude, but it gives us a guideline to refine it and build even better models.

# Summary

In this chapter, we learned about the missing link between vanilla neural networks and GNNs. We built our own GNN architecture using our intuition and a bit of linear algebra. We explored two popular graph datasets from the scientific literature to compare our two architectures. Finally, we implemented them in PyTorch and evaluated their performance. The result is clear: even our intuitive version of a GNN completely outperforms the MLP on both datasets.

In *Chapter 6, Normalizing Embeddings with Graph Convolutional Networks*, we refine our vanilla GNN architecture to correctly normalize its inputs. This graph convolutional network model is an incredibly efficient baseline we'll keep using in the rest of the book. We will compare its results on our two previous datasets and introduce a new interesting task: node regression.

# Further reading

- [1] P. Sen, G. Namata, M. Bilgic, L. Getoor, B. Galligher, and T. Eliassi-Rad, "Collective Classification in Network Data", AIMag, vol. 29, no. 3, p. 93, Sep. 2008. Available: `https://ojs.aaai.org//index.php/aimagazine/article/view/2157`

- [2] B. Rozemberczki, C. Allen, and R. Sarkar, Multi-Scale Attributed Node Embedding. arXiv, 2019. doi: 10.48550/ARXIV.1909.13021. Available: `https://arxiv.org/abs/1909.13021`

# 6

# Introducing Graph Convolutional Networks

The **Graph Convolutional Network (GCN)** architecture is the blueprint of what a GNN looks like. Introduced by Kipf and Welling in 2017 [1], it is based on the idea of creating an efficient variant of **Convolutional Neural Networks (CNNs)** applied to graphs. More accurately, it is an approximation of a graph convolution operation in graph signal processing. Thanks to its versatility and ease of use, the GCN has become the most popular GNN in scientific literature. More generally, it is the architecture of choice to create a solid baseline when dealing with graph data.

In this chapter, we'll talk about the limitations of our previous vanilla GNN layer. This will help us to understand the motivation behind GCNs. We'll detail how the GCN layer works and why it performs better than our solution. We'll test this statement by implementing a GCN on the `Cora` and `Facebook Page-Page` datasets using PyTorch Geometric. This should improve our results even further.

The last section is dedicated to a new task: **node regression**. This is not a very common task when it comes to GNNs, but it is particularly useful when you're working with tabular data. If you have the opportunity to transform your tabular dataset into a graph, this will enable you to perform regression in addition to classification.

By the end of this chapter, you will be able to implement a GCN in PyTorch Geometric for classification or regression tasks. Thanks to linear algebra, you'll understand why this model performs better than our vanilla GNN. Finally, you'll know how to plot node degrees and the density distribution of a target variable.

In this chapter, we'll cover the following topics:

- Designing the graph convolutional layer
- Comparing graph convolutional and graph linear layers
- Predicting web traffic with node regression

## Technical requirements

All the code examples from this chapter can be found on GitHub at `https://github.com/PacktPublishing/Hands-On-Graph-Neural-Networks-Using-Python/tree/main/Chapter06`.

Installation steps required to run the code on your local machine can be found in the *Preface* section of this book.

## Designing the graph convolutional layer

First, let's talk about a problem we did not anticipate in the previous chapter. Unlike tabular or image data, nodes do not always have the same number of neighbors. For instance, in *Figure 6.1*, node 1 has 3 neighbors while node 2 only has 1:

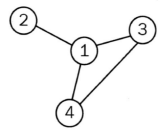

Figure 6.1 – Simple graph where nodes have different numbers of neighbors

However, if we look at our GNN layer, we don't take into account this difference in the number of neighbors. Our layer consists of a simple sum without any normalization coefficient. Here is how we calculated the embedding of a node, $i$:

$$h_i = \sum_{j \in \mathcal{N}_i} x_j W^T$$

Imagine that node 1 has 1,000 neighbors and node 2 only has 1: the embedding $h_A$ will have much larger values than $h_B$. This is an issue because we want to compare these embeddings. How are we supposed to make meaningful comparisons when their values are so vastly different?

Fortunately, there is a simple solution: dividing the embedding by the number of neighbors. Let's write $\deg(A)$, the degree of node $A$. Here is the new formula for the GNN layer:

$$h_i = \frac{1}{\deg(i)} \sum_{j \in \mathcal{N}_i} x_j W^T$$

But how do we translate it into a matrix multiplication? As a reminder, this was what we obtained for our vanilla GNN layer:

$$H = \tilde{A}^T X W^T$$

Here, $\tilde{A} = A + I$ .

The only thing that is missing from this formula is a matrix to give us the normalization coefficient, $\frac{1}{deg(i)}$. This is something that can be obtained thanks to the degree matrix $D$, which counts the number of neighbors for each node. Here is the degree matrix for the graph shown in *Figure 6.1*:

$$D = \begin{pmatrix} 3 & 0 & 0 & 0 \\ 0 & 1 & 0 & 0 \\ 0 & 0 & 2 & 0 \\ 0 & 0 & 0 & 2 \end{pmatrix}$$

Here is the same matrix in NumPy:

```
import numpy as np

D = np.array([
    [3, 0, 0, 0],
    [0, 1, 0, 0],
    [0, 0, 2, 0],
    [0, 0, 0, 2]
])
```

By definition, $D$ gives us the degree of each node, $deg(i)$. Therefore, the inverse of this matrix $D^{-1}$ directly gives us the normalization coefficients, $\frac{1}{deg(i)}$:

$$D^{-1} = \begin{pmatrix} \frac{1}{3} & 0 & 0 & 0 \\ 0 & 1 & 0 & 0 \\ 0 & 0 & \frac{1}{2} & 0 \\ 0 & 0 & 0 & \frac{1}{2} \end{pmatrix}$$

The inverse of a matrix can directly be calculated using the numpy.linalg.inv() function:

```
np.linalg.inv(D)
array([[0.33333333, 0.        , 0.        , 0.        ],
       [0.        , 1.        , 0.        , 0.        ],
       [0.        , 0.        , 0.5       , 0.        ],
       [0.        , 0.        , 0.        , 0.5       ]])
```

This is exactly what we were looking for. To be even more accurate, we added self-loops to the graph, represented by $\tilde{A} = A + I$. Likewise, we should add self-loops to the degree matrix, $\tilde{D} = D + I$. The final matrix we are actually interested in is $\tilde{D}^{-1} = (D + I)^{-1}$:

$$
\tilde{D}^{-1} = \begin{pmatrix} \frac{1}{4} & 0 & 0 & 0 \\ 0 & \frac{1}{2} & 0 & 0 \\ 0 & 0 & \frac{1}{3} & 0 \\ 0 & 0 & 0 & \frac{1}{3} \end{pmatrix}
$$

NumPy has a specific function, numpy.identity(n), to quickly create an identity matrix $I$ of $n$ dimensions. In this example, we have four dimensions:

```
np.linalg.inv(D + np.identity(4))
array([[0.25      , 0.       , 0.        , 0.        ],
       [0.       , 0.5      , 0.        , 0.        ],
       [0.       , 0.       , 0.33333333, 0.        ],
       [0.       , 0.       , 0.        , 0.33333333]])
```

Now that we have our matrix of normalization coefficients, where should we put it in the formula? There are two options:

- $\tilde{D}^{-1}\tilde{A}XW^T$ will normalize every row of features.

- $\tilde{A}\tilde{D}^{-1}XW^T$ will normalize every column of features.

We can verify this experimentally by calculating $\tilde{D}^{-1}\tilde{A}$ and $\tilde{A}\tilde{D}^{-1}$.

$$
\tilde{D}^{-1}\tilde{A} = \begin{pmatrix} \frac{1}{4} & 0 & 0 & 0 \\ 0 & \frac{1}{2} & 0 & 0 \\ 0 & 0 & \frac{1}{3} & 0 \\ 0 & 0 & 0 & \frac{1}{3} \end{pmatrix} \cdot \begin{pmatrix} 1 & 1 & 1 & 1 \\ 1 & 1 & 0 & 0 \\ 1 & 0 & 1 & 1 \\ 1 & 0 & 1 & 1 \end{pmatrix} = \begin{pmatrix} \frac{1}{4} & \frac{1}{4} & \frac{1}{4} & \frac{1}{4} \\ \frac{1}{2} & \frac{1}{2} & 0 & 0 \\ \frac{1}{3} & 0 & \frac{1}{3} & \frac{1}{3} \\ \frac{1}{3} & 0 & \frac{1}{3} & \frac{1}{3} \end{pmatrix}
$$

$$
\tilde{A}\tilde{D}^{-1} = \begin{pmatrix} 1 & 1 & 1 & 1 \\ 1 & 1 & 0 & 0 \\ 1 & 0 & 1 & 1 \\ 1 & 0 & 1 & 1 \end{pmatrix} \cdot \begin{pmatrix} \frac{1}{4} & 0 & 0 & 0 \\ 0 & \frac{1}{2} & 0 & 0 \\ 0 & 0 & \frac{1}{3} & 0 \\ 0 & 0 & 0 & \frac{1}{3} \end{pmatrix} = \begin{pmatrix} \frac{1}{4} & \frac{1}{2} & \frac{1}{3} & \frac{1}{3} \\ \frac{1}{4} & \frac{1}{2} & 0 & 0 \\ \frac{1}{4} & 0 & \frac{1}{3} & \frac{1}{3} \\ \frac{1}{4} & 0 & \frac{1}{3} & \frac{1}{3} \end{pmatrix}
$$

Indeed, in the first case, the sum of every row is equal to 1. In the second case, the sum of every column is equal to 1.

Matrix multiplications can be performed using the `numpy.matmul()` function. Even more conveniently, Python has had its own matrix multiplication operator, @, since version 3.5. Let's define the adjacency matrix $A$ and use this operator to compute our matrix multiplications:

```
A = np.array([
    [1, 1, 1, 1],
    [1, 1, 0, 0],
    [1, 0, 1, 1],
    [1, 0, 1, 1]
])
```

```
print(np.linalg.inv(D + np.identity(4)) @ A)
[[0.25       0.25       0.25       0.25      ]
 [0.5        0.5        0.         0.        ]
 [0.33333333 0.         0.33333333 0.33333333]
 [0.33333333 0.         0.33333333 0.33333333]]
```

```
print(A @ np.linalg.inv(D + np.identity(4)))
[[0.25       0.5        0.33333333 0.33333333]
 [0.25       0.5        0.         0.        ]
 [0.25       0.         0.33333333 0.33333333]
 [0.25       0.         0.33333333 0.33333333]]
```

We obtain the same results as with manual matrix multiplication.

So, which option should we use? Naturally, the first option looks more appealing because it nicely normalizes neighboring node features.

However, Kipf and Welling [1] noticed that features from nodes with a lot of neighbors spread very easily, unlike features from more isolated nodes. In the original GCN paper, the authors proposed a hybrid normalization to counterbalance this effect. In practice, they assign higher weights to nodes with few neighbors using the following formula:

$$H = \tilde{D}^{-\frac{1}{2}} \tilde{A}^T \tilde{D}^{-\frac{1}{2}} X W^T$$

In terms of individual embeddings, this operation can be written as follows:

$$h_i = \sum_{j \in \mathcal{N}_i} \frac{1}{\sqrt{\deg(i)} \sqrt{\deg(j)}} x_j W^T$$

Those are the original formulas to implement a graph convolutional layer. As with our vanilla GNN layer, we can stack these layers to create a GCN. Let's implement a GCN and verify that it performs better than our previous approaches.

## Comparing graph convolutional and graph linear layers

In the previous chapter, our vanilla GNN outperformed the Node2Vec model, but how does it compare to a GCN? In this section, we will compare their performance on the Cora and Facebook Page-Page datasets.

Compared to the vanilla GNN, the main feature of the GCN is that it considers node degrees to weigh its features. Before the real implementation, let's analyze the node degrees in both datasets. This information is relevant since it is directly linked to the performance of the GCN.

From what we know about this architecture, we expect it to perform better when node degrees vary greatly. If every node has the same number of neighbors, these architectures are equivalent: ($\sqrt{\deg(i)}\sqrt{\deg(i)} = \deg(i)$):

1.  We import the `Planetoid` class from PyTorch Geometric. To visualize the node degrees, we also import `matplotlib` and two additional classes: `degree` to get the number of neighbors of each node and `Counter` to count the number of nodes for each degree:

    ```
    from torch_geometric.datasets import Planetoid
    from torch_geometric.utils import degree
    from collections import Counter
    import matplotlib.pyplot as plt
    ```

2.  The Cora dataset is imported and its graph is stored in `data`:

    ```
    dataset = Planetoid(root=".", name="Cora")
    data = dataset[0]
    ```

3.  We compute the number of neighbors of each node in the graph:

    ```
    degrees = degree(data.edge_index[0]).numpy()
    ```

4.  To produce a more natural visualization, we count the number of nodes for each degree:

```
numbers = Counter(degrees)
```

5.  Let's plot this result using a bar plot:

```
fig, ax = plt.subplots()
ax.set_xlabel('Node degree')
ax.set_ylabel('Number of nodes')
plt.bar(numbers.keys(), numbers.values())
```

That gives us the following plot.

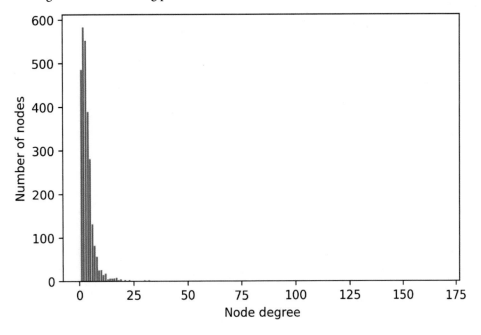

Figure 6.2 – Number of nodes with specific node degrees in the Cora dataset

This distribution looks exponential with a heavy tail: it ranges from 1 neighbor (485 nodes) to 168 neighbors (1 node)! This is exactly the kind of dataset where we want a normalization process to consider this disbalance.

The same process is repeated with the Facebook Page-Page dataset with the following result:

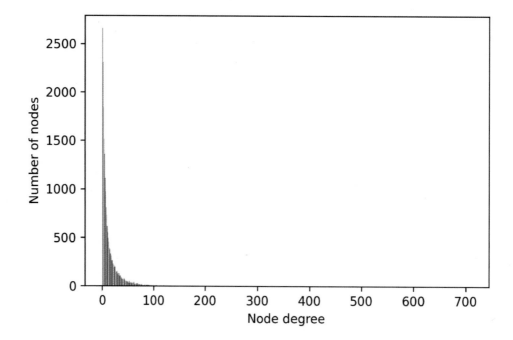

Figure 6.3 – Number of nodes with specific node degrees in the Facebook Page-Page dataset

This distribution of node degrees looks even more skewed, with a number of neighbors that ranges from 1 to 709. For the same reason, the Facebook Page-Page dataset is also a good case in which to apply a GCN.

We could build our own graph layer but, conveniently enough, PyTorch Geometric already has a predefined GCN layer. Let's implement it on the Cora dataset first:

1.  We import PyTorch and the GCN layer from PyTorch Geometric:

    ```
    import torch
    import torch.nn.functional as F
    from torch_geometric.nn import GCNConv
    ```

2.  We create a function to calculate the accuracy score:

    ```
    def accuracy(pred_y, y):
        return ((pred_y == y).sum() / len(y)).item()
    ```

3.  We create a GCN class with a `__init__()` function that takes three parameters as input: the number of input dimensions, `dim_in`, the number of hidden dimensions, `dim_h`, and the number of output dimensions, `dim_out`:

```
class GCN(torch.nn.Module):
    """Graph Convolutional Network"""
    def __init__(self, dim_in, dim_h, dim_out):
        super().__init__()
        self.gcn1 = GCNConv(dim_in, dim_h)
        self.gcn2 = GCNConv(dim_h, dim_out)
```

4.  The `forward` method is identical, and has two GCN layers. A log `softmax` function is applied to the result for classification:

```
def forward(self, x, edge_index):
    h = self.gcn1(x, edge_index)
    h = torch.relu(h)
    h = self.gcn2(h, edge_index)
    return F.log_softmax(h, dim=1)
```

5.  The `fit()` method is the same, with the exact same parameters for the Adam optimizer (a learning rate of 0.1 and L2 regularization of 0.0005):

```
def fit(self, data, epochs):
    criterion = torch.nn.CrossEntropyLoss()
    optimizer = torch.optim.Adam(self.parameters(),
                                 lr=0.01,
                                 weight_decay=5e-4)

    self.train()
    for epoch in range(epochs+1):
        optimizer.zero_grad()
        out = self(data.x, data.edge_index)
        loss = criterion(out[data.train_mask],
data.y[data.train_mask])
        acc = accuracy(out[data.train_mask].
argmax(dim=1), data.y[data.train_mask])
        loss.backward()
        optimizer.step()

        if(epoch % 20 == 0):
```

```
                    val_loss = criterion(out[data.val_mask],
        data.y[data.val_mask])

                        val_acc = accuracy(out[data.val_mask].
        argmax(dim=1), data.y[data.val_mask])

                        print(f'Epoch {epoch:>3} | Train Loss:
        {loss:.3f} | Train Acc: {acc*100:>5.2f}% | Val Loss:
        {val_loss:.2f} | Val Acc: {val_acc*100:.2f}%')
```

6.  We implement the same `test()` method:

```
    @torch.no_grad()
    def test(self, data):
        self.eval()
        out = self(data.x, data.edge_index)
        acc = accuracy(out.argmax(dim=1)[data.test_mask],
        data.y[data.test_mask])
        return acc
```

7.  Let's instantiate and train our model for `100` epochs:

```
    gcn = GCN(dataset.num_features, 16, dataset.num_classes)
    print(gcn)
    gcn.fit(data, epochs=100)
```

8.  Here is the output of the training:

```
GCN(
  (gcn1): GCNConv(1433, 16)
  (gcn2): GCNConv(16, 7)
)
Epoch   0 | Train Loss: 1.963 | Train Acc:  8.57% | Val
Loss: 1.96 | Val Acc: 9.80%
Epoch  20 | Train Loss: 0.142 | Train Acc: 100.00% | Val
Loss: 0.82 | Val Acc: 78.40%
Epoch  40 | Train Loss: 0.016 | Train Acc: 100.00% | Val
Loss: 0.77 | Val Acc: 77.40%
Epoch  60 | Train Loss: 0.015 | Train Acc: 100.00% | Val
Loss: 0.76 | Val Acc: 76.40%
Epoch  80 | Train Loss: 0.018 | Train Acc: 100.00% | Val
Loss: 0.75 | Val Acc: 76.60%
```

```
Epoch 100 | Train Loss: 0.017 | Train Acc: 100.00% | Val
Loss: 0.75 | Val Acc: 77.20%
```

9.  Finally, let's evaluate it on the test set:

```
acc = gcn.test(data)
print(f'GCN test accuracy: {acc*100:.2f}%')
GCN test accuracy: 79.70%
```

If we repeat this experiment 100 times, we obtain an average accuracy score of 80.17% (± 0.61%), which is significantly higher than the 74.98% (± 1.50%) obtained by our vanilla GNN.

The exact same model is then applied to the Facebook Page-Page dataset, where it obtains an average accuracy of 91.54% (± 0.28%). Once again, it is significantly higher than the result obtained by the vanilla GNN, with only 84.85% (± 1.68%). The following table summarizes the accuracy scores with standard deviation:

|          | MLP | GNN | GCN |
|----------|-----|-----|-----|
| **Cora** | 53.47% | 74.98% | 80.17% |
|          | (±1.81%) | (±1.50%) | (±0.61%) |
| **Facebook** | 75.21% | 84.85% | 91.54% |
|          | (±0.40%) | (±1.68%) | (±0.28%) |

Figure 6.4 – Summary of accuracy scores with standard deviation

We can attribute these high scores to the wide range of node degrees in these two datasets. By normalizing features and considering the number of neighbors of the central node and its own neighbors, the GCN gains a lot of flexibility and can work well with various types of graphs.

Nonetheless, node classification is not the only task that GNNs can perform. In the next section, we'll see a new type of application that is rarely covered in the literature.

# Predicting web traffic with node regression

In machine learning, **regression** refers to the prediction of continuous values. It is often contrasted with **classification**, where the goal is to find the correct categories (which are not continuous). In graph data, their counterparts are node classification and node regression. In this section, we will try to predict a continuous value instead of a categorical variable for each node.

The dataset we will use is the Wikipedia Network (GNU General Public License v3.0), introduced by Rozemberckzi et al. in 2019 [2]. It is composed of three page-page networks: chameleons (2,277 nodes and 31,421 edges), crocodiles (11,631 nodes and 170,918 edges), and squirrels (5,201 nodes and 198,493 edges). In these datasets, nodes represent articles and edges are mutual links between them. Node features reflect the presence of particular words in the articles. Finally, the goal is to predict the log average monthly traffic of December 2018.

In this section, we will apply a GCN to predict this traffic on the chameleon dataset:

1. We import the Wikipedia Network and download the chameleon dataset. We apply the `transform` function, `RandomNodeSplit()`, to randomly create an evaluation mask and a test mask:

```
from torch_geometric.datasets import WikipediaNetwork
import torch_geometric.transforms as T

dataset = WikipediaNetwork(root=".", name="chameleon",
transform = T.RandomNodeSplit(num_val=200, num_test=500))
data = dataset[0]
```

2. We print information about this dataset:

```
print(f'Dataset: {dataset}')
print('-------------------')
print(f'Number of graphs: {len(dataset)}')
print(f'Number of nodes: {data.x.shape[0]}')
print(f'Number of unique features: {dataset.num_
features}')
print(f'Number of classes: {dataset.num_classes}')
```

This is the output we obtain:

```
Dataset: WikipediaNetwork()
-------------------
Number of graphs: 1
Number of nodes: 2277
Number of unique features: 2325
Number of classes: 5
```

3. There is a problem with our dataset: the output says that we have five classes. However, we want to perform node regression, not classification. So what happened?

In fact, these five classes are bins of the continuous values we want to predict. Unfortunately, these labels are not the ones we want: we have to change them manually. First, let's download the `wikipedia.zip` file from the following page: `https://snap.stanford.edu/data/wikipedia-article-networks.html`. After unzipping the file, we import `pandas` and use it to load the targets:

```
import pandas as pd
df = pd.read_csv('wikipedia/chameleon/musae_chameleon_
target.csv')
```

4. We apply a log function to the target values using `np.log10()` because the goal is to predict the log average monthly traffic:

```
values = np.log10(df['target'])
```

5. We redefine `data.y` as a tensor of the continuous values from the previous step. Note that these values are not normalized in this example, which is a good practice that is usually implemented. We will not perform it here for ease of exposition:

```
data.y = torch.tensor(values)
tensor([2.2330, 3.9079, 3.9329,  ..., 1.9956, 4.3598,
2.4409], dtype=torch.float64)
```

Once again, it is a good idea to visualize the node degrees as we did for the two previous datasets. We use the exact same code to produce the following figure:

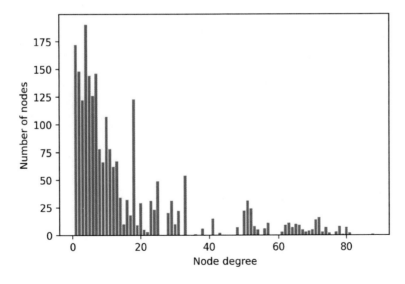

Figure 6.5 – Number of nodes with specific node degrees in the Wikipedia Network

This distribution has a shorter tail than the previous ones but keeps a similar shape: most nodes have one or a few neighbors, but some of them act as "hubs" and can connect more than 80 nodes.

In the case of node regression, the distribution of node degrees is not the only type of distribution we should check: the distribution of our target values is also essential. Indeed, non-normal distribution (such as node degrees) tends to be harder to predict. We can use the Seaborn library to plot the target values and compare them to a normal distribution provided by `scipy.stats.norm`:

```
import seaborn as sns
from scipy.stats import norm
df['target'] = values
sns.distplot(df['target'], fit=norm)
```

This gives us the following plot:

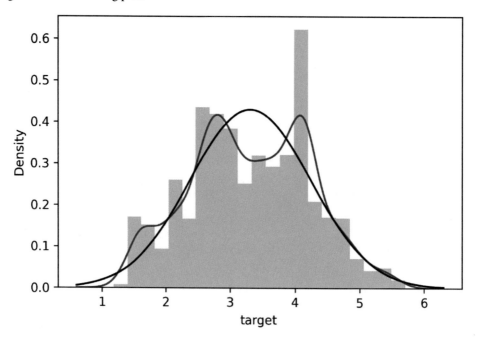

Figure 6.6 – Density plot of target values from the Wikipedia Network

This distribution is not exactly normal, but it is not exponential like the node degrees either. We can expect our model to perform well to predict these values.

Let's implement it step by step with PyTorch Geometric:

1.  We define the GCN class and the __init__() function. This time, we have three GCNConv layers with a decreasing number of neurons. The idea behind this encoder architecture is to force the model to select the most relevant features to predict the target values. We also added a linear layer to output a prediction that is not limited to a number between 0 or -1 and 1:

```
class GCN(torch.nn.Module):
    def __init__(self, dim_in, dim_h, dim_out):
        super().__init__()
        self.gcn1 = GCNConv(dim_in, dim_h*4)
        self.gcn2 = GCNConv(dim_h*4, dim_h*2)
        self.gcn3 = GCNConv(dim_h*2, dim_h)
        self.linear = torch.nn.Linear(dim_h, dim_out)
```

2.  The forward() method includes the new GCNConv and nn.Linear layers. There is no need for a log softmax function here since we're not predicting a class:

```
def forward(self, x, edge_index):
    h = self.gcn1(x, edge_index)
    h = torch.relu(h)
    h = F.dropout(h, p=0.5, training=self.training)
    h = self.gcn2(h, edge_index)
    h = torch.relu(h)
    h = F.dropout(h, p=0.5, training=self.training)
    h = self.gcn3(h, edge_index)
    h = torch.relu(h)
    h = self.linear(h)
    return h
```

3.  The main change in the fit() method is the F.mse_loss() function, which replaces the cross-entropy loss used in classification tasks. The **Mean Squared Error** (MSE) will be our main metric. It corresponds to the average of the squares of the errors and can be defined as follows:

$$MSE = \frac{1}{N} \sum_{i=1}^{N} (y_i - \hat{y}_i)^2$$

1. In code, this is how it is implemented:

```
def fit(self, data, epochs):
    optimizer = torch.optim.Adam(self.parameters(),
                                 lr=0.02,
                                 weight_decay=5e-4)

    self.train()
    for epoch in range(epochs+1):
        optimizer.zero_grad()
        out = self(data.x, data.edge_index)
        loss = F.mse_loss(out.squeeze()[data.train_
mask], data.y[data.train_mask].float())
        loss.backward()
        optimizer.step()
        if epoch % 20 == 0:
            val_loss = F.mse_loss(out.squeeze()[data.
val_mask], data.y[data.val_mask])
            print(f"Epoch {epoch:>3} | Train Loss:
{loss:.5f} | Val Loss: {val_loss:.5f}")
```

2. The MSE is also included in the `test()` method:

```
@torch.no_grad()
def test(self, data):
    self.eval()
    out = self(data.x, data.edge_index)
    return F.mse_loss(out.squeeze()[data.test_mask],
data.y[data.test_mask].float())
```

3. We instantiate the model with 128 hidden dimensions and only 1 output dimension (the target value). It is trained on 200 epochs:

```
gcn = GCN(dataset.num_features, 128, 1)
print(gcn)
gcn.fit(data, epochs=200)

GCN(
  (gcn1): GCNConv(2325, 512)
  (gcn2): GCNConv(512, 256)
```

```
    (gcn3): GCNConv(256, 128)
    (linear): Linear(in_features=128, out_features=1,
bias=True)
)
Epoch    0 | Train Loss: 12.05177 | Val Loss: 12.12162
Epoch   20 | Train Loss: 11.23000 | Val Loss: 11.08892
Epoch   40 | Train Loss: 4.59072 | Val Loss: 4.08908
Epoch   60 | Train Loss: 0.82827 | Val Loss: 0.84340
Epoch   80 | Train Loss: 0.63031 | Val Loss: 0.71436
Epoch  100 | Train Loss: 0.54679 | Val Loss: 0.75364
Epoch  120 | Train Loss: 0.45863 | Val Loss: 0.73487
Epoch  140 | Train Loss: 0.40186 | Val Loss: 0.67582
Epoch  160 | Train Loss: 0.38461 | Val Loss: 0.54889
Epoch  180 | Train Loss: 0.33744 | Val Loss: 0.56676
Epoch  200 | Train Loss: 0.29155 | Val Loss: 0.59314
```

4.  We test it to obtain the MSE on the test set:

```
loss = gcn.test(data)
print(f'GCN test loss: {loss:.5f}')
```

```
GCN test loss: 0.43005
```

This MSE loss is not the most interpretable metric by itself. We can get more meaningful results using the two following metrics:

- The RMSE, which measures the average magnitude of the error:

$$RMSE = \sqrt{MSE} = \sqrt{\frac{1}{N}\sum_{i=1}^{N}(y_i - \hat{y}_i)^2}$$

- The **Mean Absolute Error (MAE)**, which gives the mean absolute difference between the predicted and real values:

$$MAE = \frac{1}{N}\sum_{i=1}^{N}|y_i - \hat{y}_i|$$

Let's implement them in Python:

1.  We can directly import the MSE and the MAE from the scikit-learn library:

    ```
    from sklearn.metrics import mean_squared_error, mean_
    absolute_error
    ```

2.  We convert the PyTorch tensors for the predictions into the NumPy arrays given by the model using `.detach().numpy()`:

    ```
    out = gcn(data.x, data.edge_index)
    y_pred = out.squeeze()[data.test_mask].detach().numpy()
    mse = mean_squared_error(data.y[data.test_mask], y_pred)
    mae = mean_absolute_error(data.y[data.test_mask], y_pred)
    ```

3.  We compute the MSE and the MAE with their dedicated function. The RMSE is calculated as the square root of MSE using `np.sqrt()`:

    ```
    print('=' * 43)
    print(f'MSE = {mse:.4f} | RMSE = {np.sqrt(mse):.4f} | MAE
    = {mae:.4f}')
    print('=' * 43)

    ===========================================
    MSE = 0.4300 | RMSE = 0.6558 | MAE = 0.5073
    ===========================================
    ```

These metrics are useful for comparing different models, but it can be difficult to interpret the MSE and the RMSE.

The best tool to visualize the results of our model is a scatter plot, where the horizontal axis represents our predictions and the vertical axis represents the real values. Seaborn has a dedicated function (`regplot()`) for this type of visualization:

```
fig = sns.regplot(x=data.y[data.test_mask].numpy(), y=y_pred)
```

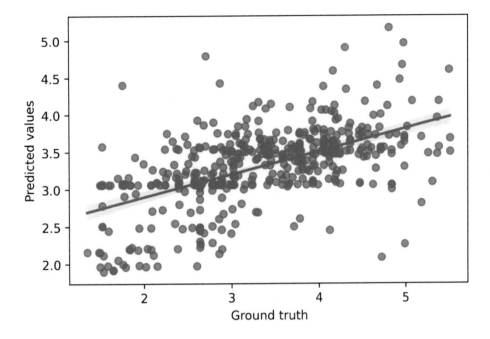

Figure 6.7 – Ground truth test values (x-axis) versus. predicted test values (y-axis)

We don't have a baseline to work with in this example, but this is a decent prediction with few outliers. It would work in a lot of applications, despite a minimalist dataset. If we wanted to improve these results, we could tune the hyperparameters and do more error analysis to understand where the outliers come from.

## Summary

In this chapter, we improved our vanilla GNN layer to correctly normalize features. This enhancement introduced the GCN layer and smart normalization. We compared this new architecture to Node2Vec and our vanilla GNN on the Cora and Facebook Page-Page datasets. Thanks to this normalization process, the GCN obtained the highest accuracy scores by a large margin in both cases. Finally, we applied it to node regression with the Wikipedia Network and learned how to handle this new task.

In *Chapter 7, Graph Attention Networks*, we will go a step further by discriminating neighboring nodes based on their importance. We will see how to automatically weigh node features through a process called self-attention. This will improve our performance, as we will see by comparing it to the GCN architecture.

# Further reading

- [1] T. N. Kipf and M. Welling, *Semi-Supervised Classification with Graph Convolutional Networks*. arXiv, 2016. DOI: 10.48550/ARXIV.1609.02907. Available: `https://arxiv.org/abs/1609.02907`.

- [2] B. Rozemberczki, C. Allen, and R. Sarkar, *Multi-scale Attributed Node Embedding*. arXiv, 2019. DOI: 10.48550/ARXIV.1909.13021. Available: `https://arxiv.org/abs/1909.13021`.

# 7

# Graph Attention Networks

**Graph Attention Networks** (**GATs**) are a theoretical improvement over GCNs. Instead of static normalization coefficients, they propose weighting factors calculated by a process called **self-attention**. The same process is at the core of one of the most successful deep learning architectures: the **transformer**, popularized by **BERT** and **GPT-3**. Introduced by Veličković et al. in 2017, GATs have become one of the most popular GNN architectures thanks to excellent out-of-the-box performance.

In this chapter, we will learn how the graph attention layer works in four steps. This is actually the perfect example for understanding how self-attention works in general. This theoretical background will allow us to implement a graph attention layer from scratch in `NumPy`. We will build the matrices by ourselves to understand how their values are calculated at each step.

In the last section, we'll use a GAT on two node classification datasets: `Cora`, and a new one called `CiteSeer`. As anticipated in the last chapter, this will be a good opportunity to analyze our results a little further. Finally, we will compare the accuracy of this architecture with a GCN.

By the end of this chapter, you will be able to implement a graph attention layer from scratch and a GAT in **PyTorch Geometric** (**PyG**). You will learn about the differences between this architecture and a GCN. Furthermore, you will master an error analysis tool for graph data.

In this chapter, we'll cover the following topics:

- Introducing the graph attention layer
- Implementing the graph attention layer in NumPy
- Implementing a GAT in PyTorch Geometric

# Technical requirements

All the code examples from this chapter can be found on GitHub at `https://github.com/PacktPublishing/Hands-On-Graph-Neural-Networks-Using-Python/tree/main/Chapter07`.

The installation steps required to run the code on your local machine can be found in the *Preface* section of this book.

# Introducing the graph attention layer

The main idea behind GATs is that some nodes are more important than others. In fact, this was already the case with the graph convolutional layer: nodes with few neighbors were more important than others, thanks to the normalization coefficient $\frac{1}{\sqrt{deg(i)}\sqrt{deg(j)}}$. This approach is limiting because it only takes into account node degrees. On the other hand, the goal of the graph attention layer is to produce weighting factors that also consider the importance of node features.

Let's call our weighting factors **attention scores** and note, $\alpha_{ij}$, the attention score between the nodes $i$ and $j$. We can define the graph attention operator as follows:

$$h_i = \sum_{j \in \mathcal{N}_i} \alpha_{ij} \mathbf{W} x_j$$

An important characteristic of GATs is that the attention scores are calculated implicitly by comparing inputs to each other (hence the name *self*-attention). In this section, we will see how to calculate these attention scores in four steps and also how to make an improvement to the graph attention layer:

- Linear transformation

- Activation function

- Softmax normalization

- Multi-head attention

- Improved graph attention layer

First things first, let's see how the linear transformation differs from previous architectures.

## Linear transformation

The attention score represents the importance between a central node $i$ and a neighbor $j$. As stated previously, it requires node features from both nodes. In the graph attention layer, it is represented by a concatenation between the hidden vectors $\mathbf{W} x_i$ and $\mathbf{W} x_j$, $[\mathbf{W} x_i \mathbin{\|} \mathbf{W} x_j]$. Here, $\mathbf{W}$ is a classic shared weight matrix to compute hidden vectors. An additional linear transformation is applied to this result with a dedicated learnable weight matrix $W_{att}$. During training, this matrix learns weights to produce attention coefficients $a_{ij}$. This process is summarized by the following formula:

$$a_{ij} = W_{att}^T [\mathbf{W}x_i \mathbin{||} \mathbf{W}x_j]$$

This output is given to an activation function like in traditional neural networks.

## Activation function

Nonlinearity is an essential component in neural networks to approximate nonlinear target functions. Such functions could not be captured by simply stacking linear layers, as their final outcome would still behave like a single linear layer.

In the official implementation (`https://github.com/PetarV-/GAT/blob/master/utils/layers.py`), the authors chose the **Leaky Rectified Linear Unit (ReLU)** activation function (see *Figure 7.1*). This function fixes the *dying ReLU* problem, where ReLU neurons only output zero:

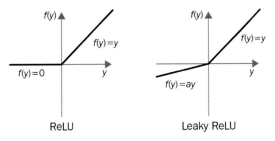

Figure 7.1 – ReLU versus Leaky ReLU functions

This is implemented by applying the Leaky ReLU function to the output of the previous step:

$$e_{ij} = LeakyReLU(a_{ij})$$

However, we are now facing a new problem: the resulting values are not normalized!

## Softmax normalization

We want to compare different attention scores, which means we need normalized values on the same scale. In machine learning, it is common to use the softmax function for this purpose. Let's call $\mathcal{N}_i$ the neighboring nodes of node $i$, including itself:

$$\alpha_{ij} = softmax_j(e_{ij}) = \frac{exp(e_{ij})}{\sum_{k \in \mathcal{N}_i} exp(e_{ik})}$$

The result of this operation gives us our final attention scores $\alpha_{ij}$. But there's another problem: self-attention is not very stable.

## Multi-head attention

This issue was already noticed by Vaswani et al. (2017) in the original transformer paper. Their proposed solution consists of calculating multiple embeddings with their own attention scores instead of a single one. This technique is called multi-head attention.

The implementation is straightforward, as we just have to repeat the three previous steps multiple times. Each instance produces an embedding $h_i^k$, where $k$ is the index of the attention head. There are two ways of combining these results:

- **Averaging**: With this, we sum the different embeddings and normalize the result by the number of attention heads $n$:

$$h_i = \frac{1}{n}\sum_{k=1}^{n} h_i^k = \frac{1}{n}\sum_{k=1}^{n}\sum_{j\in\mathcal{N}_i} \alpha_{ij}^k \mathbf{W}^k x_j$$

- **Concatenation**: Here, we concatenate the different embeddings, which will produce a larger matrix:

$$h_i = \|_{k=1}^{n} h_i^k = \|_{k=1}^{n}\sum_{j\in\mathcal{N}_i} \alpha_{ij}^k \mathbf{W}^k x_j$$

In practice, there is a simple rule to know which one to use: we choose the concatenation scheme when it's a hidden layer and the average scheme when it's the last layer of the network. The entire process can be summarized by the following diagram:

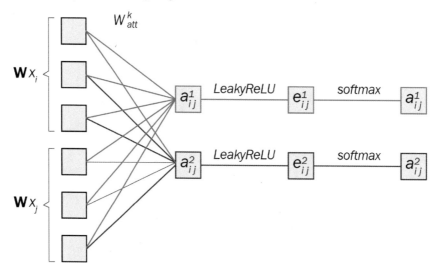

Figure 7.2 – Calculating attention scores with multi-head attention

This is all there is to know about the theoretical aspect of the graph attention layer. However, since its inception in 2017, an improvement has been suggested.

## Improved graph attention layer

Brody et al. (2021) argued that the graph attention layer only computes a static type of attention. This is an issue because there are simple graph problems we cannot express with a GAT. So they introduced an improved version, called GATv2, which computes a strictly more expressive dynamic attention.

Their solution consists of modifying the order of operations. The weight matrix $W$ is applied after the concatenation and the attention weight matrix $W_{att}$ after the *LeakyReLU* function. In summary, here is the original **Graph Attentional Operator**, also **GAT**:

$$\alpha_{ij} = \frac{exp\left(W_{att}^t \ LeakyReLU(\mathbf{W}[x_i \ || \ x_j])\right)}{\sum_{k \in \mathcal{N}_i} exp(W_{att}^t \ LeakyReLU(\mathbf{W}[x_i \ || \ x_k]))}$$

And this is the modified operator, GATv2:

$$\alpha_{ij} = \frac{exp\left(W_{att}^t \ LeakyReLU(\mathbf{W}[x_i \ || \ x_j])\right)}{\sum_{k \in \mathcal{N}_i} exp(W_{att}^t \ LeakyReLU(\mathbf{W}[x_i \ || \ x_k]))}$$

Which one should we use? According to Brody et al., GATv2 consistently outperforms the GAT and thus should be preferred. In addition to the theoretical proof, they also ran several experiments to show the performance of GATv2 compared to the original GAT. In the rest of this chapter, we will consider both options: the GAT in the second section and GATv2 in the third section.

# Implementing the graph attention layer in NumPy

As previously stated, neural networks work in terms of matrix multiplications. Therefore, we need to translate our individual embeddings into operations for the entire graph. In this section, we will implement the original graph attention layer from scratch to properly understand the inner workings of self-attention. Naturally, this process can be repeated several times to create multi-head attention.

The first step consists of translating the original graph attention operator in terms of matrices. This is how we defined it in the last section:

$$h_i = \sum_{j \in \mathcal{N}_i} \alpha_{ij} \mathbf{W} x_j$$

By taking inspiration from the graph linear layer, we can write the following:

$$H = \tilde{A}^T W_\alpha X \mathbf{W}^T$$

Where $W_\alpha$ is a matrix that stores every $\alpha_{ij}$.

In this example, we will use the following graph from the previous chapter:

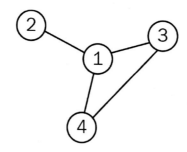

Figure 7.3 – Simple graph where nodes have different numbers of neighbors

The graph must provide two important pieces of information: the adjacency matrix with self-loops $\tilde{A}$ and the node features $X$. Let's see how to implement it in NumPy:

1.  We can build the adjacency matrix from the connections in *Figure 7.3*:

```
import numpy as np
np.random.seed(0)


A = np.array([
    [1, 1, 1, 1],
    [1, 1, 0, 0],
    [1, 0, 1, 1],
    [1, 0, 1, 1]
])


array([[1, 1, 1, 1],
       [1, 1, 0, 0],
       [1, 0, 1, 1],
       [1, 0, 1, 1]])
```

2.  For $X$, we generate a random matrix of node features using np.random.uniform():

```
X = np.random.uniform(-1, 1, (4, 4))


array([[ 0.0976270,  0.4303787,  0.2055267,  0.0897663],
       [-0.1526904,  0.2917882, -0.1248255,  0.783546 ],
       [ 0.9273255, -0.2331169,  0.5834500,  0.0577898],
       [ 0.1360891,  0.8511932, -0.8579278, -0.8257414]])
```

3.  The next step is to define our weight matrices. Indeed, in graph attention layers, there are two of them: the regular weight matrix **W**, and the attention weight matrix $W_{att}$. There are different ways to initialize them (Xavier or He initialization, for example), but we can just reuse the same random function in this example.

    The matrix **W** has to be carefully designed as its dimensions are (*nb of hidden dimensions, nb of nodes*). Notice that *nb of nodes* = 4 is already fixed because it represents the number of nodes in $X$. On the contrary, the value of *nb of hidden dimensions* is arbitrary: we'll choose 2 in this example:

    ```
    W = np.random.uniform(-1, 1, (2, 4))
    ```

    ```
    array([[-0.9595632,  0.6652396,  0.556313 ,  0.740024 ],
           [ 0.9572366,  0.5983171, -0.0770412,  0.5610583]])
    ```

4.  This attention matrix is applied to the concatenation of hidden vectors to produce a unique value. Thus, its size needs to be $(1, dim\_h \times 2)$:

    ```
    W_att = np.random.uniform(-1, 1, (1, 4))
    ```

    ```
    array([[-0.7634511,  0.2798420, -0.7132934,  0.8893378]])
    ```

5.  We want to concatenate hidden vectors from source and destination nodes. A simple way to obtain pairs of source and destination nodes is to look at our adjacency matrix $\tilde{A}$ in COO format: rows store source nodes, and columns store destination nodes. NumPy provides a quick and efficient way of doing it with np.where():

    ```
    connections = np.where(A > 0)
    ```

    ```
    (array([0, 0, 0, 0, 1, 1, 2, 2, 2, 3, 3, 3]),
     array([0, 1, 2, 3, 0, 1, 0, 2, 3, 0, 2, 3]))
    ```

6.  We can concatenate hidden vectors of source and destination nodes using np.concatenate:

    ```
    np.concatenate([(X @ W.T)[connections[0]], (X @ W.T)
    [connections[1]]], axis=1)
    ```

    ```
    array([[ 0.3733923,  0.3854852,  0.3733923,  0.3854852],
           [ 0.3733923,  0.3854852,  0.8510261,  0.4776527],
           [ 0.3733923,  0.3854852, -0.6775590,  0.7356658],
           [ 0.3733923,  0.3854852, -0.6526841,  0.2423597],
           [ 0.8510261,  0.4776527,  0.3733923,  0.3854852],
           [ 0.8510261,  0.4776527,  0.8510261,  0.4776527],
    ```

```
         [-0.6775590,   0.7356658,   0.3733923,   0.3854852],
         [-0.6775590,   0.7356658,  -0.6775590,   0.7356658],
         [-0.6775590,   0.7356658,  -0.6526841,   0.2423597],
         [-0.6526841,   0.2423597,   0.3733923,   0.3854852],
         [-0.6526841,   0.2423597,  -0.6775590,   0.7356658],
         [-0.6526841,   0.2423597,  -0.6526841,   0.2423597]])
```

7. We then apply a linear transformation to this result with the attention matrix $W_{att}$:

```
a = W_att @ np.concatenate([[(X @ W.T)[connections[0]], (X
@ W.T)[connections[1]]], axis=1).T
array([[-0.1007035 ,
-0.35942847,  0.96036209,  0.50390318,
-0.43956122, -0.69828618,  0.79964181,  1.8607074
,  1.40424849,  0.64260322,  1.70366881,  1.2472099 ]])
```

8. The second step consists of applying a Leaky ReLU function to the previous outcome:

```
def leaky_relu(x, alpha=0.2):
    return np.maximum(alpha*x, x)


e = leaky_relu(a)
array([[-0.0201407 ,
-0.07188569,  0.96036209,  0.50390318,
-0.08791224,  -0.13965724,  0.79964181,  1.8607074
,  1.40424849,  0.64260322,  1.70366881,  1.2472099 ]])
```

9. We have the right values but need to place them correctly in a matrix. This matrix should look like $\tilde{A}$ because there is no need for unnormalized attention scores when there is no connection between two nodes. To build this matrix, we know the sources $i$ and destinations $j$ thanks to connections. So, the first value in e corresponds to $e_{00}$, the second value to $e_{01}$, but the seventh value corresponds to $e_{20}$ and not to $e_{12}$. We can fill the matrix as follows:

```
E = np.zeros(A.shape)
E[connections[0], connections[1]] = e[0]


array([[-0.020140 , -0.0718856,  0.9603620,  0.5039031],
       [-0.0879122, -0.1396572,  0.        ,  0.        ],
       [ 0.7996418,  0.        ,  1.8607074,  1.4042484],
       [ 0.6426032,  0.        ,  1.7036688,  1.247209 ]])
```

10. The next step is to normalize every row of attention scores. This requires a custom `softmax` function to produce our final attention scores:

```
def softmax2D(x, axis):
    e = np.exp(x - np.expand_dims(np.max(x, axis=axis),
axis))
    sum = np.expand_dims(np.sum(e, axis=axis), axis)
    return e / sum


W_alpha = softmax2D(E, 1)


array([[0.15862414, 0.15062488, 0.42285965, 0.26789133],
       [0.24193418, 0.22973368, 0.26416607, 0.26416607],
       [0.16208847, 0.07285714, 0.46834625, 0.29670814],
       [0.16010498, 0.08420266, 0.46261506, 0.2930773 ]])
```

11. This attention matrix $W_\alpha$ provides weights for every possible connection in the network. We can use it to calculate our matrix of embeddings $H$, which should give us two-dimensional vectors for each node:

```
H = A.T @ W_alpha @ X @ W.T


array([[-1.10126376,  1.99749693],
       [-0.33950544,  0.97045933],
       [-1.03570438,  1.53614075],
       [-1.03570438,  1.53614075]])
```

Our graph attention layer is now complete! Adding multi-head attention consists of repeating these steps with different **W** and $W_{att}$ before aggregating the results.

The graph attention operator is an essential building block to developing GNNs. In the next section, we will use a PyG implementation to create a GAT.

# Implementing a GAT in PyTorch Geometric

We now have a complete picture of how the graph attention layer works. These layers can be stacked to create our new architecture of choice: the GAT. In this section, we will follow the guidelines from the original GAT paper to implement our own model using PyG. We will use it to perform node classification on the `Cora` and `CiteSeer` datasets. Finally, we will comment on these results and compare them.

Let's start with the Cora dataset:

1.  We import Cora from the Planetoid class using PyG:

    ```
    from torch_geometric.datasets import Planetoid

    dataset = Planetoid(root=".", name="Cora")
    data = dataset[0]

    Data(x=[2708, 1433], edge_index=[2, 10556], y=[2708],
    train_mask=[2708], val_mask=[2708], test_mask=[2708])
    ```

2.  We import the necessary libraries to create our own GAT class, using the GATv2 layer:

    ```
    import torch
    import torch.nn.functional as F
    from torch_geometric.nn import GATv2Conv
    from torch.nn import Linear, Dropout
    ```

3.  We implement the accuracy() function to evaluate the performance of our model:

    ```
    def accuracy(y_pred, y_true):
        return torch.sum(y_pred == y_true) / len(y_true)
    ```

4.  The class is initialized with two improved graph attention layers. Note it is important to declare the number of heads used for multi-head attention. The authors stated that eight heads improved performance for the first layer, but it didn't make any difference for the second one:

    ```
    class GAT(torch.nn.Module):
        def __init__(self, dim_in, dim_h, dim_out, heads=8):
            super().__init__()
            self.gat1 = GATv2Conv(dim_in, dim_h, heads=heads)
            self.gat2 = GATv2Conv(dim_h*heads, dim_out,
    heads=1)
    ```

5.  Compared to the previous implementation of a GCN, we're adding two dropout layers to prevent overfitting. These layers randomly zero some values from the input tensor with a predefined probability (0.6 in this case). Conforming to the original paper, we also use the **Exponential Linear Unit (ELU)** function, which is the exponential version of the Leaky ReLU:

    ```
    def forward(self, x, edge_index):
        h = F.dropout(x, p=0.6, training=self.training)
    ```

```
h = self.gat1(h, edge_index)
h = F.elu(h)
h = F.dropout(h, p=0.6, training=self.training)
h = self.gat2(h, edge_index)
return F.log_softmax(h, dim=1)
```

6. The `fit()` function is identical to the GCN's. The parameters of the Adam optimizer have been tuned to match the best values for the `Cora` dataset, according to the authors:

```
def fit(self, data, epochs):
    criterion = torch.nn.CrossEntropyLoss()
    optimizer = torch.optim.Adam(self.parameters(),
lr=0.01, weight_decay=0.01)

    self.train()
    for epoch in range(epochs+1):
        optimizer.zero_grad()
        out = self(data.x, data.edge_index)
        loss = criterion(out[data.train_mask],
data.y[data.train_mask])
        acc = accuracy(out[data.train_mask].
argmax(dim=1), data.y[data.train_mask])
        loss.backward()
        optimizer.step()

        if(epoch % 20 == 0):
            val_loss = criterion(out[data.val_mask],
data.y[data.val_mask])
            val_acc = accuracy(out[data.val_mask].
argmax(dim=1), data.y[data.val_mask])
            print(f'Epoch {epoch:>3} | Train Loss:
{loss:.3f} | Train Acc: {acc*100:>5.2f}% | Val Loss:
{val_loss:.2f} | Val Acc: {val_acc*100:.2f}%')
```

7. The `test()` function is exactly the same:

```
@torch.no_grad()
def test(self, data):
    self.eval()
    out = self(data.x, data.edge_index)
```

```
        acc = accuracy(out.argmax(dim=1)[data.test_mask],
    data.y[data.test_mask])
        return acc
```

8.  We create a GAT and train it for 100 epochs:

```
gat = GAT(dataset.num_features, 32, dataset.num_classes)
gat.fit(data, epochs=100)


GAT(
   (gat1): GATv2Conv(1433, 32, heads=8)
   (gat2): GATv2Conv(256, 7, heads=1)
)
Epoch 0 | Train Loss: 1.978 | Train Acc: 12.86% | Val
Loss: 1.94 | Val Acc: 13.80%
Epoch 20 | Train Loss: 0.238 | Train Acc: 96.43% | Val
Loss: 1.04 | Val Acc: 67.40%
Epoch 40 | Train Loss: 0.165 | Train Acc: 98.57% | Val
Loss: 0.95 | Val Acc: 71.00%
Epoch 60 | Train Loss: 0.209 | Train Acc: 96.43% | Val
Loss: 0.91 | Val Acc: 71.80%
Epoch 80 | Train Loss: 0.172 | Train Acc: 100.00% | Val
Loss: 0.93 | Val Acc: 70.80%
Epoch 100 | Train Loss: 0.190 | Train Acc: 97.86% | Val
Loss: 0.96 | Val Acc: 70.80%
```

9.  This outputs the final test accuracy:

```
acc = gat.test(data)
print(f'GAT test accuracy: {acc*100:.2f}%')


GAT test accuracy: 81.10%
```

This accuracy score is slightly better than the average score we obtained with a GCN. We'll make a proper comparison after applying the GAT architecture to the second dataset.

We will use a new popular dataset for node classification called CiteSeer (MIT License). Like Cora, it represents a network of research papers where each connection is a citation. CiteSeer involves 3327 nodes, whose features represent the presence (1) or absence (0) of 3703 words in a paper. The goal of this dataset is to correctly classify these nodes into six categories. *Figure 7.4* shows a plot of CiteSeer made with yEd Live:

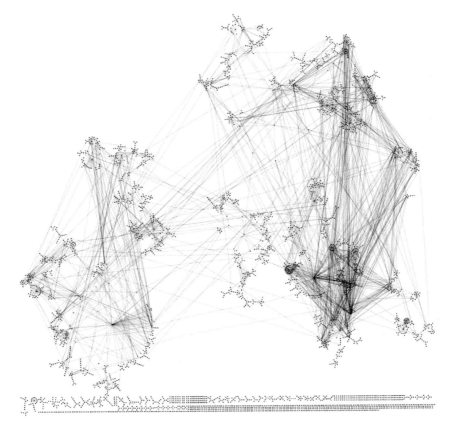

Figure 7.4 – The CiteSeer dataset (made with yEd Live)

Compared to `Cora`, this dataset is larger in terms of the number of nodes (from 2,708 to 3,327) and also in terms of feature dimensionality (from 1,433 to 3,703). However, the exact same process can be applied to it:

1.  First, we load the `CiteSeer` dataset:

```
dataset = Planetoid(root=".", name="CiteSeer")
data = dataset[0]
Data(x=[3327, 3703], edge_index=[2, 9104], y=[3327],
train_mask=[3327], val_mask=[3327], test_mask=[3327])
```

2.  For good measure, we plot the number of nodes per node degree, using the code from the last chapter:

```python
import matplotlib.pyplot as plt
from torch_geometric.utils import degree
from collections import Counter

degrees = degree(dataset[0].edge_index[0]).numpy()

numbers = Counter(degrees)

fig, ax = plt.subplots(dpi=300)
ax.set_xlabel('Node degree')
ax.set_ylabel('Number of nodes')
plt.bar(numbers.keys(), numbers.values())
```

3.  It gives us the following output:

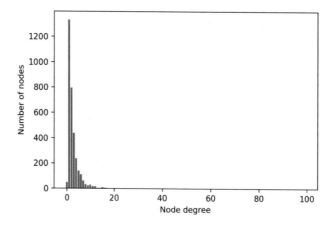

Figure 7.5 – Number of nodes per node degree (CiteSeer)

*Figure 7.5* looks like a typical heavy-tailed distribution but with a twist: some nodes have a degree of zero! In other words, they are not connected to any other node. We can assume that they will be much more difficult to classify than the rest.

4.  We initialize a new GAT model with the correct number of input and output nodes and train it for 100 epochs:

```python
gat = GAT(dataset.num_features, 16, dataset.num_classes)
gat.fit(data, epochs=100)
```

```
Epoch    0 | Train Loss: 1.815 | Train Acc: 15.00% | Val
Loss: 1.81 | Val Acc: 14.20%
Epoch   20 | Train Loss: 0.173 | Train Acc: 99.17% | Val
Loss: 1.15 | Val Acc: 63.80%
Epoch   40 | Train Loss: 0.113 | Train Acc: 99.17% | Val
Loss: 1.12 | Val Acc: 64.80%
Epoch   60 | Train Loss: 0.099 | Train Acc: 98.33% | Val
Loss: 1.12 | Val Acc: 62.40%
Epoch   80 | Train Loss: 0.130 | Train Acc: 98.33% | Val
Loss: 1.19 | Val Acc: 62.20%
Epoch  100 | Train Loss: 0.158 | Train Acc: 98.33% | Val
Loss: 1.10 | Val Acc: 64.60%
```

5.  We obtain the following test accuracy score:

```
acc = gat.test(data)
print(f'GAT test accuracy: {acc*100:.2f}%')
```

```
GAT test accuracy: 68.10%
```

Is it a good result? This time, we have no point of comparison.

According to Schur et al. in *Pitfalls of Graph Neural Network Evaluation*, the GAT is slightly better than the GCN (82.8% ± 0.6% versus 81.9% ± 0.8%) on `Cora` and `CiteSeer` (71.0 ± 0.6% versus 69.5% ± 0.9%). The authors also note that the accuracy scores are not normally distributed, making the usage of standard deviation less relevant. It is important to keep that in mind in this type of benchmark.

Previously, I speculated that poorly connected nodes might negatively impact performance. We can verify this hypothesis by plotting the average accuracy score for each node degree:

1.  We get the model's classifications:

```
out = gat(data.x, data.edge_index)
```

2.  We calculate the degree of each node:

```
degrees = degree(data.edge_index[0]).numpy()
```

3.  We store the accuracy scores and sample sizes:

```
accuracies = []
sizes = []
```

4.  We get the average accuracy for each node degree between zero and five using a mask with np.where():

```
for i in range(0, 6):
    mask = np.where(degrees == i)[0]
    accuracies.append(accuracy(out.argmax(dim=1)[mask],
data.y[mask]))
    sizes.append(len(mask))
```

5.  We repeat this process for every node with a degree higher than five:

```
mask = np.where(degrees > 5)[0]
accuracies.append(accuracy(out.argmax(dim=1)[mask],
data.y[mask]))
sizes.append(len(mask))
```

6.  We plot these accuracy scores with the corresponding node degrees:

```
fig, ax = plt.subplots(dpi=300)
ax.set_xlabel('Node degree')
ax.set_ylabel('Accuracy score')
plt.bar(['0','1','2','3','4','5','6+'], accuracies)
for i in range(0, 7):
    plt.text(i, accuracies[i],
f'{accuracies[i]*100:.2f}%', ha='center', color='black')
for i in range(0, 7):
    plt.text(i, accuracies[i]//2, sizes[i], ha='center',
color='white')
```

7.   It outputs the following graph:

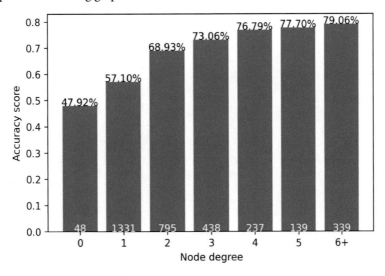

Figure 7.6 – Accuracy score per node degree (CiteSeer)

*Figure 7.6* confirms our hypothesis: nodes with few neighbors are harder to classify correctly. Furthermore, it even shows that, in general, the higher the node degree, the better the accuracy score. This is quite natural because a higher number of neighbors will provide more information to the GNN to make its predictions.

## Summary

In this chapter, we introduced a new essential architecture: the GAT. We saw its inner workings with four main steps, from linear transformation to multi-head attention. We saw how it works in practice by implementing a graph attention layer in NumPy. Finally, we applied a GAT model (with GATv2) to the `Cora` and `CiteSeer` datasets, where it provided excellent accuracy scores. We showed that these scores were dependent on the number of neighbors, which is a first step toward error analysis.

In *Chapter 8, Scaling Graph Neural Networks with GraphSAGE*, we will introduce a new architecture dedicated to managing large graphs. To test this claim, we will implement it on a new dataset several times bigger than what we've seen so far. We will talk about transductive and inductive learning, which is an important distinction for GNN practitioners.

# Part 3:
# Advanced Techniques

In this third part of the book, we will delve into the more advanced and specialized GNN architectures that have been developed to solve a variety of graph-related problems. We will cover state-of-the-art GNN models designed for specific tasks and domains, which can address challenges and requirements more effectively. In addition, we will provide an overview of several new graph-based tasks that can be tackled using GNNs, such as link prediction and graph classification, and demonstrate their applications through practical code examples and implementations.

By the end of this part, you will be able to understand and implement advanced GNN architectures and apply them to solve your own graph-based problems. You will have a comprehensive understanding of specialized GNNs and their respective strengths, as well as hands-on experience with code examples. This knowledge will equip you with the skills to apply GNNs to real-world use cases and potentially contribute to the development of new and innovative GNN architectures.

This part comprises the following chapters:

- *Chapter 8, Scaling Up Graph Neural Networks with GraphSAGE*
- *Chapter 9, Defining Expressiveness for Graph Classification*
- *Chapter 10, Predicting Links with Graph Neural Networks*
- *Chapter 11, Generating Graphs Using Graph Neural Networks*
- *Chapter 12, Learning from Heterogeneous Graphs*
- *Chapter 13, Temporal Graph Neural Networks*
- *Chapter 14, Explaining Graph Neural Networks*

# 8

# Scaling Up Graph Neural Networks with GraphSAGE

**GraphSAGE** is a GNN architecture designed to handle large graphs. In the tech industry, **scalability** is a key driver for growth. As a result, systems are inherently designed to accommodate millions of users. This ability requires a fundamental shift in how the GNN model works compared to GCNs and GATs. Thus, it is no surprise that GraphSAGE is the architecture of choice for tech companies such as Uber Eats and Pinterest.

In this chapter, we will learn about the two main ideas behind GraphSAGE. First, we will describe its **neighbor sampling** technique, which is at the core of its performance in terms of scalability. We will then explore three aggregation operators used to produce node embeddings. Besides the original approach, we will also detail the variants proposed by Uber Eats and Pinterest.

Moreover, GraphSAGE offers new possibilities in terms of training. We will implement two ways of training a GNN for two tasks – node classification with `PubMed` and **multi-label classification** for **protein-protein interactions**. Finally, we will discuss the benefits of a new **inductive** approach and how to use it.

By the end of this chapter, you will understand how and why the neighbor sampling algorithm works. You will be able to implement it to create mini-batches and speed up training on most GNN architectures using a GPU. Furthermore, you will master inductive learning and multi-label classification on graphs.

In this chapter, we will cover the following topics:

- Introducing GraphSAGE
- Classifying nodes on PubMed
- Inductive learning on protein-protein interactions

# Technical requirements

All the code examples from this chapter can be found on GitHub at `https://github.com/PacktPublishing/Hands-On-Graph-Neural-Networks-Using-Python/tree/main/Chapter08`.

The installation steps required to run the code on your local machine can be found in the *Preface* chapter of this book.

# Introducing GraphSAGE

Hamilton et al. introduced GraphSAGE in 2017 (see item [1] of the *Further reading* section) as a framework for inductive representation learning on large graphs (with over 100,000 nodes). Its goal is to generate node embeddings for downstream tasks, such as node classification. In addition, it solves two issues with GCNs and GATs – scaling to large graphs and efficiently generalizing to unseen data. In this section, we will explain how to implement it by describing the two main components of GraphSAGE:

- Neighbor sampling
- Aggregation

Let's take a look at them.

## Neighbor sampling

So far, we haven't discussed an essential concept in traditional neural networks – **mini-batching**. It consists of dividing our dataset into smaller fragments, called batches. They are used in **gradient descent**, the optimization algorithm that finds the best weights and biases during training. There are three types of gradient descent:

- **Batch gradient descent**: Weights and biases are updated after a whole dataset has been processed (every epoch). This is the technique we have implemented so far. However, it is a slow process that requires the dataset to fit in memory.

- **Stochastic gradient descent**: Weights and biases are updated for each training example in the dataset. This is a noisy process because the errors are not averaged. However, it can be used to perform online training.

- **Mini-batch gradient descent**: Weights and biases are updated at the end of every mini-batch of $n$ training examples. This technique is faster (mini-batches can be processed in parallel using a GPU) and leads to more stable convergence. In addition, the dataset can exceed the available memory, which is essential for handling large graphs.

In practice, we use more advanced optimizers such as **RMSprop** or Adam, which also implement mini-batching.

Dividing a tabular dataset is straightforward; it simply consists of selecting $n$ samples (rows). However, this is an issue regarding graph datasets – how do we choose $n$ nodes without breaking essential connections? If we're not careful, we could end up with a collection of isolated nodes where we cannot perform any aggregation.

We have to think about how GNNs use datasets. Every GNN layer computes node embeddings based on their neighbors. This means that computing an embedding only requires the direct neighbors of this node (**1 hop**). If our GNN has two GNN layers, we need these neighbors and their own neighbors (**2 hops**), and so on (see *Figure 8.1*). The rest of the network is irrelevant to computing these individual node embeddings.

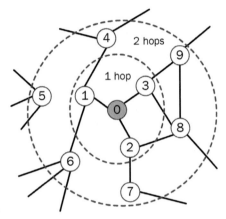

Figure 8.1 – A graph with node 0 as the target node and the 1-hop and 2-hop neighbors

This technique allows us to fill batches with computation graphs, which describe the entire sequence of operations for calculating a node embedding. *Figure 8.2* shows the computation graph of node 0 in a more intuitive representation.

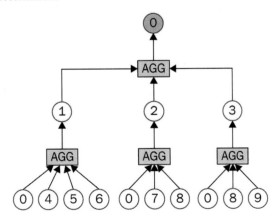

Figure 8.2 – A computation graph for node 0

We need to aggregate 2-hop neighbors in order to compute the embedding of 1-hop neighbors. These embeddings are then aggregated to obtain the embedding of node 0. However, there are two problems with this design:

- The computation graph becomes exponentially large with respect to the number of hops

- Nodes with very high degrees of connectivity (such as celebrities on an online social network a social network), also called **hub nodes**, create enormous computation graphs

To solve these issues, we have to limit the size of our computation graphs. In GraphSAGE, the authors propose a technique called neighbor sampling. Instead of adding every neighbor in the computation graph, we sample a predefined number of them. For instance, we choose only to keep (at most) three neighbors during the first hop and five neighbors during the second hop. Hence, the computation graph cannot exceed $3 \times 5 = 15$ nodes in this case.

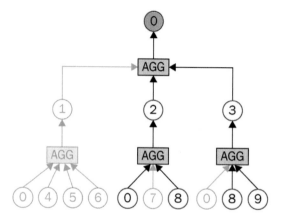

Figure 8.3 – A computation graph with neighbor sampling to keep
two 1-hop neighbors and two 2-hop neighbors

A low sampling number is more efficient but makes the training more random (higher variance). Additionally, the number of GNN layers (hops) must stay low to avoid exponentially large computation graphs. Neighbor sampling can handle large graphs, but it causes a trade-off by pruning important information, which can negatively impact performance such as accuracy. Note that computation graphs involve a lot of redundant calculations, which makes the entire process computationally less efficient.

Nonetheless, this random sampling is not the only technique we can use. Pinterest has its own version of GraphSAGE, called PinSAGE, to power its recommender system (see *Further reading* [2]). It implements another sampling solution using random walks. PinSAGE keeps the idea of a fixed number of neighbors but implements random walks to see which nodes are the most frequently encountered. This frequency determines their relative importance. PinSAGE's sampling strategy allows it to select the most critical nodes and proves more efficient in practice.

## Aggregation

Now that we've seen how to select the neighboring nodes, we still need to compute embeddings. This is performed by the aggregation operator (or aggregator). In GraphSAGE, the authors have proposed three solutions:

- A mean aggregator
- A **long short-term memory** (**LSTM**) aggregator
- A pooling aggregator

We will focus on the mean aggregator, as it is the easiest to understand. First, the mean aggregator takes the embeddings of target nodes and their sampled neighbors to average them. Then, a linear transformation with a weight matrix, $\mathbf{W}$, is applied to this result:

The mean aggregator can be summarized by the following formula, where $\sigma$ is a non-linear function such as ReLU or tanh:

$$h_i' = \sigma \left( \mathbf{W} \cdot mean_{j \in \mathcal{N}_i}(h_j) \right)$$

In the case of PyG's and Uber Eats' implementation of GraphSAGE [3], we use two weight matrices instead of one; the first one is dedicated to the target node, and the second to the neighbors. This aggregator can be written as follows:

$$h_i' = \sigma \left( \mathbf{W}_1 h_i + \mathbf{W}_2 \cdot mean_{j \in \mathcal{N}_i}(h_j) \right)$$

The LSTM aggregator is based on LSTM architecture, a popular recurrent neural network type. Compared to the mean aggregator, the LSTM aggregator can, in theory, discriminate between more graph structures and, thus, produce better embeddings. The issue is that recurrent neural networks only consider sequences of inputs, such as a sentence with a beginning and an end. However, nodes do not have any sequence. Therefore, we perform random permutations of the node's neighbors to address this problem. This solution allows us to use the LSTM architecture without relying on any sequence of inputs.

Finally, the pooling aggregator works in two steps. First, every neighbor's embedding is fed to an MLP to produce a new vector. Secondly, an elementwise max operation is performed to only keep the highest value for each feature.

We are not limited to these three options and could implement other aggregators in the GraphSAGE framework. Indeed, the main idea behind GraphSAGE resides in its efficient neighbor sampling. In the next section, we will use it to perform node classification on a new dataset.

# Classifying nodes on PubMed

In this section, we will implement a GraphSAGE architecture to perform node classification on the PubMed dataset (available under the MIT license from `https://github.com/kimiyoung/planetoid`) [4].

Previously, we saw two other citation network datasets from the same Planetoid family – `Cora` and `CiteSeer`. The `PubMed` dataset displays a similar but larger graph, with 19,717 nodes and 88,648 edges. *Figure 8.3* shows a visualization of this dataset as created by Gephi (`https://gephi.org/`).

Figure 8.4 – A visualization of the PubMed dataset

Node features are TF-IDF-weighted word vectors with 500 dimensions. The goal is to correctly classify nodes into three categories – diabetes mellitus experimental, diabetes mellitus type 1, and diabetes mellitus type 2. Let's implement it step by step using PyG:

1.  We load the `PubMed` dataset from the `Planetoid` class and print some information about the graph:

```
from torch_geometric.datasets import Planetoid

dataset = Planetoid(root='.', name="Pubmed")
data = dataset[0]

print(f'Dataset: {dataset}')
```

```
print('-------------------')
print(f'Number of graphs: {len(dataset)}')
print(f'Number of nodes: {data.x.shape[0]}')
print(f'Number of features: {dataset.num_features}')
print(f'Number of classes: {dataset.num_classes}')

print('Graph:')
print('------')
print(f'Training nodes: {sum(data.train_mask).item()}')
print(f'Evaluation nodes: {sum(data.val_mask).item()}')
print(f'Test nodes: {sum(data.test_mask).item()}')
print(f'Edges are directed: {data.is_directed()}')
print(f'Graph has isolated nodes: {data.has_isolated_
nodes()}')
print(f'Graph has loops: {data.has_self_loops()}')
```

2.  This produces the following output:

```
Dataset: Pubmed()
-------------------
Number of graphs: 1
Number of nodes: 19717
Number of features: 500
Number of classes: 3

Graph:
------
Training nodes: 60
Evaluation nodes: 500
Test nodes: 1000
Edges are directed: False
Graph has isolated nodes: False
Graph has loops: False
```

As you can see, there are only 60 training nodes for 1,000 test nodes, which is quite challenging (a 6/94 split). Fortunately for us, with only 19,717 nodes, PubMed will be extremely fast to process with GraphSAGE.

3.  The first step in the GraphSAGE framework is neighbor sampling. PyG implements the `NeighborLoader` class to perform it. Let's keep 10 neighbors of our target node and 10 of their own neighbors. We will group our 60 target nodes into batches of 16 nodes, which should result in four batches:

```
from torch_geometric.loader import NeighborLoader

train_loader = NeighborLoader(
    data,
    num_neighbors=[10,10],
    batch_size=16,
    input_nodes=data.train_mask,
)
```

4.  By printing their information, let's verify that we obtained four subgraphs (batches):

```
for i, subgraph in enumerate(train_loader):
    print(f'Subgraph {i}: {subgraph}')

Subgraph 0: Data(x=[400, 500], edge_index=[2, 455],
y=[400], train_mask=[400], val_mask=[400], test_
mask=[400], batch_size=16)
Subgraph 1: Data(x=[262, 500], edge_index=[2, 306],
y=[262], train_mask=[262], val_mask=[262], test_
mask=[262], batch_size=16)
Subgraph 2: Data(x=[275, 500], edge_index=[2, 314],
y=[275], train_mask=[275], val_mask=[275], test_
mask=[275], batch_size=16)
Subgraph 3: Data(x=[194, 500], edge_index=[2, 227],
y=[194], train_mask=[194], val_mask=[194], test_
mask=[194], batch_size=12)
```

5.  These subgraphs contain more than 60 nodes, which is normal, since any neighbor can be sampled. We can even plot them like graphs using `matplotlib`'s subplots:

```
import numpy as np
import networkx as nx
import matplotlib.pyplot as plt
from torch_geometric.utils import to_networkx

fig = plt.figure(figsize=(16,16))
```

```
for idx, (subdata, pos) in enumerate(zip(train_loader,
[221, 222, 223, 224])):
    G = to_networkx(subdata, to_undirected=True)
    ax = fig.add_subplot(pos)
    ax.set_title(f'Subgraph {idx}', fontsize=24)
    plt.axis('off')
    nx.draw_networkx(G,
                     pos=nx.spring_layout(G, seed=0),
                     with_labels=False,
                     node_color=subdata.y,
                     )
plt.show()
```

6.    We obtain the following plot:

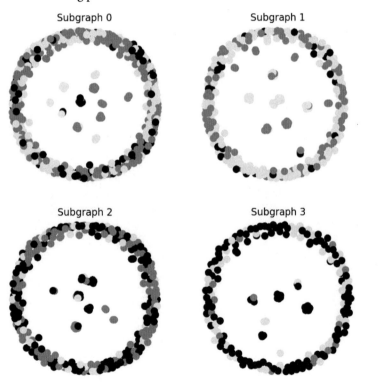

Figure 8.5 – A plot of the subgraphs obtained with neighbor sampling

Most of these nodes have a degree of 1 because of the way neighbor sampling works. In this case, it's not an issue, since their embeddings are only used once in the computation graph to calculate the embeddings of the second layer.

7.  We implement the following function to evaluate the accuracy of our model:

```
def accuracy(pred_y, y):
    return ((pred_y == y).sum() / len(y)).item()
```

8.  Let's create a GraphSAGE class using two SAGEConv layers (the mean aggregator is selected by default):

```
import torchmport torch.nn.functional as F
from torch_geometric.nn import SAGEConv


class GraphSAGE(torch.nn.Module):
    def __init__(self, dim_in, dim_h, dim_out):
        super().__init__()
        self.sage1 = SAGEConv(dim_in, dim_h)
        self.sage2 = SAGEConv(dim_h, dim_out)
```

9.  Embeddings are computed using two mean aggregators. We also use a nonlinear function (ReLU) and a dropout layer:

```
def forward(self, x, edge_index):
    h = self.sage1(x, edge_index)
    h = torch.relu(h)
    h = F.dropout(h, p=0.5, training=self.training)
    h = self.sage2(h, edge_index)
    return F.log_softmax(h, dim=1)
```

10. Now that we have to consider batches, the fit() function has to change to loop through epochs and then through batches. The metrics we want to measure have to be reinitialized at every epoch:

```
def fit(self, data, epochs):
    criterion = torch.nn.CrossEntropyLoss()
    optimizer = torch.optim.Adam(self.parameters(),
lr=0.01)
    self.train()
    for epoch in range(epochs+1):
```

```
                total_loss, val_loss, acc, val_acc = 0, 0, 0,
     0
```

11. The second loop trains the model on every batch:

```
            for batch in train_loader:
                optimizer.zero_grad()
                out = self(batch.x, batch.edge_index)
                loss = criterion(out[batch.train_mask],
    batch.y[batch.train_mask])
                total_loss += loss
                acc += accuracy(out[batch.train_mask].
    argmax(dim=1), batch.y[batch.train_mask])
                loss.backward()
                optimizer.step()

                # Validation
                val_loss += criterion(out[batch.val_
    mask], batch.y[batch.val_mask])
                val_acc += accuracy(out[batch.val_mask].
    argmax(dim=1), batch.y[batch.val_mask])
```

12. We also want to print our metrics. They must be divided by the number of batches to represent an epoch:

```
            if epoch % 20 == 0:
                print(f'Epoch {epoch:>3} | Train
    Loss: {loss/len(train_loader):.3f} | Train Acc: {acc/
    len(train_loader)*100:>6.2f}% | Val Loss: {val_loss/
    len(train_loader):.2f} | Val Acc: {val_acc/len(train_
    loader)*100:.2f}%')
```

13. The test() function does not change, since we don't use batches for the test set:

```
        @torch.no_grad()
        def test(self, data):
            self.eval()
            out = self(data.x, data.edge_index)
            acc = accuracy(out.argmax(dim=1)[data.test_mask],
    data.y[data.test_mask])
            return acc
```

14. Let's create a model with a hidden dimension of 64 and train it for 200 epochs:

```
graphsage = GraphSAGE(dataset.num_features, 64, dataset.
num_classes)
print(graphsage)
graphsage.fit(data, 200)
```

15. This gives us the following output:

```
GraphSAGE(
    (sage1): SAGEConv(500, 64, aggr=mean)
    (sage2): SAGEConv(64, 3, aggr=mean)
)
Epoch 0 | Train Loss: 0.317 | Train Acc: 28.77% | Val
Loss: 1.13 | Val Acc: 19.55%
Epoch 20 | Train Loss: 0.001 | Train Acc: 100.00% | Val
Loss: 0.62 | Val Acc: 75.07%
Epoch 40 | Train Loss: 0.000 | Train Acc: 100.00% | Val
Loss: 0.55 | Val Acc: 80.56%
Epoch 60 | Train Loss: 0.000 | Train Acc: 100.00% | Val
Loss: 0.35 | Val Acc: 86.11%
Epoch 80 | Train Loss: 0.002 | Train Acc: 100.00% | Val
Loss: 0.64 | Val Acc: 73.58%
Epoch 100 | Train Loss: 0.000 | Train Acc: 100.00% | Val
Loss: 0.79 | Val Acc: 74.72%
Epoch 120 | Train Loss: 0.000 | Train Acc: 100.00% | Val
Loss: 0.71 | Val Acc: 76.75%
Epoch 140 | Train Loss: 0.000 | Train Acc: 100.00% | Val
Loss: 0.75 | Val Acc: 67.50%
Epoch 160 | Train Loss: 0.000 | Train Acc: 100.00% | Val
Loss: 0.63 | Val Acc: 73.54%
Epoch 180 | Train Loss: 0.000 | Train Acc: 100.00% | Val
Loss: 0.47 | Val Acc: 86.11%
Epoch 200 | Train Loss: 0.000 | Train Acc: 100.00% | Val
Loss: 0.48 | Val Acc: 78.37%
```

Note that the mean aggregator was automatically selected for both SAGEConv layers.

16. Finally, let's test it on the test set:

```
acc = graphsage.test(data)
print(f'GraphSAGE test accuracy: {acc*100:.2f}%')
```

```
GraphSAGE test accuracy: 74.70%
```

Considering this dataset's unfavorable train/test split, we obtain a decent test accuracy of 74.70%. However, GraphSAGE gets a lower average accuracy than a GCN (-0.5%) or a GAT (-1.4%) on PubMed. So why should we use it?

The answer is evident when you train the three models – GraphSAGE is extremely fast. On a consumer GPU, it is 4 times faster than a GCN and 88 times faster than a GAT. Even if GPU memory was not an issue, GraphSAGE could handle larger graphs, producing better results than small networks.

To complete this deep-dive into GraphSAGE's architecture, we must discuss one more feature – its inductive capabilities.

## Inductive learning on protein-protein interactions

In GNNs, we distinguish two types of learning – **transductive** and **inductive**. They can be summarized as follows:

- In inductive learning, the GNN only sees data from the training set during training. This is the typical supervised learning setting in machine learning. In this situation, labels are used to tune the GNN's parameters.

- In transductive learning, the GNN sees data from the training and test sets during training. However, it only learns data from the training set. In this situation, the labels are used for information diffusion.

The transductive situation should be familiar, since it is the only one we have covered so far. Indeed, you can see in the previous example that GraphSAGE makes predictions using the whole graph during training (`self(batch.x, batch.edge_index)`). We then mask part of these predictions to calculate the loss and train the model only using training data (`criterion(out[batch.train_mask], batch.y[batch.train_mask])`).

Transductive learning can only generate embeddings for a fixed graph; it does not generalize for unseen nodes or graphs. However, thanks to neighbor sampling, GraphSAGE is designed to make predictions at a local level with pruned computation graphs. It is considered an inductive framework, since it can be applied to any computation graph with the same feature schema.

Let's apply it to a new dataset – the protein-protein interaction (PPI) network, described by Agrawal et al. [5]. This dataset is a collection of 24 graphs, where nodes (21,557) are human proteins and edges (342,353) are physical interactions between proteins in a human cell. *Figure 8.6* shows a representation of PPI made with Gephi.

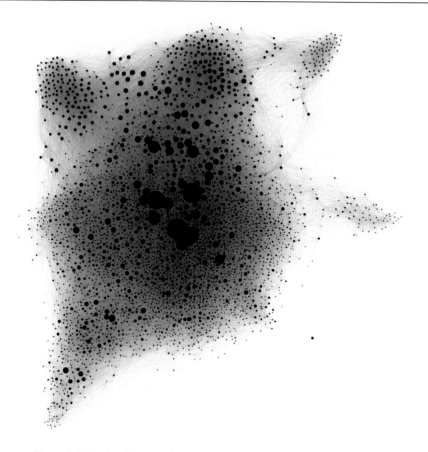

Figure 8.6 – A visualization of the protein-protein interaction network

The goal of the dataset is to perform multi-label classification with 121 labels. This means that every node can range from 0 to 121 labels. This differs from a multi-class classification, where every node would only have one class.

Let's implement a new GraphSAGE model using PyG:

1. We load the PPI dataset with three different splits – train, validation, and test:

```
from torch_geometric.datasets import PPI

train_dataset = PPI(root=".", split='train')
val_dataset = PPI(root=".", split='val')
test_dataset = PPI(root=".", split='test')
```

2. The training set comprises 20 graphs, while the validation and test sets only have two. We want to apply neighbor sampling to the training set. For convenience, let's unify all the training graphs in a single set, using `Batch.from_data_list()`, and then apply neighbor sampling:

```
from torch_geometric.data import Batch
from torch_geometric.loader import NeighborLoader


train_data = Batch.from_data_list(train_dataset)
loader = NeighborLoader(train_data, batch_size=2048,
shuffle=True, num_neighbors=[20, 10], num_workers=2,
persistent_workers=True)
```

3. The training set is ready. We can create our batches using the `DataLoader` class. We define a `batch_size` value of 2, corresponding to the number of graphs in each batch:

```
from torch_geometric.loader import DataLoader


train_loader = DataLoader(train_dataset, batch_size=2)
val_loader = DataLoader(val_dataset, batch_size=2)
test_loader = DataLoader(test_dataset, batch_size=2)
```

4. One of the main benefits of these batches is that they can be processed on a GPU. We can get a GPU if one is available, or take a CPU otherwise:

```
device = torch.device('cuda' if torch.cuda.is_available()
else 'cpu')
```

5. Instead of implementing GraphSAGE by ourselves, we can directly use PyTorch Geometric's implementation from `torch_geometric.nn`. We initialize it with two layers and a hidden dimension of 512. In addition, we need to place the model on the same device as our data, using `to(device)`:

```
from torch_geometric.nn import GraphSAGE


model = GraphSAGE(
    in_channels=train_dataset.num_features,
    hidden_channels=512,
    num_layers=2,
    out_channels=train_dataset.num_classes,
).to(device)
```

6.  The `fit()` function is similar to the one we used in the previous section, with two exceptions. First, we want to move the data to a GPU when possible. Secondly, we have two graphs per batch, so we multiply the individual loss by two (`data.num_graphs`):

```
criterion = torch.nn.BCEWithLogitsLoss()
optimizer = torch.optim.Adam(model.parameters(),
lr=0.005)


def fit():
    model.train()

    total_loss = 0
    for data in train_loader:
        data = data.to(device)
        optimizer.zero_grad()
        out = model(data.x, data.edge_index)
        loss = criterion(out, data.y)
        total_loss += loss.item() * data.num_graphs
        loss.backward()
        optimizer.step()
    return total_loss / len(train_loader.dataset)
```

In the `test()` function, we take advantage of the fact that `val_loader` and `test_loader` have two graphs and a `batch_size` value of 2. That means that the two graphs are in the same batch; we don't need to loop through the loaders like during training.

7.  Instead of accuracy, let's use another metric – the F1 score. It corresponds to the harmonic mean of precision and recall. However, our predictions are 121-dim vectors of real numbers. We need to transform them into binary vectors, using `out > 0` to compare them to `data.y`:

```
from sklearn.metrics import f1_score
@torch.no_grad()
def test(loader):
    model.eval()
    data = next(iter(loader))
    out = model(data.x.to(device), data.edge_index.
to(device))
    preds = (out > 0).float().cpu()
    y, pred = data.y.numpy(), preds.numpy()
```

```
        return f1_score(y, pred, average='micro') if pred.
sum() > 0 else 0
```

8. Let's train our model for 300 epochs and print the validation F1 score during training:

```
for epoch in range(301):
    loss = fit()
    val_f1 = test(val_loader)
    if epoch % 50 == 0:
        print(f'Epoch {epoch:>3} | Train Loss: {loss:.3f}
| Val F1 score: {val_f1:.4f}')
```

```
Epoch   0 | Train Loss: 0.589 | Val F1-score: 0.4245
Epoch  50 | Train Loss: 0.194 | Val F1-score: 0.8400
Epoch 100 | Train Loss: 0.143 | Val F1-score: 0.8779
Epoch 150 | Train Loss: 0.123 | Val F1-score: 0.8935
Epoch 200 | Train Loss: 0.107 | Val F1-score: 0.9013
Epoch 250 | Train Loss: 0.104 | Val F1-score: 0.9076
Epoch 300 | Train Loss: 0.090 | Val F1-score: 0.9154
```

9. Finally, we calculate the F1 score on the test set:

```
print(f'Test F1 score: {test(test_loader):.4f}')
Test F1 score: 0.9360
```

We obtain an excellent F1 score of 0.9360 in an inductive setting. This value dramatically changes when you increase or decrease the size of the hidden channels. You can try it for yourself with different values, such as 128 and 1,024 instead of 512.

If you look carefully at the code, there is no masking involved. Indeed, inductive learning is forced by the PPI dataset; the training, validation, and test data are in different graphs and loaders. Naturally, we could merge them using Batch.from_data_list() and fall back into a transductive situation.

We could also train GraphSAGE without labels using unsupervised learning. This is particularly useful when labels are scarce or provided by downstream applications. However, it requires a new loss function to encourage nearby nodes to have similar representations while ensuring that distant nodes have distant embeddings:

$$J_G(h_i) = -log\left(\sigma(h_i^T h_j)\right) - Q \cdot E_{j_n \sim P_n(j)} \, log\left(\sigma(-h_i^T h_{j_n})\right)$$

Here, $j$ is a neighbor of $u$ in a random walk, $\sigma$ is the sigmoid function, $P_n(j)$ is the negative sampling distribution for $j$, and $Q$ is the number of negative samples:

Finally, PinSAGE and Uber Eats' versions of GraphSAGE are recommender systems. They combine the unsupervised setting with a different loss because of this application. Their objective is to rank the most relevant entities (food, restaurants, pins, and so on) for each user, which is an entirely different task. To perform that, they implement a max-margin ranking loss that considers pairs of embeddings.

If you need to scale up GNNs, other solutions can be considered. Here are short descriptions of two standard techniques:

- **Cluster-GCN** [6] provides a different answer to the question of how to create mini-batches. Instead of neighbor sampling, it divides the graph into isolated communities. These communities are then processed as independent graphs, which can negatively impact the quality of the resulting embeddings.

- Simplifying GNNs can decrease training and inference times. In practice, simplification consists of discarding nonlinear activation functions. Linear layers can then be compressed into one matrix multiplication using linear algebra. Naturally, these simplified versions are not as accurate as real GNNs on small datasets but are efficient for large graphs, such as Twitter [7].

As you can see, GraphSAGE is a flexible framework that can be tweaked and fine-tuned to suit your goals. Even if you don't reuse its exact formulation, it introduces key concepts that greatly influence GNN architectures in general.

## Summary

This chapter introduced the GraphSAGE framework and its two components – the neighbor sampling algorithm and three aggregation operators. Neighbor sampling is at the core of GraphSAGE's ability to process large graphs in a short amount of time. It is also responsible for its inductive setting, which allows it to generalize predictions to unseen nodes and graphs. We tested a transductive situation on PubMed and an inductive one to perform a new task on the PPI dataset – multi-label classification. While not as accurate as a GCN or a GAT, GraphSAGE is a popular and efficient framework for processing massive amounts of data.

In *Chapter 9, Defining Expressiveness for Graph Classification*, we will try to define what makes a GNN powerful in terms of representation. We will introduce a famous graph algorithm called the Weisfeiler-Lehman isomorphism test. It will act as a benchmark to evaluate the theoretical performance of numerous GNN architectures, including the graph isomorphism network. We will apply this GNN to perform a new prevalent task – graph classification.

## Further reading

- [1] W. L. Hamilton, R. Ying, and J. Leskovec. *Inductive Representation Learning on Large Graphs.* arXiv, 2017. DOI: 10.48550/ARXIV.1706.02216.

- [2] R. Ying, R. He, K. Chen, P. Eksombatchai, W. L. Hamilton, and J. Leskovec. *Graph Convolutional Neural Networks for Web-Scale Recommender Systems.* Jul. 2018. DOI: 10.1145/3219819.3219890.

- [3] Ankit Jain. *Food Discovery with Uber Eats: Using Graph Learning to Power Recommendations*: `https://www.uber.com/en-US/blog/uber-eats-graph-learning/`.

- [4] Galileo Mark Namata, Ben London, Lise Getoor, and Bert Huang. *Query-Driven Active Surveying for Collective Classification.* International Workshop on Mining and Learning with Graphs. 2012.

- [5] M. Agrawal, M. Zitnik, and J. Leskovec. *Large-scale analysis of disease pathways in the human interactome.* Nov. 2017. DOI: 10.1142/9789813235533_0011.

- [6] W.-L. Chiang, X. Liu, S. Si, Y. Li, S. Bengio, and C.-J. Hsieh. *Cluster-GCN.* Jul. 2019. DOI: 10.1145/3292500.3330925.

- [7] F. Frasca, E. Rossi, D. Eynard, B. Chamberlain, M. Bronstein, and F. Monti. *SIGN: Scalable Inception Graph Neural Networks.* arXiv, 2020. DOI: 10.48550/ARXIV.2004.11198.

# 9

# Defining Expressiveness for Graph Classification

In the previous chapter, we traded accuracy for scalability. We saw that it was instrumental in applications such as recommender systems. However, it raises several questions about what makes GNNs "accurate." Where does this precision come from? Can we use this knowledge to design better GNNs?

This chapter will clarify what makes a GNN powerful by introducing the **Weisfeiler-Leman (WL)** test. This test will give us the framework to understand an essential concept in GNNs – **expressiveness**. We will use it to compare different GNN layers and see which one is the most expressive. This result will then be used to design a more powerful GNN than GCNs, GATs, and GraphSAGE.

Finally, we will implement it using PyTorch Geometric to perform a new task – graph classification. We will implement a new GNN on the PROTEINS dataset, comprising 1,113 graphs representing proteins. We will compare different methods for graph classification and analyze our results.

By the end of this chapter, you will understand what makes a GNN expressive and how to measure it. You will be able to implement a new GNN architecture based on the WL test and perform graph classification using various techniques.

In this chapter, we will cover the following main topics:

- Defining expressiveness
- Introducing the GIN
- Classifying graphs with GIN

# Technical requirements

All the code examples from this chapter can be found on GitHub at `https://github.com/PacktPublishing/Hands-On-Graph-Neural-Networks-Using-Python/tree/main/Chapter09`.

Installation steps required to run the code on your local machine can be found in the *Preface* section of this book.

# Defining expressiveness

Neural networks are used to approximate functions. This is justified by the **universal approximation theorem**, which states that a feedforward neural network with only one layer can approximate any smooth function. But what about universal function approximation on graphs? This is a more complex problem that requires the ability to distinguish graph structures.

With GNNs, our goal is to produce the best node embeddings possible. This means that different nodes must have different embeddings, and similar nodes must have similar embeddings. But how do we know that two nodes are similar? Embeddings are computed using node features and connections. Therefore, we have to compare their features and neighbors to distinguish nodes.

In graph theory, this is referred to as the graph **isomorphism** problem. Two graphs are isomorphic ("the same") if they have the same connections, and their only difference is a permutation of their nodes (see *Figure 9.1*). In 1968, Weisfeiler and Lehman [1] proposed an efficient algorithm to solve this problem, now known as the WL test.

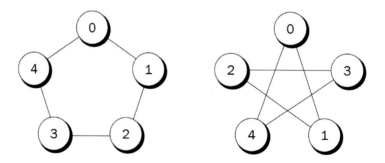

Figure 9.1 – An example of two isomorphic graphs

The WL test aims to build the **canonical form** of a graph. We can then compare the canonical form of two graphs to check whether they are isomorphic or not. However, this test is not perfect, and non-isomorphic graphs can share the same canonical form. This can be surprising, but it is an intricate problem that is still not completely understood; for instance, the complexity of the WL algorithm is unknown.

The WL test works as follows:

1. At the beginning, each node in the graph receives the same color.

2. Each node aggregates its own color and the colors of its neighbors.

3. The result is fed to a hash function that produces a new color.

4. Each node aggregates its new color and the new colors of its neighbors.

5. The result is fed to a hash function that produces a new color.

6. These steps are repeated until no more nodes change color.

The following figure summarizes the WL algorithm.

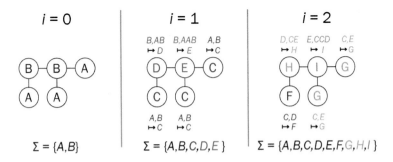

Figure 9.2 – An application of the WL algorithm to get the canonical form of a graph

The resulting colors give us the canonical form of the graph. If two graphs do not share the same colors, they are not isomorphic. Conversely, we cannot be sure they are isomorphic if they obtain the same colors.

The steps we described should be familiar; they are surprisingly close to what GNNs perform. Colors are a form of embeddings, and the hash function is an aggregator. But it is not just any aggregator; the hash function is particularly suited for this task. Would it still be as efficient if we were to replace it with another function, such as a mean or max aggregator (as seen in *Chapter 8*)?

Let's see the result for each operator:

- With the mean aggregator, having 1 blue node and 1 red node, or 10 blue nodes and 10 red nodes, results in the same embedding (half blue and half red).

- With the max aggregator, half of the nodes would be ignored in the previous example; the embedding would only consider the blue or red color.

- With the sum aggregator, however, every node contributes to the final embedding; having 1 red node and 1 blue node is different from having 10 blue nodes and 10 red nodes.

Indeed, the sum aggregator can discriminate more graph structures than the other two. If we follow this logic, this can only mean one thing – the aggregators we have been using so far are suboptimal, since they are strictly less expressive than a sum. Can we use this knowledge to build better GNNs? In the next section, we will introduce the **Graph Isomorphism Network (GIN)** based on this idea.

## Introducing the GIN

In the previous section, we saw that the GNNs introduced in the previous chapters were less expressive than the WL test. This is an issue because the ability to distinguish more graph structures seems to be connected to the quality of the resulting embeddings. In this section, we will translate the theoretical framework into a new GNN architecture – the GIN.

Introduced in 2018 by Xu et al. in a paper called *"How Powerful are Graph Neural Networks?"* [2], the GIN is designed to be as expressive as the WL test. The authors generalized our observations on aggregation by dividing it into two functions:

- **Aggregate**: This function, $f$, selects the neighboring nodes that the GNN considers
- **Combine**: This function, $\phi$, combines the embeddings from the selected nodes to produce the new embedding of the target node

The embedding of the $i$ node can be written as the following:

$$h_i^{'} = \phi \left( h_i, f \left( \{ h_j : j \in \mathcal{N}_i \} \right) \right)$$

In the case of a GCN, the $f$ function aggregates every neighbor of the $i$ node, and $\phi$ applies a specific mean aggregator. In the case of GraphSAGE, the neighborhood sampling is the $f$ function, and we saw three options for $\phi$ – the mean, LSTM, and max aggregators.

So, what are these functions in the GIN? Xu et al. argue that they have to be **injective**. As shown in *Figure 9.3*, injective functions map distinct inputs to distinct outputs. This is precisely what we want to distinguish graph structures. If the functions were not injective, we would end up with the same output for different inputs. In this case, our embeddings would be less valuable because they would contain less information.

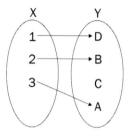

Figure 9.3 – A mapping diagram of an injective function

The GIN's authors use a clever trick to design these two functions – they simply approximate them. In the GAT layer, we learned the self-attention weights. In this example, we can learn both functions using a single MLP, thanks to the universal approximation theorem:

$$h_i' = MLP\left( (1 + \varepsilon) \cdot h_i + \sum_{j \in \mathcal{N}_i} h_j \right)$$

Here, $\varepsilon$ is a learnable parameter or a fixed scalar, representing the importance of the target node's embedding compared to its neighbors'. The authors also emphasize that the MLP must have more than one layer to distinguish specific graph structures.

We now have a GNN that is as expressive as the WL test. Can we do even better? The answer is yes. The WL test can be generalized to a hierarchy of higher-level tests known as **k-WL**. Instead of considering individual nodes, $k$-WL tests look at $k$-tuples of nodes. It means that they are non-local, since they can look at distant nodes. This is also why $(k + 1)$-WL tests can distinguish more graph structures than $k$-WL tests for $k \geq 2$.

Several architectures based on $k$-WL tests have been proposed, such as the **k-GNN** by Morris et al. [3]. While these architectures help us better understand how GNNs work, they tend to underperform in practice compared to less expressive models, such as GNNs or GATs [4]. But all hope is not lost, as we will see in the next section in the particular context of graph classification.

# Classifying graphs using GIN

We could directly implement a GIN model for node classification, but this architecture is more interesting for performing graph classification. In this section, we will see how to transform node embeddings into graph embeddings using **global pooling** techniques. We will then apply these techniques to the PROTEINS dataset and compare our results using GIN and GCN models.

## Graph classification

Graph classification is based on the node embeddings that a GNN produces. This operation is often called global pooling or **graph-level readout**. There are three simple ways of implementing it:

- **Mean global pooling**: The graph embedding $h_G$ is obtained by averaging the embeddings of every node in the graph:

$$h_G = \frac{1}{N} \sum_{i=0}^{N} h_i$$

- **Max global pooling**: The graph embedding is obtained by selecting the highest value for each node dimension:

$$h_G = \max_{i=0}^{N}(h_i)$$

- **Sum global pooling**: The graph embedding is obtained by summing the embeddings of every node in the graph:

$$h_G = \sum_{i=0}^{N} h_i$$

According to what we saw in the first section, the sum global pooling is strictly more expressive than the two other techniques. The GIN's authors also note that to consider all structural information, it is necessary to consider embeddings produced by every layer of the GNN. In summary, we concatenate the sum of node embeddings produced by each of the $k$ layers of our GNN:

$$h_G = \sum_{i=0}^{N} h_i^0 \; || \; \dots \; || \sum_{i=0}^{N} h_i^k$$

This solution elegantly combines the expressive power of the sum operator with the memory of each layer provided by the concatenation.

## Implementing the GIN

We will now implement a GIN model with the previous graph-level readout function on the PROTEINS [5, 6, 7] dataset.

This dataset comprises 1,113 graphs representing proteins, where every node is an amino acid. An edge connects two nodes when their distance is lower than 0.6 nanometers. The goal of this dataset is to classify each protein as an **enzyme**. Enzymes are a particular type of protein that act as catalysts to speed up chemical reactions in a cell. For instance, enzymes called lipases aid in the digestion of food. *Figure 9.4* shows the 3D plot of a protein.

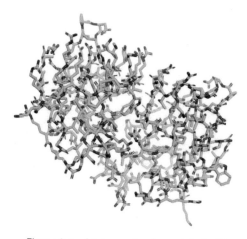

Figure 9.4 – An example of a protein in 3D

Let's implement a GIN model on this dataset:

1.  First, we import the PROTEINS dataset using the TUDataset class from PyTorch Geometric and print the information:

```
from torch_geometric.datasets import TUDataset


dataset = TUDataset(root='.', name='PROTEINS').shuffle()


print(f'Dataset: {dataset}')
print('-----------------------')
print(f'Number of graphs: {len(dataset)}')
print(f'Number of nodes: {dataset[0].x.shape[0]}')
print(f'Number of features: {dataset.num_features}')
print(f'Number of classes: {dataset.num_classes}')


Dataset: PROTEINS(1113)
-----------------------
Number of graphs: 1113
Number of nodes: 30
Number of features: 0
Number of classes: 2
```

2.  We split the data (graphs) into training, validation, and test sets with an 80/10/10 split respectively:

```
from torch_geometric.loader import DataLoader


train_dataset = dataset[:int(len(dataset)*0.8)]
val_dataset   =
dataset[int(len(dataset)*0.8):int(len(dataset)*0.9)]
test_dataset  = dataset[int(len(dataset)*0.9):]


print(f'Training set   = {len(train_dataset)} graphs')
print(f'Validation set = {len(val_dataset)} graphs')
print(f'Test set       = {len(test_dataset)} graphs')
```

3.  This gives us the following output:

```
Training set   = 890 graphs
Validation set = 111 graphs
Test set       = 112 graphs
```

4.  We convert these splits into mini-batches using the `DataLoader` object with a batch size of 64. This means that each batch will contain up to 64 graphs:

```
train_loader = DataLoader(train_dataset, batch_size=64,
shuffle=True)
val_loader   = DataLoader(val_dataset, batch_size=64,
shuffle=True)
test_loader  = DataLoader(test_dataset, batch_size=64,
shuffle=True)
```

5.  We can verify that by printing information about each batch, as follows:

```
print('\nTrain loader:')
for i, batch in enumerate(train_loader):
    print(f' - Batch {i}: {batch}')

print('\nValidation loader:')
for i, batch in enumerate(val_loader):
    print(f' - Batch {i}: {batch}')

print('\nTest loader:')
for i, batch in enumerate(test_loader):
    print(f' - Batch {i}: {batch}')


Train loader:
  - Batch 0: DataBatch(edge_index=[2, 8622], x=[2365, 0],
y=[64], batch=[2365], ptr=[65])
  - Batch 1: DataBatch(edge_index=[2, 6692], x=[1768, 0],
y=[64], batch=[1768], ptr=[65])
...
  - Batch 13: DataBatch(edge_index=[2, 7864], x=[2102, 0],
y=[58], batch=[2102], ptr=[59])


Validation loader:
```

```
  - Batch 0: DataBatch(edge_index=[2, 8724], x=[2275, 0],
y=[64], batch=[2275], ptr=[65])
  - Batch 1: DataBatch(edge_index=[2, 8388], x=[2257, 0],
y=[47], batch=[2257], ptr=[48])


Test loader:
  - Batch 0: DataBatch(edge_index=[2, 7906], x=[2187, 0],
y=[64], batch=[2187], ptr=[65])
  - Batch 1: DataBatch(edge_index=[2, 9442], x=[2518, 0],
y=[48], batch=[2518], ptr=[49])
```

Let's start implementing a GIN model. The first question we have to answer is the composition of our GIN layer. We need an MLP with at least two layers. Following the authors' guidelines, we can also introduce batch normalization to standardize the inputs of each hidden layer, which stabilizes and speeds up training. In summary, our GIN layer has the following composition:

$$Linear \rightarrow BatchNorm \rightarrow ReLU \rightarrow Linear \rightarrow ReLU$$

In code, it is defined as follows:

```
import torch
torch.manual_seed(0)
import torch.nn.functional as F
from torch.nn import Linear, Sequential, BatchNorm1d,
ReLU, Dropout
from torch_geometric.nn import GINConv
from torch_geometric.nn import global_add_pool


class GIN(torch.nn.Module):
    def __init__(self, dim_h):
        super(GIN, self).__init__()
        self.conv1 = GINConv(
            Sequential(Linear(dataset.num_node_features,
dim_h), BatchNorm1d(dim_h), ReLU(), Linear(dim_h, dim_h),
ReLU()))
        self.conv2 = GINConv(
            Sequential(Linear(dim_h, dim_h),
BatchNorm1d(dim_h), ReLU(), Linear(dim_h, dim_h),
ReLU()))
        self.conv3 = GINConv(
            Sequential(Linear(dim_h, dim_h),
```

```
BatchNorm1d(dim_h), ReLU(), Linear(dim_h, dim_h),
ReLU()))
```

> **Note**
>
> PyTorch Geometric also offers the GINE layer, a modified version of the GIN layer. It was introduced in 2019 by Hu et al. in *"Strategies for Pre-training Graph Neural Networks"* [8]. Its major improvement over the previous GIN version is the ability to consider edge features during the aggregation process. The PROTEINS dataset does not have edge features, which is why we will implement the classic GIN model instead.

6. Our model is not complete yet. We must not forget that we want to perform graph classification. It requires the sum of every node embedding in the graph for each layer. In other words, we will need to store one vector of dim_h size per layer – three, in this example. This is why we add a linear layer with 3*dim_h size before the final linear layer for binary classification (data.num_classes = 2):

```
self.lin1 = Linear(dim_h*3, dim_h*3)
self.lin2 = Linear(dim_h*3, dataset.num_classes)
```

7. We must implement the logic to connect our initialized layers. Each layer produces a different embedding tensor – h1, h2, and h3. We sum them using the global_add_pool() function and then concatenate them with torch.cat(). This gives us the input to our classifier, which acts as a regular neural network with a dropout layer:

```
def forward(self, x, edge_index, batch):
    # Node embeddings
    h1 = self.conv1(x, edge_index)
    h2 = self.conv2(h1, edge_index)
    h3 = self.conv3(h2, edge_index)

    # Graph-level readout
    h1 = global_add_pool(h1, batch)
    h2 = global_add_pool(h2, batch)
    h3 = global_add_pool(h3, batch)

    # Concatenate graph embeddings
    h = torch.cat((h1, h2, h3), dim=1)

    # Classifier
    h = self.lin1(h)
```

```
        h = h.relu()
        h = F.dropout(h, p=0.5, training=self.training)
        h = self.lin2(h)

        return F.log_softmax(h, dim=1)
```

8.  We can now implement a regular training loop with mini-batching for 100 epochs:

```
def train(model, loader):
    criterion = torch.nn.CrossEntropyLoss()
    optimizer = torch.optim.Adam(model.parameters(),
lr=0.01)
    epochs = 100

    model.train()
    for epoch in range(epochs+1):
        total_loss = 0
        acc = 0
        val_loss = 0
        val_acc = 0

        # Train on batches
        for data in loader:
            optimizer.zero_grad()
            out = model(data.x, data.edge_index, data.
batch)
            loss = criterion(out, data.y)
            total_loss += loss / len(loader)
            acc += accuracy(out.argmax(dim=1), data.y) /
len(loader)
            loss.backward()
            optimizer.step()

        # Validation
        val_loss, val_acc = test(model, val_loader)
```

9. We print the training and validation accuracy every 20 epochs and return the trained model:

```
# Print metrics every 20 epochs
if (epoch % 20 == 0):
    print(f'Epoch {epoch:>3} | Train Loss:
{total_loss:.2f} | Train Acc: {acc*100:>5.2f}% | Val
Loss: {val_loss:.2f} | Val Acc: {val_acc*100:.2f}%')

return model
```

10. Unlike the `test` function from the previous chapter, this one must also include mini-batching, since our validation and test loaders contain more than one batch:

```
@torch.no_grad()
def test(model, loader):
    criterion = torch.nn.CrossEntropyLoss()
    model.eval()
    loss = 0
    acc = 0

    for data in loader:
        out = model(data.x, data.edge_index, data.batch)
        loss += criterion(out, data.y) / len(loader)
        acc += accuracy(out.argmax(dim=1), data.y) /
len(loader)

    return loss, acc
```

11. We define the function we will use to calculate the accuracy score:

```
def accuracy(pred_y, y):
    return ((pred_y == y).sum() / len(y)).item()
```

12. Let's instantiate and train our GIN model:

```
gin = GIN(dim_h=32)
gin = train(gin, train_loader)

Epoch 0 | Train Loss: 1.33 | Train Acc: 58.04% | Val
Loss: 0.70 | Val Acc: 59.97%
Epoch 20 | Train Loss: 0.54 | Train Acc: 74.50% | Val
```

```
Loss: 0.55 | Val Acc: 76.86%
Epoch 40 | Train Loss: 0.50 | Train Acc: 76.28% | Val
Loss: 0.56 | Val Acc: 74.73%
Epoch 60 | Train Loss: 0.50 | Train Acc: 76.77% | Val
Loss: 0.54 | Val Acc: 72.04%
Epoch 80 | Train Loss: 0.49 | Train Acc: 76.95% | Val
Loss: 0.57 | Val Acc: 73.67%
Epoch 100 | Train Loss: 0.50 | Train Acc: 76.04% | Val
Loss: 0.53 | Val Acc: 69.55%
```

13. Finally, let's test it using the test loader:

```
test_loss, test_acc = test(gin, test_loader)
print(f'Test Loss: {test_loss:.2f} | Test Acc: {test_
acc*100:.2f}%')
```

```
Test Loss: 0.44 | Test Acc: 81.77%
```

To better understand this final test score, we can implement a GCN that performs graph classification with a simple global mean pooling (global_mean_pool() in PyTorch Geometric). With the exact same setting, it achieves an average accuracy score of 53.72% ($\pm$ 0.73%) on 100 experiments. This is much lower than the average 76.56% ($\pm$ 1.77%) obtained by the GIN model.

We can conclude that the entire GIN architecture is much more suited for this graph classification task than GCNs. According to the theoretical framework we used, this is explained by the fact that GCNs are strictly less expressive than GINs. In other words, GINs can distinguish more graph structures than GCNs, which is why they are more accurate. We can verify this assumption by visualizing the mistakes made by both models:

1. We import the matplotlib and networkx libraries to make a 4x4 plot of proteins:

```
import numpy as np
import networkx as nx
import matplotlib.pyplot as plt
from torch_geometric.utils import to_networkx

fig, ax = plt.subplots(4, 4)
```

2. For each protein, we get the final classification from our GNN (the GIN in this case). We give the prediction a green color if it is correct (red otherwise):

```
for i, data in enumerate(dataset[-16:]):
    out = gcn(data.x, data.edge_index, data.batch)
```

```
      color = "green" if out.argmax(dim=1) == data.y else
"red"
```

3. We convert our protein into a `networkx` graph for convenience. We can then draw it using the `nx.draw_networkx()` function:

```
ix = np.unravel_index(i, ax.shape)
ax[ix].axis('off')
G = to_networkx(dataset[i], to_undirected=True)
nx.draw_networkx(G,
                 pos=nx.spring_layout(G, seed=0),
                 with_labels=False,
                 node_size=10,
                 node_color=color,
                 width=0.8,
                 ax=ax[ix]
                 )
```

4. We obtain the following plot for the GIN model.

Figure 9.5 – Graph classifications produced by the GIN model

5.   We repeat this process for the GCN and get the following visualization.

Figure 9.6 – Graph classifications produced by the GCN model

As expected, the GCN model makes more mistakes. Understanding which graph structures are not adequately captured would require extensive analysis for each protein correctly classified by GIN. However, we can see that the GIN also makes different mistakes. This is interesting because it shows that these models can be complementary.

Creating ensembles from models that make different mistakes is a common technique in machine learning. We could use different approaches, such as a third model trained on our final classifications. As creating ensembles is not the goal of this chapter, we will implement a simple model-averaging technique instead:

1.   First, we set the models in evaluation mode and define the variables to store accuracy scores:

```
gcn.eval()
gin.eval()
acc_gcn = 0
acc_gin = 0
acc_ens = 0
```

2. We get the final classifications for each model and combine them to get the ensemble's predictions:

```
for data in test_loader:
    out_gcn = gcn(data.x, data.edge_index, data.batch)
    out_gin = gin(data.x, data.edge_index, data.batch)
    out_ens = (out_gcn + out_gin)/2
```

3. We calculate the accuracy scores for the three sets of predictions:

```
    acc_gcn += accuracy(out_gcn.argmax(dim=1), data.y) /
len(test_loader)
    acc_gin += accuracy(out_gin.argmax(dim=1), data.y) /
len(test_loader)
    acc_ens += accuracy(out_ens.argmax(dim=1), data.y) /
len(test_loader)
```

4. Finally, let's print the results:

```
print(f'GCN accuracy:     {acc_gcn*100:.2f}%')
print(f'GIN accuracy:     {acc_gin*100:.2f}%')
print(f'GCN+GIN accuracy: {acc_ens*100:.2f}%')
```

```
GCN accuracy: 72.14%
GIN accuracy: 80.99%
GCN+GIN accuracy: 81.25%
```

In this example, our ensemble outperforms both models with an accuracy score of 81.25% (compared to 72.14% for the GCN and 80.99% for the GIN). This result is significant, as it shows the possibilities offered by this kind of technique. However, this is not necessarily the case in general; even with this example, the ensemble model does not consistently outperform the GIN. We could enrich it with embeddings from other architectures, such as Node2Vec, and see whether it improves the final accuracy.

## Summary

In this chapter, we defined the expressive power of GNNs. This definition is based on another algorithm, the WL method, which outputs the canonical form of a graph. This algorithm is not perfect, but it can distinguish most graph structures. It inspired the GIN architecture, designed to be as expressive as the WL test and, therefore, strictly more expressive than GCNs, GATs, or GraphSAGE.

We then implemented this architecture for graph classification. We saw different methods to combine node embeddings into graph embeddings. GIN offers a new technique, which incorporates a sum operator and the concatenation of graph embeddings produced by every GIN layer. It significantly outperformed the classic global mean pooling obtained with GCN layers. Finally, we combined predictions made by both models into a simple ensemble, which increased the accuracy score even further.

In *Chapter 10, Predicting Links with Graph Neural Networks*, we will explore another popular task with GNNs – link prediction. In fact, this is not entirely new, as previous techniques we saw such as `DeepWalk` and `Node2Vec` were already based on this idea. We will explain why and introduce two new GNN frameworks – the Graph (Variational) Autoencoder and SEAL. Finally, we will implement and compare them on the `Cora` dataset on a link prediction task.

# Further reading

- [1] Weisfeiler and Lehman, A.A. (1968) A Reduction of a Graph to a Canonical Form and an Algebra Arising during This Reduction. Nauchno-Technicheskaya Informatsia, 9.

- [2] K. Xu, W. Hu, J. Leskovec, and S. Jegelka, *How Powerful are Graph Neural Networks?* arXiv, 2018. doi: 10.48550/ARXIV.1810.00826.

- [3] C. Morris et al., *Weisfeiler and Leman Go Neural: Higher-order Graph Neural Networks.* arXiv, 2018. doi: 10.48550/ARXIV.1810.02244.

- [4] V. P. Dwivedi et al. *Benchmarking graph neural networks.* arXiv, 2020. doi: 10.48550/ARXIV.2003.00982.

- [5] K. M. Borgwardt, C. S. Ong, S. Schoenauer, S. V. N. Vishwanathan, A. J. Smola, and H. P. Kriegel. *Protein function prediction via graph kernels.* Bioinformatics, 21(Suppl 1):i47–i56, Jun 2005.

- [6] P. D. Dobson and A. J. Doig. *Distinguishing enzyme structures from non-enzymes without alignments.* J. Mol. Biol., 330(4):771–783, Jul 2003.

- [7] Christopher Morris and Nils M. Kriege and Franka Bause and Kristian Kersting and Petra Mutzel and Marion Neumann. *TUDataset: A collection of benchmark datasets for learning with graphs.* In ICML 2020 Workshop on Graph Representation Learning and Beyond.

- [8] W. Hu et al., *Strategies for Pre-training Graph Neural Networks.* arXiv, 2019. doi: 10.48550/ARXIV.1905.12265.

# 10

# Predicting Links with Graph Neural Networks

**Link prediction** is one of the most popular tasks performed with graphs. It is defined as the problem of predicting the existence of a link between two nodes. This ability is at the core of social networks and recommender systems. A good example is how social media networks display friends and followers you have in common with others. Intuitively, if this number is high, you are more likely to connect with these people. This likelihood is precisely what link prediction tries to estimate.

In this chapter, we will first see how to perform link prediction without any machine learning. These traditional techniques are essential to understanding what GNNs learn. We will then refer to previous chapters about DeepWalk and Node2Vec to link prediction through **matrix factorization**. Unfortunately, these techniques have significant limitations, which is why we will transition to GNN-based methods.

We will explore three methods from two different families. The first family is based on node embeddings and performs a GNN-based matrix factorization. The second method focuses on subgraph representation. The neighborhood around each link (fake or real) is considered an input to predict the link probability. Finally, we will implement a model of each family in PyTorch Geometric.

By the end of this chapter, you will be able to implement various link prediction techniques. Given a link prediction problem, you will know which technique is the best suited to address it – heuristics, matrix factorization, GNN-based embeddings, or subgraph-based techniques.

In this chapter, we will cover the following main topics:

- Predicting links with traditional methods
- Predicting links with node embeddings
- Predicting links with SEAL

## Technical requirements

All the code examples from this chapter can be found on GitHub at `https://github.com/PacktPublishing/Hands-On-Graph-Neural-Networks-Using-Python/tree/main/Chapter10`.

Installation steps required to run the code on your local machine can be found in the *Preface* section of this book.

## Predicting links with traditional methods

The link prediction problem has been around for a long time, which is why numerous techniques have been proposed to solve it. First, this section will describe popular heuristics based on local and global neighborhoods. Then, we will introduce matrix factorization and its connection to DeepWalk and Node2Vec.

### Heuristic techniques

Heuristic techniques are a simple and practical way to predict links between nodes. They are easy to implement and offer strong baselines for this task. We can classify them based on the number of hops they perform (see *Figure 10.1*). Some of them only require 1-hop neighbors that are adjacent to the target nodes. More complex techniques also consider 2-hop neighbors or an entire graph. In this section, we will divide them into two categories – *local* (1-hop and 2-hop) and *global* heuristics.

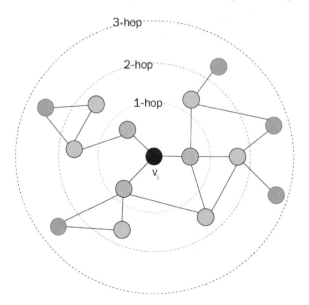

Figure 10.1 – Graph with 1-hop, 2-hop, and 3-hop neighbors

Local heuristics measure the similarity between two nodes by considering their local neighborhoods. We use $\mathcal{N}(u)$ to denote the neighbors of node $u$. Here are three examples of popular local heuristics:

- **Common neighbors** simply counts the number of neighbors two nodes have in common (1-hop neighbors). The idea is similar to our previous example with social networks – the more neighbors you have in common, the more likely you are to be connected:

$$f(u, v) = |\mathcal{N}(u) \cap \mathcal{N}(v)|$$

- **Jaccard's coefficient** measures the proportion of neighbors shared by two nodes (1-hop neighbors). It relies on the same idea as common neighbors but normalizes the result by the total number of neighbors. This rewards nodes with few interconnected neighbors instead of nodes with high degrees:

$$f(u, v) = \frac{|\mathcal{N}(u) \cap \mathcal{N}(v)|}{|\mathcal{N}(u) \cup \mathcal{N}(v)|}$$

- The **Adamic–Adar index** sums the inverse logarithmic degree of neighbors shared by the two target nodes (2-hop neighbors). The idea is that common neighbors with large neighborhoods are less significant than those with small neighborhoods. This is why they should have less importance in the final score:

$$f(u, v) = \sum_{x \in \mathcal{N}(u) \cap \mathcal{N}(v)} \frac{1}{\log|\mathcal{N}(x)|}$$

All these techniques rely on neighbors' node degrees, whether they are direct (common neighbors or Jaccard's coefficient) or indirect (the Adamic–Adar index). This is beneficial for speed and explainability but also limits the complexity of the relationships they can capture.

Global heuristics offer a solution to this problem by considering an entire network instead of a local neighborhood. Here are two well-known examples:

- The **Katz index** computes the weighted sum of every possible path between two nodes. Weights correspond to a discount factor, $\beta \in [0,1]$ (usually between 0.8 and 0.9), to penalize longer paths. With this definition, two nodes are more likely to be connected if there are many (preferably short) paths between them. Paths of any length can be calculated using adjacency matrix powers, $A^n$, which is why the Katz index is defined as follows:

$$f(u, v) = \sum_{i=1}^{\infty} \beta^i A^i$$

- **Random walk with restart** [1] performs random walks, starting from a target node. After each walk, it increases the visit count of the current node. With an α probability, it restarts the walk at the target node. Otherwise, it continues its random walk. After a predefined number of iterations, we stop the algorithm, and we can suggest links between the target node and nodes with the highest visit counts. This idea is also essential in `DeepWalk` and `Node2Vec` algorithms.

Global heuristics are usually more accurate but require knowing the entirety of a graph. However, they are not the only way to predict links with this knowledge.

## Matrix factorization

Matrix factorization for link prediction is inspired by the previous work on recommender systems [2]. With this technique, we indirectly predict links by predicting the entire adjacency matrix, $\hat{A}$. This is performed using node embeddings – similar nodes, $u$ and $v$, should have similar embeddings, $z_u$ and $z_v$ respectively. Using the dot product, we can write it as follows:

- If these nodes are similar, $z_v^T z_u$ should be maximal
- If these nodes are different, $z_v^T z_u$ should be minimal

So far, we have assumed that similar nodes should be connected. This is why we can use this dot product to approximate each element (link) of the adjacency matrix, $A$:

$$A_{uv} \approx z_v^T z_u$$

In terms of matrix multiplication, we have the following:

$$A \approx Z^T Z$$

Here, $Z$ is the node embedding matrix. The following figure shows a visual explanation of how matrix factorization works:

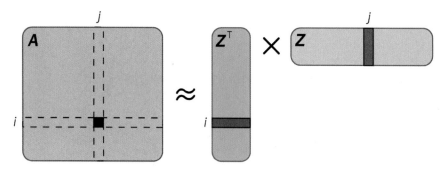

Figure 10.2 – Matrix multiplication with node embeddings

This technique is called matrix factorization because the adjacency matrix, $A$, is decomposed into a product of two matrices. The goal is to learn relevant node embeddings that minimize the L2 norm between true and predicted elements, $A_{uv}$, for the graph, $G = (V, E)$:

$$\underset{z}{\text{minimize}} \sum_{i \in V, j \in V} (A_{uv} - z_v^T z_u)^2$$

There are more advanced variants of matrix factorization that include the Laplacian matrix and powers of $A$. Another solution consists of using models such as `DeepWalk` and `Node2Vec`. They produce node embeddings that can be paired to create link representations. According to Qiu, et al. [3], these algorithms implicitly approximate and factorize complex matrices. For example, here is the matrix computed by `DeepWalk`:

$$\log\left( \sum_{i=1}^{|V|} \sum_{j=1}^{|V|} A_{ij} \left( \frac{1}{T} \sum_{r=1}^{T} (D^{-1}A)^r \right) D^{-1} \right) - \log b$$

Here, $b$ is the parameter for negative sampling. The same can be said for similar algorithms, such as LINE and PTE. Although they can capture more complex relationships, they suffer from the same limitations that we saw in *Chapters 3* and *4*:

- **They cannot use node features**: They only use topological information to create embeddings
- **They have no inductive capabilities**: They cannot generalize to nodes that were not in the training set
- **They cannot capture structural similarity**: Structurally similar nodes in the graph can obtain vastly different embeddings

These limitations motivate the need for GNN-based techniques, as we will see in the next sections.

## Predicting links with node embeddings

In the previous chapters, we saw how to use GNNs to produce node embeddings. A popular link prediction technique consists of using these embeddings to perform matrix factorization. This section will discuss two GNN architectures for link prediction – the **Graph Autoencoder (GAE)** and the **Variational Graph Autoencoder (VGAE)**.

## Introducing Graph Autoencoders

Both architectures were introduced by Kipf and Welling in 2016 [5] in a three-page paper. They represent the GNN counterparts of two popular neural network architectures – the autoencoder and the variational autoencoder. Prior knowledge about these architectures is helpful but not necessary. For ease of understanding, we will first focus on the GAE.

The GAE is composed of two modules:

- The **encoder** is a classic two-layer GCN that computes node embeddings as follows:

$$Z = \text{GCN}(X, A)$$

- The **decoder** approximates the adjacency matrix, $\hat{A}$, using matrix factorization and a sigmoid function, $\sigma$, to output probabilities:

$$\hat{A} = \sigma(Z^T Z)$$

Note that we are not trying to classify nodes or graphs. The goal is to predict a probability (between 0 and 1) for each element of the adjacency matrix, $\hat{A}$. This is why the GAE is trained using the binary cross-entropy loss (negative log-likelihood) between the elements of both adjacency matrices:

$$\mathcal{L}_{BCE} = \sum_{i \in V, j \in V} -A_{ij} \log(\hat{A}_{ij}) - (1 - A_{ij}) \log(1 - \hat{A}_{ij})$$

However, adjacency matrices are often very sparse, which biases the GAE toward predicting zero values. There are two simple techniques to fix this bias. First, we can add a weight to favor $A_{ij} = 1$ in the previous loss function. Secondly, we can sample fewer zero values during training, making labels more balanced. The latter technique is the one implemented by Kipf and Welling.

This architecture is flexible – the encoder can be replaced with another type of GNN (GraphSAGE, for example), and an MLP can take the role of a decoder, for instance. Another possible improvement involves transforming the GAE into a probabilistic variant – the Variational GAE.

## Introducing VGAEs

The difference between GAEs and VGAEs is the same as between autoencoders and variational autoencoders. Instead of directly learning node embeddings, VGAEs learn normal distributions that are then sampled to produce embeddings. They are also divided into two modules:

- The **encoder** is composed of two GCNs that share their first layer. The objective is to learn the parameters of each latent normal distribution – a mean, $\mu_i$ (learned by $\text{GCN}_\mu$), and a variance, $\sigma_i^2$ (in practice, $\log \sigma$ learned by $\text{GCN}_\sigma$).

- The **decoder** samples embeddings, $z_i$, from the learned distributions, $\mathcal{N}(\mu_i, \sigma_i^2)$, using the reparametrization trick [4]. Then, it uses the same inner product between latent variables to approximate the adjacency matrix, $\hat{A} = \sigma(Z^T Z)$.

With VGAEs, it is important to ensure that the encoder's output follows a normal distribution. This is why we add a new term to the loss function – the **Kullback-Leibler** (**KL**) divergence, which measures the divergence between two distributions. We obtain the following loss, also called the **evidence lower bound** (**ELBO**):

$$\mathcal{L}_{ELBO} = \mathcal{L}_{BCE} - \text{KL}[q(Z|X,A) \,||\, p(Z)]$$

Here, $q(Z|X,A)$ represents the encoder and $p(Z)$ is the prior distribution of $Z$.

The model's performance is generally evaluated using two metrics – the area under the ROC (**AUROC**) curve and the **average precision** (**AP**).

Let's see how to implement a VGAE using PyTorch Geometric.

## Implementing a VGAE

There are two main differences with previous GNN implementations:

- We will preprocess the dataset to remove links to predict randomly.
- We will create an encoder model that we will feed to a VGAE class, instead of directly implementing a VGAE from scratch.

The following code is inspired by PyTorch Geometric's VGAE example:

1. First, we import the required libraries:

```
import numpy as np
np.random.seed(0)
import torch
torch.manual_seed(0)
import matplotlib.pyplot as plt
import torch_geometric.transforms as T
from torch_geometric.datasets import Planetoid
```

2. We try to use the GPU if it's available:

```
device = torch.device('cuda' if torch.cuda.is_available()
else 'cpu')
```

3.  We create a `transform` object that normalizes input features, directly performs tensor device conversion, and randomly splits links. In this example, we have an 85/5/10 split. The `add_negative_train_samples` parameter is set to `False` because the model already performs negative sampling, so it is not needed in the dataset:

```
transform = T.Compose([
    T.NormalizeFeatures(),
    T.ToDevice(device),
    T.RandomLinkSplit(num_val=0.05, num_test=0.1, is_
undirected=True, split_labels=True, add_negative_train_
samples=False),
])
```

4.  We load the `Cora` dataset with the previous `transform` object:

```
dataset = Planetoid('.', name='Cora',
transform=transform)
```

5.  The `RandomLinkSplit` produces a train/val/test split by design. We store these splits as follows:

```
train_data, val_data, test_data = dataset[0]
```

6.  Now, let's implement the encoder. First, we need to import GCNConv and VGAE:

```
from torch_geometric.nn import GCNConv, VGAE
```

7.  We declare a new class. In this class, we want three GCN layers – a shared layer, a second layer to approximate mean values, $\mu_i$, and a third layer to approximate variance values (in practice, the log standard deviation, $\log \sigma$):

```
class Encoder(torch.nn.Module):
    def __init__(self, dim_in, dim_out):
        super().__init__()
        self.conv1 = GCNConv(dim_in, 2 * dim_out)
        self.conv_mu = GCNConv(2 * dim_out, dim_out)
        self.conv_logstd = GCNConv(2 * dim_out, dim_out)

    def forward(self, x, edge_index):
        x = self.conv1(x, edge_index).relu()
        return self.conv_mu(x, edge_index), self.conv_
logstd(x, edge_index)
```

8. We can initialize our VGAE and give the encoder as input. By default, it will use the inner product as a decoder:

```
model = VGAE(Encoder(dataset.num_features, 16)).
to(device)
optimizer = torch.optim.Adam(model.parameters(), lr=0.01)
```

9. The `train()` function includes two important steps. First, the embedding matrix, $Z$, is computed using `model.encode()`; the name might be counter-intuitive, but this function does sample embeddings from the learned distributions. Then, the ELBO loss is computed with `model.recon_loss()` (binary cross-entropy loss) and `model.kl_loss()` (KL divergence). The decoder is implicitly called to calculate the cross-entropy loss:

```
def train():
    model.train()
    optimizer.zero_grad()
    z = model.encode(train_data.x, train_data.edge_index)
    loss = model.recon_loss(z, train_data.pos_edge_label_
index) + (1 / train_data.num_nodes) * model.kl_loss()
    loss.backward()
    optimizer.step()
    return float(loss)
```

10. The `test()` function simply calls the VGAE's dedicated method:

```
@torch.no_grad()
def test(data):
    model.eval()
    z = model.encode(data.x, data.edge_index)
    return model.test(z, data.pos_edge_label_index, data.
neg_edge_label_index)
```

11. We train this model for 301 epochs and print the two built-in metrics – the AUC and the AP:

```
for epoch in range(301):
    loss = train()
    val_auc, val_ap = test(val_data)
    if epoch % 50 == 0:
        print(f'Epoch {epoch:>2} | Loss: {loss:.4f} | Val
AUC: {val_auc:.4f} | Val AP: {val_ap:.4f}')
```

12.  We obtain the following output:

```
Epoch 0 | Loss: 3.4210 | Val AUC: 0.6772 | Val AP: 0.7110
Epoch 50 | Loss: 1.3324 | Val AUC: 0.6593 | Val AP:
0.6922
Epoch 100 | Loss: 1.1675 | Val AUC: 0.7366 | Val AP:
0.7298
Epoch 150 | Loss: 1.1166 | Val AUC: 0.7480 | Val AP:
0.7514
Epoch 200 | Loss: 1.0074 | Val AUC: 0.8390 | Val AP:
0.8395
Epoch 250 | Loss: 0.9541 | Val AUC: 0.8794 | Val AP:
0.8797
Epoch 300 | Loss: 0.9509 | Val AUC: 0.8833 | Val AP:
0.8845
```

13.  We evaluate our model on the test set:

```
test_auc, test_ap = test(test_data)
print(f'Test AUC: {test_auc:.4f} | Test AP {test_
ap:.4f}')
```

```
Test AUC: 0.8833 | Test AP 0.8845
```

14.  Finally, we can manually calculate the approximated adjacency matrix, $\hat{A}$:

```
z = model.encode(test_data.x, test_data.edge_index)
Ahat = torch.sigmoid(z @ z.T)
```

```
tensor([[0.8846, 0.5068, ..., 0.5160, 0.8309, 0.8378],
        [0.5068, 0.8741, ..., 0.3900, 0.5367, 0.5495],
        [0.7074, 0.7878, ..., 0.4318, 0.7806, 0.7602],
        ...,
        [0.5160, 0.3900, ..., 0.5855, 0.5350, 0.5176],
        [0.8309, 0.5367, ..., 0.5350, 0.8443, 0.8275],
        [0.8378, 0.5495, ..., 0.5176, 0.8275, 0.8200]
    ], device='cuda:0', grad_fn=<SigmoidBackward0>)
```

Training a VGAE is fast and outputs results that are easily understandable. However, we saw that the GCN is not the most expressive operator. In order to improve the model's expressiveness, we need to incorporate better techniques.

# Predicting links with SEAL

The previous section introduced node-based methods, which learn relevant node embeddings to compute link likelihoods. Another approach consists of looking at the local neighborhood around the target nodes. These techniques are called subgraph-based algorithms and were popularized by **SEAL** (which could be said to stand for **Subgraphs, Embeddings, and Attributes for Link prediction** – though not always!). In this section, we will describe the SEAL framework and implement it using PyTorch Geometric.

## Introducing the SEAL framework

Introduced in 2018 by Zhang and Chen [6], SEAL is a framework that learns graph structure features for link prediction. It defines the subgraph formed by the target nodes $(x, y)$ and their $k$-hop neighbors as the **enclosing subgraph**. Each enclosing subgraph is used as input (instead of the entire graph) to predict a link likelihood. Another way to look at it is that SEAL automatically learns a local heuristic for link prediction.

The framework involves three steps:

1. **Enclosing subgraph extraction**, which consists of taking a set of real links and a set of fake links (negative sampling) to form the training data.

2. **Node information matrix construction**, which involves three components – node labels, node embeddings, and node features.

3. **GNN training**, which takes the node information matrices as input and outputs link likelihoods.

These steps are summarized in the following figure:

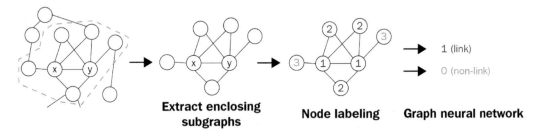

Figure 10.3 – The SEAL framework

The enclosing subgraph extraction is a straightforward process. It consists of listing the target nodes and their $k$-hop neighbors to extract their edges and features. A high $k$ will improve the quality of the heuristics SEAL can learn, but it also creates larger subgraphs that are more computationally expensive.

The first component of the node information construction is node labeling. This process assigns a specific number to each node. Without it, the GNN would be unable to differentiate between target and contextual nodes (their neighbors). It also embeds distances, which describe nodes' relative positions and structural importance.

In practice, the target nodes, $x$ and $y$, must share a unique label to identify them as target nodes. For contextual nodes, $i$ and $j$, they must share the same label if they have the same distance as the target nodes – $d(i, x) = d(j, x)$ and $d(i, y) = d(j, y)$. We call this distance the double radius, noted as $(d(i, x), d(i, y))$.

Different solutions can be considered, but SEAL's authors propose the **Double-Radius Node Labeling** **(DRNL)** algorithm. It works as follows:

1.   First, assign label 1 to $x$ and $y$.

2.   Assign label 1 to nodes with a radius – (1,1).

3.   Assign label 3 to nodes with a radius – (1,2) or (2,1).

4.   Assign label 4 to nodes with a radius – (1,3), (3,1), and so on.

The DRNL function can be written as follows:

$$f(i) = 1 + min(d(i, x), d(i, y)) + (d/2)[(d/2) + (d\%2) - 1]$$

Here, $d = d(i, x) + d(i, y)$, and $(d/2)$ and $(d\%2)$ are the integer quotient and remainder of $d$ divided by 2 respectively. Finally, these node labels are one-hot encoded.

> **Note**
>
> The two other components are easier to obtain. The node embeddings are optional but can be calculated using another algorithm, such as Node2Vec. Then, they are concatenated with the node features and one-hot encoded labels to build the final node information matrix.

Finally, a GNN is trained to predict links, using enclosing subgraphs' information and adjacency matrices. For this task, SEAL's authors chose the **Deep Graph Convolutional Neural Network** **(DGCNN)** [7]. This architecture performs three steps:

1.   Several GCN layers compute node embeddings that are then concatenated (like a GIN).

2.   A global sort pooling layer sorts these embeddings in a consistent order before feeding them into convolutional layers, which are not permutation-invariant.

3.   Traditional convolutional and dense layers are applied to the sorted graph representations and output a link probability.

The DGCNN model is trained using the binary cross-entropy loss and outputs probabilities between 0 and 1.

## Implementing the SEAL framework

The SEAL framework requires extensive preprocessing to extract and label the enclosing subgraphs. Let's implement it using PyTorch Geometric:

1.  First, we import all the necessary libraries:

    ```
    import numpy as np
    from sklearn.metrics import roc_auc_score, average_
    precision_score
    from scipy.sparse.csgraph import shortest_path


    import torch
    import torch.nn.functional as F
    from torch.nn import Conv1d, MaxPool1d, Linear, Dropout,
    BCEWithLogitsLoss


    from torch_geometric.datasets import Planetoid
    from torch_geometric.transforms import RandomLinkSplit
    from torch_geometric.data import Data
    from torch_geometric.loader import DataLoader
    from torch_geometric.nn import GCNConv, aggr
    from torch_geometric.utils import k_hop_subgraph, to_
    scipy_sparse_matrix
    ```

2.  We load the `Cora` dataset and apply a link-level random split, like in the previous section:

    ```
    transform = RandomLinkSplit(num_val=0.05, num_test=0.1,
    is_undirected=True, split_labels=True)
    dataset = Planetoid('.', name='Cora',
    transform=transform)
    train_data, val_data, test_data = dataset[0]
    ```

3.  The link-level random split creates new fields in the `Data` object to store the labels and index of each positive (real) and negative (fake) edge:

    ```
    train_data


    Data(x=[2708, 1433], edge_index=[2, 8976], y=[2708],
    train_mask=[2708], val_mask=[2708], test_mask=[2708],
    pos_edge_label=[4488], pos_edge_label_index=[2, 4488],
    neg_edge_label=[4488], neg_edge_label_index=[2, 4488])
    ```

4.  We create a function to process each split and obtain enclosing subgraphs with one-hot encoded node labels and node features. We declare a list to store these subgraphs:

```
def seal_processing(dataset, edge_label_index, y):
    data_list = []
```

5.  For each (source and destination) pair in the dataset, we extract the k-hop neighbors (here, $k = 2$):

```
for src, dst in edge_label_index.t().tolist():
    sub_nodes, sub_edge_index, mapping, _ = k_hop_
subgraph([src, dst], 2, dataset.edge_index, relabel_
nodes=True)
    src, dst = mapping.tolist()
```

6.  We calculate the distances using the DRNL function. First, we remove the target nodes from the subgraph:

```
    mask1 = (sub_edge_index[0] != src) | (sub_edge_
index[1] != dst)
    mask2 = (sub_edge_index[0] != dst) | (sub_edge_
index[1] != src)
    sub_edge_index = sub_edge_index[:, mask1 & mask2]
```

7.  We compute the adjacency matrices for source and destination nodes based on the previous subgraph:

```
    src, dst = (dst, src) if src > dst else (src,
dst)
    adj = to_scipy_sparse_matrix(sub_edge_index, num_
nodes=sub_nodes.size(0)).tocsr()

    idx = list(range(src)) + list(range(src + 1, adj.
shape[0]))
    adj_wo_src = adj[idx, :][:, idx]

    idx = list(range(dst)) + list(range(dst + 1, adj.
shape[0]))
    adj_wo_dst = adj[idx, :][:, idx]
```

8.  We calculate the distance between every node and the source/destination target node:

```
    d_src = shortest_path(adj_wo_dst, directed=False,
unweighted=True, indices=src)
```

```
        d_src = np.insert(d_src, dst, 0, axis=0)
        d_src = torch.from_numpy(d_src)
        d_dst = shortest_path(adj_wo_src, directed=False,
unweighted=True, indices=dst-1)
        d_dst = np.insert(d_dst, src, 0, axis=0)
        d_dst = torch.from_numpy(d_dst)
```

9. We calculate the node labels, z, for every node in the subgraph:

```
        dist = d_src + d_dst
        z = 1 + torch.min(d_src, d_dst) + dist // 2 *
(dist // 2 + dist % 2 - 1)
        z[src], z[dst], z[torch.isnan(z)] = 1., 1., 0.
        z = z.to(torch.long)
```

10. In this example, we will not use node embeddings, but we still concatenate features and one-hot-encoded labels to build the node information matrix:

```
        node_labels = F.one_hot(z, num_classes=200).
to(torch.float)
        node_emb = dataset.x[sub_nodes]
        node_x = torch.cat([node_emb, node_labels],
dim=1)
```

11. We create a Data object and append it to the list, which is the final output of this function:

```
        data = Data(x=node_x, z=z, edge_index=sub_edge_
index, y=y)
        data_list.append(data)

    return data_list
```

12. Let's use it to extract enclosing subgraphs for each dataset. We separate positive and negative examples to get the correct label to predict:

```
train_pos_data_list = seal_processing(train_data, train_
data.pos_edge_label_index, 1)
train_neg_data_list = seal_processing(train_data, train_
data.neg_edge_label_index, 0)

val_pos_data_list = seal_processing(val_data, val_data.
pos_edge_label_index, 1)
```

```
val_neg_data_list = seal_processing(val_data, val_data.
neg_edge_label_index, 0)


test_pos_data_list = seal_processing(test_data, test_
data.pos_edge_label_index, 1)
test_neg_data_list = seal_processing(test_data, test_
data.neg_edge_label_index, 0)
```

13. Next, we merge positive and negative data lists to reconstruct the training, validation, and test datasets:

```
train_dataset = train_pos_data_list + train_neg_data_list
val_dataset = val_pos_data_list + val_neg_data_list
test_dataset = test_pos_data_list + test_neg_data_list
```

14. We create data loaders to train the GNN using batches:

```
train_loader = DataLoader(train_dataset, batch_size=32,
shuffle=True)
val_loader = DataLoader(val_dataset, batch_size=32)
test_loader = DataLoader(test_dataset, batch_size=32)
```

15. We create a new class for the DGCNN model. The k parameter represents the number of nodes to hold for each subgraph:

```
class DGCNN(torch.nn.Module):
    def __init__(self, dim_in, k=30):
        super().__init__()
```

16. We create four GCN layers with a fixed hidden dimension of 32:

```
        self.gcn1 = GCNConv(dim_in, 32)
        self.gcn2 = GCNConv(32, 32)
        self.gcn3 = GCNConv(32, 32)
        self.gcn4 = GCNConv(32, 1)
```

17. We instantiate the global sort pooling at the core of the DGCNN architecture:

```
        self.global_pool = aggr.SortAggregation(k=k)
```

18. The node ordering provided by global pooling allows us to use traditional convolutional layers:

```
        self.conv1 = Conv1d(1, 16, 97, 97)
```

```
        self.conv2 = Conv1d(16, 32, 5, 1)
        self.maxpool = MaxPool1d(2, 2)
```

19. Finally, the prediction is managed by an MLP:

```
        self.linear1 = Linear(352, 128)
        self.dropout = Dropout(0.5)
        self.linear2 = Linear(128, 1)
```

20. In the forward() function, we calculate node embeddings for each GCN and concatenate the results:

```
    def forward(self, x, edge_index, batch):
        h1 = self.gcn1(x, edge_index).tanh()
        h2 = self.gcn2(h1, edge_index).tanh()
        h3 = self.gcn3(h2, edge_index).tanh()
        h4 = self.gcn4(h3, edge_index).tanh()
        h = torch.cat([h1, h2, h3, h4], dim=-1)
```

21. The global sort pooling, convolutional layers, and dense layers are sequentially applied to this result:

```
        h = self.global_pool(h, batch)
        h = h.view(h.size(0), 1, h.size(-1))
        h = self.conv1(h).relu()
        h = self.maxpool(h)
        h = self.conv2(h).relu()
        h = h.view(h.size(0), -1)
        h = self.linear1(h).relu()
        h = self.dropout(h)
        h = self.linear2(h).sigmoid()
        return h
```

22. We instantiate the model on a GPU if available, and train it using the Adam optimizer and the binary cross-entropy loss:

```
device = torch.device('cuda' if torch.cuda.is_available()
else 'cpu')
model = DGCNN(train_dataset[0].num_features).to(device)
optimizer = torch.optim.Adam(params=model.parameters(),
lr=0.0001)
```

```
criterion = BCEWithLogitsLoss()
```

23. We create a traditional `train()` function for batch training:

```
def train():
    model.train()
    total_loss = 0

    for data in train_loader:
        data = data.to(device)
        optimizer.zero_grad()
        out = model(data.x, data.edge_index, data.batch)
        loss = criterion(out.view(-1), data.y.to(torch.
float))
        loss.backward()
        optimizer.step()
        total_loss += float(loss) * data.num_graphs

    return total_loss / len(train_dataset)
```

24. In the `test()` function, we calculate the ROC AUC score and the average precision to compare the SEAL performance with the VGAE performance:

```
@torch.no_grad()
def test(loader):
    model.eval()
    y_pred, y_true = [], []

    for data in loader:
        data = data.to(device)
        out = model(data.x, data.edge_index, data.batch)
        y_pred.append(out.view(-1).cpu())
        y_true.append(data.y.view(-1).cpu().to(torch.
float))

    auc = roc_auc_score(torch.cat(y_true), torch.cat(y_
pred))
    ap = average_precision_score(torch.cat(y_true),
torch.cat(y_pred))
```

```
    return auc, ap
```

25. We train the DGCNN for 31 epochs:

```
for epoch in range(31):
    loss = train()
    val_auc, val_ap = test(val_loader)
    print(f'Epoch {epoch:>2} | Loss: {loss:.4f} | Val
AUC: {val_auc:.4f} | Val AP: {val_ap:.4f}')
```

```
Epoch 0 | Loss: 0.6925 | Val AUC: 0.8215 | Val AP: 0.8357
Epoch 1 | Loss: 0.6203 | Val AUC: 0.8543 | Val AP: 0.8712
Epoch 2 | Loss: 0.5888 | Val AUC: 0.8783 | Val AP:
0.8877...

Epoch 29 | Loss: 0.5461 | Val AUC: 0.8991 | Val AP:
0.8973
Epoch 30 | Loss: 0.5460 | Val AUC: 0.9005 | Val AP:
0.8992
```

26. Finally, we test it on the test dataset:

```
test_auc, test_ap = test(test_loader)
print(f'Test AUC: {test_auc:.4f} | Test AP {test_
ap:.4f}')
```

```
Test AUC: 0.8808 | Test AP 0.8863
```

We obtain results that are similar to those observed using the VGAE (test AUC – 0.8833 and test AP – 0.8845). In theory, subgraph-based methods such as SEAL are more expressive than node-based methods such as VGAEs. They capture more information by explicitly considering the entire neighborhood around target nodes. SEAL's accuracy can also be improved by increasing the number of neighbors taken into account with the k parameter.

# Summary

In this chapter, we explored a new task with link prediction. We gave an overview of this field by presenting heuristic and matrix factorization techniques. Heuristics can be classified according to the k-hop neighbors they consider – from local with 1-hop neighbors to global with the knowledge of the entire graph. Conversely, matrix factorization approximates the adjacency matrix using node embeddings. We also explained how this technique was connected to algorithms described in previous chapters (DeepWalk and Node2Vec).

After this introduction to link prediction, we saw how to implement it using GNNs. We outlined two kinds of techniques, based on node embeddings (GAE and VGAE) and subgraph representations (SEAL). Finally, we implemented a VGAE and SEAL on the Cora dataset with an edge-level random split and negative sampling. Both models obtained comparable performance, although SEAL is strictly more expressive.

In *Chapter 11, Generating Graphs with Graph Neural Networks*, we will see different strategies to produce realistic graphs. First, we will describe traditional techniques with the popular Erdős–Rényi model. Then, we will see how deep generative methods work by reusing the GVAE and introducing a new architecture – the **Graph Recurrent Neural Network (GraphRNN)**.

# Further reading

- [1] H. Tong, C. Faloutsos and J. -y. Pan. "Fast Random Walk with Restart and Its Applications" in *Sixth International Conference on Data Mining (ICDM'06)*, 2006, pp. 613-622, doi: 10.1109/ICDM.2006.70.

- [2] Yehuda Koren, Robert Bell, and Chris Volinsky. 2009. *Matrix Factorization Techniques for Recommender Systems.* Computer 42, 8 (August 2009), 30–37. https://doi.org/10.1109/MC.2009.263.

- [3] J. Qiu, Y. Dong, H. Ma, J. Li, K. Wang, and J. Tang. *Network Embedding as Matrix Factorization.* Feb. 2018. doi: 10.1145/3159652.3159706.

- [4] D. P. Kingma and M. Welling. *Auto-Encoding Variational Bayes.* arXiv, 2013. doi: 10.48550/ARXIV.1312.6114.

- [5] T. N. Kipf and M. Welling. *Variational Graph Auto-Encoders.* arXiv, 2016. doi: 10.48550/ARXIV.1611.07308.

- [6] M. Zhang and Y. Chen. *Link Prediction Based on Graph Neural Networks.* arXiv, 2018. doi: 10.48550/ARXIV.1802.09691.

- [7] Muhan Zhang, Zhicheng Cui, Marion Neumann, and Yixin Chen. 2018. *An end-to-end deep learning architecture for graph classification.* In Proceedings of the Thirty-Second AAAI Conference on Artificial Intelligence and Thirtieth Innovative Applications of Artificial Intelligence Conference and Eighth AAAI Symposium on Educational Advances in Artificial Intelligence (AAAI'18/IAAI'18/EAAI'18). AAAI Press, Article 544, 4438–4445.

# 11

# Generating Graphs Using Graph Neural Networks

Graph generation consists of finding methods to create new graphs. As a field of study, it provides insights into understanding how graphs work and evolve. It also has direct applications in data augmentation, anomaly detection, drug discovery, and so on. We can distinguish two types of generation: **realistic graph generation**, which imitates a given graph (for example, in data augmentation), and **goal-directed graph generation**, which creates graphs that optimize a specific metric (for instance, in molecule generation).

In this chapter, we will explore traditional techniques to understand how graph generation works. We will focus on two popular algorithms: the **Erdős–Rényi** and the **small-world** models. They present interesting properties but also issues that motivate the need for GNN-based graph generation. In the second section, we will describe three families of solutions: **variational autoencoder** (**VAE**)-based, autoregressive, and **GAN**-based models. Finally, we will implement a GAN-based framework with **Reinforcement Learning** (**RL**) to generate new chemical compounds. Instead of PyTorch Geometric, we will use the **DeepChem** library with TensorFlow.

By the end of this chapter, you will be able to generate graphs using traditional and GNN-based techniques. You will have a good overview of this field and the different applications you can build with it. You will know how to implement a hybrid architecture to guide the generation into generating valid molecules with your desired properties.

In this chapter, we will cover the following main topics:

- Generating graphs with traditional techniques
- Generating graphs with graph neural networks
- Generating molecules with MolGAN

# Technical requirements

All the code examples from this chapter can be found on GitHub at `https://github.com/PacktPublishing/Hands-On-Graph-Neural-Networks-Using-Python/tree/main/Chapter11`.

Installation steps required to run the code on your local machine can be found in the *Preface* of this book.

# Generating graphs with traditional techniques

Traditional graph generation techniques have been studied for decades. This is why they are well understood and can be used as baselines in various applications. However, they are often limited in the type of graphs they can generate. Most of them are specialized to output certain topologies, which is why they cannot simply imitate a given network.

In this section, we will introduce two classical techniques: the Erdős–Rényi and the small-world models.

## The Erdős–Rényi model

The Erdős–Rényi model is the simplest and most popular random graph model. It was introduced by Hungarian mathematicians Paul Erdős and Alfréd Rényi in 1959 [1] and was independently proposed by Edgar Gilbert the same year [2]. This model has two variants: $G(n, p)$ and $G(n, M)$.

The $G(n, p)$ model is straightforward: we are given $n$ nodes and a probability $p$ of connecting a pair of nodes. We try to randomly connect every node to each other to create the final graph. It means that there are $\binom{n}{2}$ possible links. Another way of understanding the probability $p$ is to consider it as a parameter to change the density of the network.

The `networkx` library has a direct implementation of the $G(n, p)$ model:

1.  We import the `networkx` library:

    ```
    import networkx as nx
    import matplotlib.pyplot as plt
    ```

2.  We generate a G graph using the `nx.erdos_renyi_graph()` function with 10 nodes ( $n = 10$) and a probability for edge creation of 0.5 ($p = 0.5$):

    ```
    G = nx.erdos_renyi_graph(10, 0.5, seed=0)
    ```

3.  We position the resulting nodes using the `nx.circular_layout()` function. Other layouts can be used, but this one is handy for comparing different values of $p$:

    ```
    pos = nx.circular_layout(G)
    ```

4.  We draw the G graph with the pos layout using nx.draw(). Global heuristics are usually more accurate but require knowing the entirety of the graph. However, it is not the only way to predict links with this knowledge:

```
nx.draw(G, pos=pos, with_labels=True)
```

This gives us the following graph:

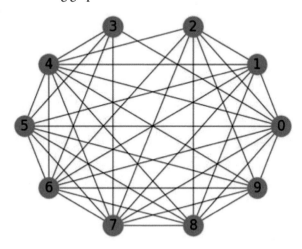

Figure 11.1 – An Erdős–Rényi graph with 10 nodes and p=0.5

We can repeat this process with a probability of **0.1** and **0.9** to obtain the following diagram:

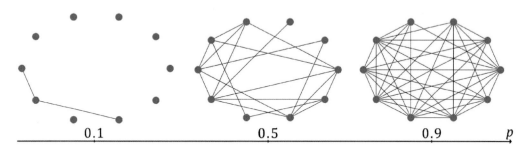

Figure 11.2 – Erdős–Rényi graphs with different probabilities for edge creation

We can see that many nodes are isolated when $p$ is low, while the graph is highly interconnected when $p$ is high.

In the $G(n, M)$ model, we randomly choose a graph from all graphs with $n$ nodes and $M$ links. For instance, if $n = 3$ and $M = 2$, there are three possible graphs (see *Figure 11.3*). The $G(n, M)$ model will just randomly select one of these graphs. This is a different approach to the same problem, but it is not as popular as the $G(n, p)$ model because it is more challenging to analyze in general:

Figure 11.3 – A set of graphs with three nodes and two links

We can also implement the $G(n, M)$ model in Python using the nx.gnm_random_graph() function:

```
G = nx.gnm_random_graph(3, 2, seed=0)
pos = nx.circular_layout(G)
nx.draw(G, pos=pos, with_labels=True)
```

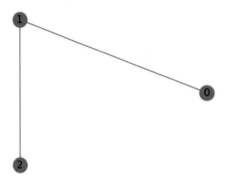

Figure 11.4 – A graph randomly sampled from the set of graphs with three nodes and two links

The strongest and most interesting assumption made by the $G(n, p)$ model is that links are independent (meaning that they do not interfere with each other). Unfortunately, it is not true for most real-world graphs, where we observe clusters and communities that contradict this rule.

## The small-world model

Introduced in 1998 by Duncan Watts and Steven Strogatz [3], the small-world model tries to imitate the behavior of biological, technological, and social networks. The main concept is that real-world networks are not completely random (as in the Erdős–Rényi model) but not totally regular either (as in a grid). This kind of topology is somewhere in between, which is why we can interpolate it using a coefficient. The small-world model produces graphs that have both:

- **Short paths**: The average distance between any two nodes in the network is relatively small, which makes it easy for information to spread quickly throughout the network

- **High clustering coefficients**: Nodes in the network tend to be closely connected to one another, creating dense clusters of nodes

Many algorithms display small-world properties. In the following, we will describe the original **Watts–Strogatz** model proposed in [3]. It can be implemented using the following steps:

1. We initialize a graph with $n$ nodes.

2. Each node is connected to its $k$ nearest neighbors (or $k − 1$ neighbors if $k$ is odd).

3. Each link between nodes $i$ and $j$ has a probability $p$ of being rewired between $i$ and $k$, where $k$ is another random node.

In Python, we can implement it by calling the nx.watts_strogatz_graph() function:

```
G = nx.watts_strogatz_graph(10, 4, 0.5, seed=0)
pos = nx.circular_layout(G)
nx.draw(G, pos=pos)
```

This produces the following graph:

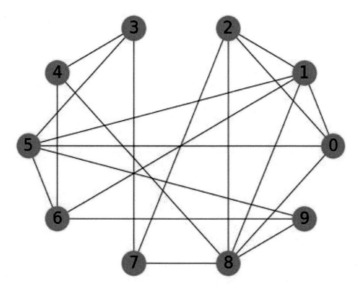

Figure 11.5 – A small-world network obtained with the Watts–Strogatz model

As with the Erdős–Rényi model, we can repeat the same process with different probabilities $p$ to obtain *Figure 11.6*:

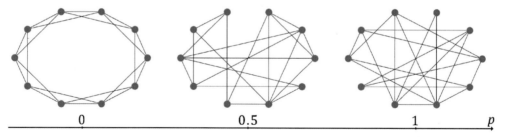

Figure 11.6 – A small-world model with different probabilities for rewiring

We can see that when $p = 0$, the graph is completely regular. On the opposite end, when $p = 1$, the graph is completely random as every link has been rewired. We obtain a balanced graph between these two extremes with hubs and local clustering.

Nonetheless, the Watts–Strogatz model does not produce a realistic degree distribution. It also requires a fixed number of nodes, which means it cannot be used for network growth. In general, classical methods fail to capture real-world graphs' full diversity and complexity. This motivated the creation of a new family of techniques, often referred to as deep graph generation.

# Generating graphs with graph neural networks

Deep graph generative models are GNN-based architectures that are more expressive than traditional techniques. However, it comes at a cost: they are often too complex to be analyzed and understood, like classical methods. We list three main families of architecture for deep graph generation: VAEs, GANs, and autoregressive models. Other techniques exist, such as normalizing flows or diffusion models, but they are less popular and mature than these three.

This section will describe how to use VAEs, GANs, and autoregressive models to generate graphs.

## Graph variational autoencoders

As seen in the last chapter, VAEs can be used to approximate an adjacency matrix. The **Graph Variational Autoencoder (GVAE)** model we saw has two components: an encoder and a decoder. The encoder uses two GCNs that share their first layer to learn the mean and the variance of each latent normal distribution. The decoder then samples the learned distributions to perform the inner product between latent variables $Z$. In the end, we obtained the approximated adjacency matrix $\hat{A} = \sigma(Z^T Z)$.

In the previous chapter, we used $\hat{A}$ to predict links. However, it is not its only application: it directly gives us the adjacency matrix of a network that imitates graphs seen during training. Instead of predicting links, we can use this output to generate new graphs. Here is an example of the adjacency matrix created by the VGAE model from *Chapter 10*:

```
z = model.encode(test_data.x, test_data.edge_index)
adj = torch.where((z @ z.T) > 0.9, 1, 0)
adj
```

```
tensor([[1, 0, 0,  ..., 0, 1, 1],
        [0, 1, 1,  ..., 0, 0, 0],
        [0, 1, 1,  ..., 0, 1, 1],
        ...,
        [0, 0, 0,  ..., 1, 0, 0],
        [1, 0, 1,  ..., 0, 1, 1],
        [1, 0, 1,  ..., 0, 1, 1]])
```

Since 2016, this technique has been expanded beyond the GVAE model to also output node and edge features. A good example is one of the most popular VAE-based graph generative models: **GraphVAE** [4]. Introduced in 2018 by Simonovsky and Komodakis, it is designed to generate realistic molecules. This requires the ability to differentiate nodes (atoms) and edges (chemical bonds).

GraphVAE considers graphs $G = (A, E, F)$, where $A$ is the adjacency matrix, $E$ is the edge attribute tensor, and $F$ is the node attribute matrix. It learns a probabilistic version of the graph $\tilde{G} = (\tilde{A}, \tilde{E}, \tilde{F})$ with a predefined number of nodes. In this probabilistic version, $\hat{A}$ contains node ($\tilde{A}_{a,a}$) and edge ($\tilde{A}_{a,b}$) probabilities, $\tilde{E}$ indicates class probabilities for edges, and $\tilde{F}$ contains class probabilities for nodes. Compared to GVAE, GraphVAE's encoder is a feed forward network with **edge-conditional graph convolutions** (ECC), and its decoder is a **multilayer perceptron** (MLP) with three outputs. The entire architecture is summarized in the following figure:

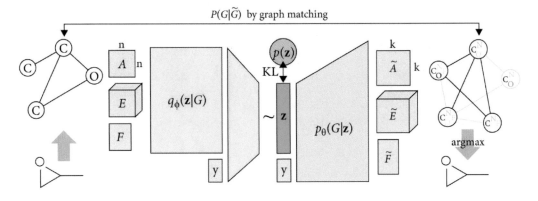

Figure 11.7 – GraphVAE's inference process

There are many other VAE-based graph generative architectures. However, their role is not limited to imitating graphs: they can also embed constraints to guide the type of graphs they produce.

A popular way of adding these constraints is to check them during the decoding phase, such as the **Constrained Graph Variational Autoencoder (CGVAE)** [5]. In this architecture, the encoder is a **Gated Graph Convolutional Network (GGCN)**, and the decoder is an autoregressive model. Autoregressive decoders are particularly suited for this task, as they can verify every constraint for each step of the process. Finally, another technique to add constraints consists of using Lagrangian-based regularizers that are faster to compute but less strict in terms of generation [6].

## Autoregressive models

Autoregressive models can also be used on their own. The difference with other models is that past outputs become part of the current input. In this framework, graph generation becomes a sequential decision-making process that considers both data and past decisions. For instance, at each step, the autoregressive model can create a new node or a new link. Then, the resulting graph is fed to the model for the next generation step until we stop it. The following diagram illustrates this process:

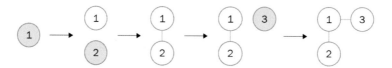

Figure 11.8 – The autoregressive process for graph generation

In practice, we use **Recurrent Neural Networks (RNNs)** to implement this autoregressive ability. In this architecture, previous outputs are used as inputs to compute the current hidden state. In addition, they can process inputs of arbitrary length, which is crucial for generating graphs iteratively. However, this computation is slower than feedforward networks, as the entire sequence must be processed to obtain the final output. The two most popular types of RNNs are the **Gated Recurrent Unit (GRU)** and **Long Short-Term Memory (LSTM)** networks.

Introduced in 2018 by You et al., **GraphRNN** [7] is a direct implementation of these techniques for deep graph generation. This architecture uses two RNNs:

- A *graph-level RNN* to generate a sequence of nodes (including the initial state)

- An *edge-level RNN* to predict connections for each newly added node

The edge-level RNN takes the hidden state of the graph-level RNN as input and then feeds it with its own output. This mechanism is illustrated in the following diagram at inference time:

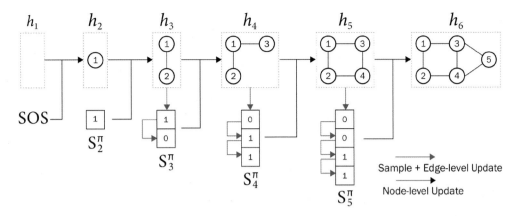

Figure 11.9 – GraphRNN's architecture at inference time

Both RNNs are actually completing an adjacency matrix: each new node created by the graph-level RNN adds a row and a column, which are filled with zeros and ones by the edge-level RNN. In summary, GraphRNN performs the following steps:

1. *Add new node*: The graph-level RNN initializes the graph and its output if fed to the edge-level RNN.

2. *Add new connections*: The edge-level RNN predicts if the new node is connected to each of the previous nodes.

3. *Stop graph generation*: The two first steps are repeated until the edge-level RNN outputs an EOS token, marking the end of the process.

The GraphRNN can learn different types of graphs (grids, social networks, proteins, and so on) and completely outperform traditional techniques. It is an architecture of choice to imitate given graphs that should be preferred to GraphVAE.

## Generative adversarial networks

Like VAEs, GANs are a well-known generative model in **ML**. In this framework, two neural networks compete in a zero-sum game with two different goals. The first neural network is a generator that creates new data, and the second one is a discriminator that classifies each sample as real (from the training set) or fake (made by the generator).

Over the years, two main improvements to the original architecture have been proposed. The first one is called the **Wasserstein GAN (WGAN)**. It improves learning stability by minimizing the Wasserstein distance (or Earth Mover's distance) between two probability distributions. This variant is further refined by introducing a gradient penalty instead of the original gradient clipping scheme.

Multiple works applied this framework to deep graph generation. Like previous techniques, GANs can imitate graphs or generate networks that optimize certain constraints. The latter option is handy in applications such as finding new chemical compounds with specific properties. This problem is exceptionally vast (over $10^{60}$ possible combinations) and complex due to its discrete nature.

Proposed by De Cao and Kipf in 2018 [8], the **molecular GAN (MolGAN)** is a popular solution to this problem. It combines a WGAN with a gradient penalty that directly processes graph-structured data and an RL objective to generate molecules with desired chemical properties. This RL objective is based on the **Deep Deterministic Policy Gradient (DDPG)** algorithm, an off-policy actor-critic model that uses deterministic policy gradients. MolGAN's architecture is summarized in the following diagram:

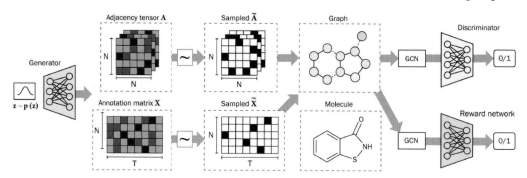

Figure 11.10 – MolGAN's architecture at inference time

This framework is divided into three main components:

- The **generator** is an MLP that outputs a node matrix $X$ containing the atom types and an adjacency matrix $A$, which is actually a tensor containing both the edges and bond types. The generator is trained using a linear combination of the WGAN and RL loss. We translate these dense representations into sparse objects ($\tilde{X}$ and $\tilde{A}$) via categorical sampling.

- The **discriminator** receives graphs from the generator and the dataset and learns to distinguish them. It is solely trained using the WGAN loss.

- The **reward network** scores each graph. It is trained using the MSE loss based on the real score provided by an external system (RDKit in this case).

The discriminator and the reward network use the GNN mode: the Relational-GCN, a GCN variant that supports multiple edge types. After several layers of graph convolutions, node embeddings are aggregated into a graph-level vector output:

$$h_G = \tanh\left(\sum_{i \in V} \sigma\big(MLP_1(h_i, x_i)\big) \odot \tanh\big(MLP_2(h_i, x_i)\big)\right)$$

Here, σ denotes the logistic sigmoid function, *MLP*$_1$ and *MLP*$_2$ are two MLPs with linear output, and ⊙ is the element-wise multiplication. A third MLP further processes this graph embedding to produce a value between 0 and 1 for the reward network and between $-\infty$ and $+\infty$ for the discriminator.

MolGAN produces valid chemical compounds that optimize properties such as drug likeliness, synthesizability, and solubility. We will implement this architecture in the next section to generate new molecules.

# Generating molecules with MolGAN

Deep graph generation is not well covered by PyTorch Geometric. Drug discovery is the main application of this subfield, which is why generative models can be found in specialized libraries. More specifically, there are two popular Python libraries for ML-based drug discovery: DeepChem and torchdrug. In this section, we will use DeepChem as it is more mature and directly implements MolGAN.

Let's see how we can use it with DeepChem and tensorflow. The following procedure is based on DeepChem's example:

1.  We install DeepChem (https://deepchem.io), which requires the following libraries: tensorflow, joblib, NumPy, pandas, scikit-learn, SciPy, and rdkit:

    ```
    !pip install deepchem==2.7.1
    ```

2.  Then, we import the required packages:

    ```
    import numpy as np
    import tensorflow as tf

    import pandas as pd
    from tensorflow import one_hot

    import deepchem as dc
    from deepchem.models.optimizers import ExponentialDecay
    from deepchem.models import BasicMolGANModel as MolGAN
    from deepchem.feat.molecule_featurizers.molgan_featurizer
    import GraphMatrix

    from rdkit import Chem
    from rdkit.Chem import Draw
    from rdkit.Chem import rdmolfiles
    from rdkit.Chem import rdmolops
    from rdkit.Chem.Draw import IpythonConsole
    ```

3.  We download the `tox21` (*Toxicology in the 21st Century*) dataset, which comprises over 6,000 chemical compounds, to analyze their toxicity. We only need their **simplified molecular-input line-entry system (SMILES)** representations in this example:

```
_, datasets, _ = dc.molnet.load_tox21()
df = pd.DataFrame(datasets[0].ids, columns=['smiles'])
```

4.  Here is an output of these `smiles` strings:

```
0     CC(O)(P(=O)(O)O)P(=O)(O)O
1     CC(C)(C)OOC(C)(C)CCC(C)(C)OOC(C)(C)C
2     OC[C@H](O)[C@@H](O)[C@H](O)CO
3     CCCCCCCC(=O)[O-].CCCCCCCC(=O)[O-].[Zn+2]
...   ...
6260  Cc1cc(CCCOc2c(C)cc(-c3noc(C(F)(F)F)n3)cc2C)on1
6261  O=C1OC(OC(=O)c2cccnc2Nc2cccc(C(F)(F)F)c2)c2ccc...
6262  CC(=O)C1(C)CC2=C(CCCC2(C)C)CC1C
6263  CC(C)CCC[C@@H](C)[C@H]1CC(=O)C2=C3CC[C@H]4C[C@...
```

5.  We only consider molecules with a maximum number of 15 atoms. We filter our dataset and create a `featurizer` to convert the `smiles` strings into input features:

```
max_atom = 15
molecules = [x for x in df['smiles'].values if Chem.
MolFromSmiles(x).GetNumAtoms() < max_atom]

featurizer = dc.feat.MolGanFeaturizer(max_atom_count=max_
atom)
```

6.  We manually loop through our dataset to convert the `smiles` strings:

```
features = []
for x in molecules:
    mol = Chem.MolFromSmiles(x)
    new_order = rdmolfiles.CanonicalRankAtoms(mol)
    mol = rdmolops.RenumberAtoms(mol, new_order)
    feature = featurizer.featurize(mol)
    if feature.size != 0:
        features.append(feature[0])
```

7. We remove invalid molecules from the dataset:

```
features = [x for x in features if type(x) is
GraphMatrix]
```

8. Then, we create the `MolGAN` model. It will be trained with a learning rate that has an exponential delay schedule:

```
gan = MolGAN(learning_rate=ExponentialDecay(0.001, 0.9,
5000), vertices=max_atom)
```

9. We create the dataset to feed to `MolGAN` in DeepChem's format:

```
dataset = dc.data.NumpyDataset(X=[x.adjacency_matrix for
x in features], y=[x.node_features for x in features])
```

10. `MolGAN` uses batch training, which is why we need to define an iterable as follows:

```
def iterbatches(epochs):
    for i in range(epochs):
        for batch in dataset.iterbatches(batch_size=gan.
batch_size, pad_batches=True):
            adjacency_tensor = one_hot(batch[0], gan.
edges)
            node_tensor = one_hot(batch[1], gan.nodes)
            yield {gan.data_inputs[0]: adjacency_tensor,
gan.data_inputs[1]: node_tensor}
```

11. We train the model for 25 epochs:

```
gan.fit_gan(iterbatches(25), generator_steps=0.2)
```

12. We generate 1000 molecules:

```
generated_data = gan.predict_gan_generator(1000)
nmols = feat.defeaturize(generated_data)
```

13. Then, we check whether these molecules are valid or not:

```
valid_mols = [x for x in generated_mols if x is not None]
print (f'{len(valid_mols)} valid molecules (out of
{len((generated_mols))} generated molecules)')
```

**31 valid molecules (out of 1000 generated molecules)**

14. We compare them to see how many molecules are unique:

```
generated_smiles = [Chem.MolToSmiles(x) for x in valid_
mols]
generated_smiles_viz = [Chem.MolFromSmiles(x) for x in
set(generated_smiles)]
print(f'{len(generated_smiles_viz)} unique valid
molecules ({len(generated_smiles)-len(generated_smiles_
viz)} redundant molecules)')
```

**24 unique valid molecules (7 redundant molecules)**

15. We print the generated molecules in a grid:

```
img = Draw.MolsToGridImage(generated_smiles_viz,
molsPerRow=6, subImgSize=(200, 200), returnPNG=False)
```

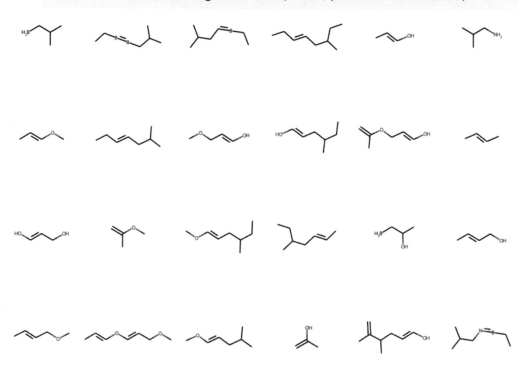

Figure 11.11 – Molecules generated with MolGAN

Despite the GAN's improvements, this training process is quite unstable and can fail to produce any meaningful result. The code we presented is sensitive to hyperparameter changes and does not generalize well to other datasets, including the QM9 dataset used in the original paper.

Nonetheless, MolGAN's concept of mixing RL and GANs can be employed beyond drug discovery to optimize any type of graph, such as computer networks, recommender systems, and so on.

# Summary

In this chapter, we saw different techniques to generate graphs. First, we explored traditional methods based on probabilities with interesting mathematical properties. However, due to their lack of expressiveness, we switched to GNN-based techniques that are much more flexible. We covered three families of deep generative models: VAE-based, autoregressive, and GAN-based methods. We introduced a model from each family to understand how they work in real life.

Finally, we implemented a GAN-based model that combines a generator, a discriminator, and a reward network from RL. Instead of simply imitating graphs seen during training, this architecture can also optimize desired properties such as solubility. We used DeepChem and TensorFlow to create 24 unique and valid molecules. Nowadays, this pipeline is common in the drug discovery industry, where ML can drastically speed up drug development.

In *Chapter 12, Handling Heterogeneous Graphs*, we will explore a new kind of graph that we previously encountered in recommender systems and molecules. These heterogeneous graphs contain multiple types of nodes and/or links, which requires specific processing. They are more general than the regular graphs we talked about and particularly useful in applications such as knowledge graphs.

# Further reading

- [1] P. Erdös and A. Rényi. *On random graphs I*, Publicationes Mathematicae Debrecen, vol. 6, p. 290, 1959. Available at `https://snap.stanford.edu/class/cs224w-readings/erdos59random.pdf`.

- [2] E. N. Gilbert, *Random Graphs*, The Annals of Mathematical Statistics, vol. 30, no. 4, pp. 1141–1144, 1959, DOI: 10.1214/aoms/1177706098. Available at: `https://projecteuclid.org/journals/annals-of-mathematical-statistics/volume-30/issue-4/Random-Graphs/10.1214/aoms/1177706098.full`.

- [3] Duncan J. Watts and Steven H. Strogatz. *Collective dynamics of small-world networks*, Nature, 393, pp. 440–442, 1998. Available at `http://snap.stanford.edu/class/cs224w-readings/watts98smallworld.pdf`.

- [4] M. Simonovsky and N. Komodakis. *GraphVAE: Towards Generation of Small Graphs Using Variational Autoencoders* CoRR, vol. abs/1802.03480, 2018, [Online]. Available at `http://arxiv.org/abs/1802.03480`.

- [5] Q. Liu, M. Allamanis, M. Brockschmidt, and A. L. Gaunt. *Constrained Graph Variational Autoencoders for Molecule Design*. arXiv, 2018. DOI: 10.48550/ARXIV.1805.09076. Available at `https://arxiv.org/abs/1805.09076`.

- [6] T. Ma, J. Chen, and C. Xiao, Constrained Generation of Semantically Valid Graphs via Regularizing Variational Autoencoders. arXiv, 2018. DOI: 10.48550/ARXIV.1809.02630. Available at https://arxiv.org/abs/1809.02630.

- [7] J. You, R. Ying, X. Ren, W. L. Hamilton, and J. Leskovec. *GraphRNN: Generating Realistic Graphs with Deep Auto-regressive Models*. arXiv, 2018. DOI: 10.48550/ARXIV.1802.08773. Available at https://arxiv.org/abs/1802.08773.

- [8] N. De Cao and T. Kipf. *MolGAN: An implicit generative model for small molecular graphs*. arXiv, 2018. DOI: 10.48550/ARXIV.1805.11973. Available at https://arxiv.org/abs/1805.11973.

# 12

# Learning from Heterogeneous Graphs

In the previous chapter, we tried to generate realistic molecules that contain different types of nodes (atoms) and edges (bonds). We also observe this kind of behavior in other applications, such as recommender systems (users and items), social networks (followers and followees), or cybersecurity (routers and servers). We call these kinds of graphs **heterogeneous**, as opposed to homogeneous graphs, which only involve one type of node and one type of edge.

In this chapter, we will recap everything we know about homogeneous GNNs. We will introduce the message passing neural network framework to generalize the architectures we have seen so far. This summary will allow us to understand how to expand our framework to heterogeneous networks. We will start by creating our own heterogeneous dataset. Then, we will transform homogeneous architectures into heterogeneous ones.

In the last section, we will take a different approach and discuss an architecture specifically designed to process heterogeneous networks. We will describe how it works to understand better the difference between this architecture and a classic GAT. Finally, we will implement it in PyTorch Geometric and compare our results with the previous techniques.

By the end of this chapter, you will have a strong understanding of the differences between homogeneous and heterogeneous graphs. You will be able to create your own heterogeneous datasets and convert traditional models to use them in this context. You will also be able to implement architectures specifically designed to make the most of heterogeneous networks.

In this chapter, we will cover the following main topics:

- The message passing neural network framework
- Introducing heterogeneous graphs
- Transforming homogeneous GNNs to heterogeneous GNNs
- Implementing a hierarchical self-attention network

# Technical requirements

All the code examples from this chapter can be found on GitHub at `https://github.com/PacktPublishing/Hands-On-Graph-Neural-Networks-Using-Python/tree/main/Chapter12`.

The installation steps required to run the code on your local machine can be found in the *Preface* of this book.

# The message passing neural network framework

Before exploring heterogeneous graphs, let's recap what we have learned about homogeneous GNNs. In the previous chapters, we saw different functions for aggregating and combining features from different nodes. As seen in *Chapter 5*, the simplest GNN layer consists of summing the linear combination of features from neighboring nodes (including the target node itself) with a weight matrix. The output of the previous sum then replaces the previous target node embedding.

The node-level operator can be written as follows:

$$h_i^{'} = \sum_{j \in \mathcal{N}_i} h_j W^T$$

$\mathcal{N}_i$ is the set of neighboring nodes of the $i$ node (including itself), $h_i$ is the embedding of the $i$ node, and $W$ is a weight matrix:

GCN and GAT layers added fixed and dynamic weights to node features but kept the same idea. Even GraphSAGE's LSTM operator or GIN's max aggregator did not change the main concept of a GNN layer. If we look at all these variants, we can generalize GNN layers into a common framework called the **Message Passing Neural Network** (**MPNN** or **MP-GNN**). Introduced in 2017 by Gilmer et al. [1], this framework consists of three main operations:

- **Message**: Every node uses a function to create a message for each neighbor. It can simply consist of its own features (as in the previous example) or also consider the neighboring node's features and edge features.

- **Aggregate**: Every node aggregates messages from its neighbors using a permutation-equivariant function, such as the sum in the previous example.

- **Update**: Every node updates its features using a function to combine its current features and the aggregated messages. In the previous example, we introduced a self-loop to aggregate the current features of the $i$ node, such as a neighbor.

These steps can be summarized in a single equation:

$$h_i^{'} = \gamma \left( h_i, \bigoplus_{j \in \mathcal{N}_i} \phi(h_i, h_j, e_{j,i}) \right)$$

Here, $h_i$ is the node embedding of the $i$ node, $e_{j,i}$ is the edge embedding of the $j \rightarrow i$ link, $\phi$ is the message function, $\bigoplus$ is the aggregation function, and $\gamma$ is the update function. You can find an illustrated version of this framework in the following figure:

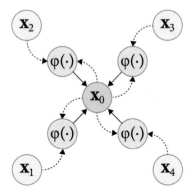

Figure 12.1 – The MPNN framework

PyTorch Geometric directly implements this framework with the `MessagePassing` class. For instance, here is how to implement the GCN layer using this class:

1.  First, we import the required libraries:

    ```
    import torch
    from torch.nn import Linear
    from torch_geometric.nn import MessagePassing
    from torch_geometric.utils import add_self_loops, degree
    ```

2.  We declare the GCN class that inherits from `MessagePassing`:

    ```
    class GCNConv(MessagePassing):
    ```

3.  This takes two parameters – the input dimensionality and the output (hidden) dimensionality. `MessagePassing` is initialized with the "add" aggregation. We define a single PyTorch linear layer without bias:

    ```
    def __init__(self, dim_in, dim_h):
        super().__init__(aggr='add')
        self.linear = Linear(dim_in, dim_h, bias=False)
    ```

4.  The `forward()` function contains the logic. First, we add self-loops to the adjacency matrix to consider target nodes:

    ```
    def forward(self, x, edge_index):
        edge_index, _ = add_self_loops(edge_index, num_
    nodes=x.size(0))
    ```

5.  Then, we apply a linear transformation using the linear layer we previously defined:

```
x = self.linear(x)
```

6.  We compute the normalization factor – $\dfrac{1}{\sqrt{\deg(i)} \cdot \sqrt{\deg(j)}}$ :

```
row, col = edge_index
deg = degree(col, x.size(0), dtype=x.dtype)
deg_inv_sqrt = deg.pow(-0.5)
deg_inv_sqrt[deg_inv_sqrt == float('inf')] = 0
norm = deg_inv_sqrt[row] * deg_inv_sqrt[col]
```

7.  We call the `propagate()` method with our updated `edge_index` (including self-loops) and our normalization factors, stored in the `norm` tensor. Internally, this method calls `message()`, `aggregate()`, and `update()`. We do not need to redefine `update()` because we already included the self-loops. The `aggregate()` function is already specified in *step 3* with `aggr='add'`:

```
out = self.propagate(edge_index, x=x, norm=norm)
return out
```

8.  We redefine the `message()` function to normalize the neighboring node features x with `norm`:

```
def message(self, x, norm):
    return norm.view(-1, 1) * x
```

9.  We can now initialize and use this object as a GCN layer:

```
conv = GCNConv(16, 32)
```

This example shows how you can create your own GNN layers in PyTorch Geometric. You can also read how the GCN or GAT layers are implemented in the source code.

The MPNN framework is an important concept that will help us to transform our GNNs into heterogeneous models.

## Introducing heterogeneous graphs

Heterogeneous graphs are a powerful tool to represent general relationships between different entities. Having different types of nodes and edges creates graph structures that are more complex but also more difficult to learn. In particular, one of the main problems with heterogeneous networks is that features from different types of nodes or edges do not necessarily have the same meaning or dimensionality.

Therefore, merging different features would destroy a lot of information. This is not the case with homogeneous graphs, where each dimension has the exact same meaning for every node or edge.

Heterogeneous graphs are a more general kind of network that can represent different types of nodes and edges. Formally, it is defined as a graph, $G = (V, E)$, comprising $V$, a set of nodes, and $E$, a set of edges. In the heterogeneous setting, it is associated with a node-type mapping function, $\phi: V \rightarrow A$ (where $A$ denotes the set of node types), and a link-type mapping function, $\psi: E \rightarrow R$ (where $R$ denotes the set of edge types).

The following figure is an example of a heterogeneous graph.

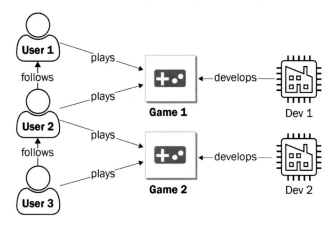

Figure 12.2 – An example of a heteregeneous graph with three types of nodes and three types of edges

In this graph, we see three types of nodes (users, games, and developers) and three types of edges (**follows**, **plays**, and **develops**). It represents a network involving people (users and developers) and games that could be used for various applications, such as recommending games. If this graph contained millions of elements, it could be used as a graph-structured knowledge database, or a knowledge graph. Knowledge graphs are used by Google or Bing to answer queries such as, "Who plays games developed by **Dev 1**?"

Similar queries can extract useful homogeneous graphs. For example, we might want only to consider users who play **Game 1**. The output would be **User 1** and **User 2**. We can create more complex queries, such as, "Who are the users who play games developed by **Dev 1**?" The result is the same, but we traversed two relations to obtain our users. This kind of query is called a meta-path.

In the first example, our meta-path was *User → Game → User* (commonly denoted as **UGU**), and in the second one, our meta-path was *User → Game → Dev → Game → User* (or **UGDGU**). Note that the start node type and the end node type are the same. Meta-paths are an essential concept in heterogeneous graphs, often used to measure the similarity of different nodes.

Now, let's see how to implement the previous graph with PyTorch Geometric. We will use a special data object called `HeteroData`. The following steps create a data object to store the graph from *Figure 12.2*:

1.  We import the `HeteroData` class from `torch_geometric.data` and create a `data` variable:

    ```
    from torch_geometric.data import HeteroData
    data = HeteroData()
    ```

2.  First, let's store node features. We can access user features with `data['user'].x`, for instance. We feed it a tensor with the `[num_users, num_features_users]` dimensions. The content does not matter in this example, so we will create feature vectors filled with ones for user 1, twos for user 2, and threes for user 3:

    ```
    data['user'].x = torch.Tensor([[1, 1, 1, 1], [2, 2, 2,
    2], [3, 3, 3, 3]])
    ```

3.  We repeat this process with `games` and `devs`. Note that the dimensionality of feature vectors is not the same; this is an important benefit of heterogeneous graphs when handling different representations:

    ```
    data['game'].x = torch.Tensor([[1, 1], [2, 2]])
    data['dev'].x = torch.Tensor([[1], [2]])
    ```

4.  Let's create connections between our nodes. Links have different meanings, which is why we will create three sets of edge indices. We can declare each set using a triplet (*source node type, edge type, destination node type*), such as `data['user', 'follows', 'user'].edge_index`. Then, we store the connections in a tensor with the `[2, number of edges]` dimensions:

    ```
    data['user', 'follows', 'user'].edge_index = torch.
    Tensor([[0, 1], [1, 2]]) # [2, num_edges_follows]
    data['user', 'plays', 'game'].edge_index = torch.
    Tensor([[0, 1, 1, 2], [0, 0, 1, 1]])
    data['dev', 'develops', 'game'].edge_index = torch.
    Tensor([[0, 1], [0, 1]])
    ```

5.  Edges can also have features – for example, the `plays` edges could include the number of hours the user played the corresponding game. In the following, we assume that user 1 played game 1 for 2 hours, user 2 played game 1 for half an hour and game 2 for 10 hours, and user 3 played game 2 for 12 hours:

    ```
    data['user', 'plays', 'game'].edge_attr = torch.
    Tensor([[2], [0.5], [10], [12]])
    ```

6.  Finally, we can print the `data` object to see the result:

```
HeteroData(
  user={ x=[3, 4] },
  game={ x=[2, 2] },
  dev={ x=[2, 1] },
  (user, follows, user)={ edge_index=[2, 2] },
  (user, plays, game)={
    edge_index=[2, 4],
    edge_attr=[4, 1]
  },
  (dev, develops, game)={ edge_index=[2, 2] }
)
```

As you can see in this implementation, different types of nodes and edges do not share the same tensors. In fact, it is impossible because they don't share the same dimensionality either. This raises a new issue – how do we aggregate information from multiple tensors using GNNs?

So far, we have only focused our efforts on a single type. In practice, our weight matrices have the right size to be multiplied with a predefined dimension. However, how do we implement GNNs when we get inputs with different dimensionalities?

# Transforming homogeneous GNNs to heterogeneous GNNs

To better understand the problem, let's take a real dataset as an example. The DBLP computer science bibliography offers a dataset, [2-3], that contains four types of nodes – `papers` (14,328), `terms` (7,723), `authors` (4,057), and `conferences` (20). This dataset's goal is to correctly classify the authors into four categories – database, data mining, artificial intelligence, and information retrieval. The authors' node features are a bag-of-words ("0" or "1") of 334 keywords they might have used in their publications. The following figure summarizes the relations between the different node types.

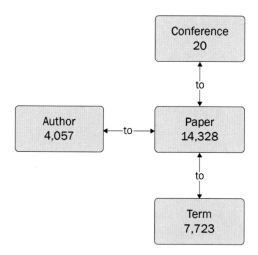

Figure 12.3 – Relationships between node types in the DBLP dataset

These node types do not have the same dimensionalities and semantic relationships. In heterogeneous graphs, relations between nodes are essential, which is why we want to consider node pairs. For example, instead of feeding author nodes to a GNN layer, we would consider a pair such as (`author`, `paper`). It means we now need a GNN layer per relation; in this case, the "to" relations are bidirectional, so we would get six layers.

These new layers have independent weight matrices with the right size for each node type. Unfortunately, we have only solved half of the problem. Indeed, we now have six distinct layers that do not share any information. We can fix that by introducing **skip-connections**, **shared layers**, **jumping knowledge**, and so on [4].

Before we transform a homogeneous model into a heterogeneous one, let's implement a classic GAT on the DBLP dataset. The GAT cannot take into account different relations; we have to give it a unique adjacency matrix that connects authors to each other. Fortunately, we now have a technique to generate this adjacency matrix easily – we can create a meta-path, such as `author-paper-author`, that will connect authors from the same papers.

> **Note**
>
> We can also build a good adjacency matrix through random walks. Even if the graph is heterogeneous, we can explore it and connect nodes that often appear in the same sequences.

The code is a little more verbose, but we can implement a regular GAT as follows:

1. We import the required libraries:

```
from torch import nn
import torch.nn.functional as F

import torch_geometric.transforms as T
from torch_geometric.datasets import DBLP
from torch_geometric.nn import GAT
```

2. We define the meta-path we will use using this specific syntax:

```
metapaths = [[('author', 'paper'), ('paper', 'author')]]
```

3. We use the `AddMetaPaths` transform function to automatically calculate our meta-path. We use `drop_orig_edge_types=True` to remove the other relations from the dataset (the GAT can only consider one):

```
transform = T.AddMetaPaths(metapaths=metapaths, drop_
orig_edge_types=True)
```

4. We load the DBLP dataset and print it:

```
dataset = DBLP('.', transform=transform)
data = dataset[0]
print(data)
```

5. We obtain the following output. Note the `(author, metapath_0, author)` relation that was created with our transform function:

```
HeteroData(
  metapath_dict={ (author, metapath_0, author)=[2] },
  author={
    x=[4057, 334],
    y=[4057],
    train_mask=[4057],
    val_mask=[4057],
    test_mask=[4057]
  },
  paper={ x=[14328, 4231] },
```

```
    term={ x=[7723, 50] },
    conference={ num_nodes=20 },
    (author, metapath_0, author)={ edge_index=[2, 11113] }
)
```

6.  We directly create a one-layer GAT model with `in_channels=-1` to perform lazy initialization (the model will automatically calculate the value) and `out_channels=4` because we need to classify the author nodes into four categories:

```
model = GAT(in_channels=-1, hidden_channels=64, out_
channels=4, num_layers=1)
```

7.  We implement the Adam optimizer and store the model and the data on a GPU if possible:

```
optimizer = torch.optim.Adam(model.parameters(),
lr=0.001, weight_decay=0.001)
device = torch.device('cuda' if torch.cuda.is_available()
else 'cpu')
data, model = data.to(device), model.to(device)
```

8.  The `test()` function measures the accuracy of the prediction:

```
@torch.no_grad()
def test(mask):
    model.eval()
    pred = model(data.x_dict['author'], data.edge_index_
dict[('author', 'metapath_0', 'author')]).argmax(dim=-1)
    acc = (pred[mask] == data['author'].y[mask]).sum() /
mask.sum()
    return float(acc)
```

9.  We create a classic training loop, where the node features (`author`) and edge indexes (`author`, `metapath_0`, and `author`) are carefully selected:

```
for epoch in range(101):
    model.train()
    optimizer.zero_grad()
    out = model(data.x_dict['author'], data.edge_index_
dict[('author', 'metapath_0', 'author')])
    mask = data['author'].train_mask
```

```
        loss = F.cross_entropy(out[mask],
data['author'].y[mask])
        loss.backward()
        optimizer.step()


        if epoch % 20 == 0:
            train_acc = test(data['author'].train_mask)
            val_acc = test(data['author'].val_mask)
            print(f'Epoch: {epoch:>3} | Train Loss:
{loss:.4f} | Train Acc: {train_acc*100:.2f}% | Val Acc:
{val_acc*100:.2f}%')
```

10. We test it on the test set with the following output:

```
test_acc = test(data['author'].test_mask)
print(f'Test accuracy: {test_acc*100:.2f}%')
```

**Test accuracy: 73.29%**

We reduced our heterogeneous dataset into a homogeneous one using a meta-path and applied a traditional GAT. We obtained a test accuracy of 73.29%, which provides a good baseline to compare it to other techniques.

Now, let's create a heterogeneous version of this GAT model. Following the method we described previously, we need six GAT layers instead of one. We don't have to do it manually, since PyTorch Geometric can do it automatically using the to_hetero() or to_hetero_bases() functions. The to_hetero() function takes three important parameters:

- module: The homogeneous model we want to convert

- metadata: Information about the heterogeneous nature of the graph, represented by a tuple, (node_types, edge_types)

- aggr: The aggregator to combine node embeddings generated by different relations (for instance, sum, max, or mean)

The following figure shows our homogeneous GAT (left) and its heterogeneous version (right), obtained with to_hetero().

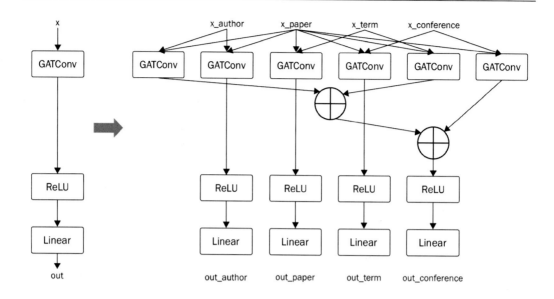

Figure 12.4 – Architecture of a homogeneous GAT (left) and a heterogeneous GAT (right) on the DBLP dataset

As shown in the following steps, the heterogeneous GAT's implementation is similar:

1.  First, we import GNN layers from PyTorch Geometric:

    ```
    from torch_geometric.nn import GATConv, Linear, to_hetero
    ```

2.  We load the DBLP dataset:

    ```
    dataset = DBLP(root='.')
    data = dataset[0]
    ```

3.  When we printed information about this dataset, you might have noticed that conference nodes do not have any features. This is an issue because our architecture assumes that each node type has its own features. We can fix this problem by generating zero values as features, as follows:

    ```
    data['conference'].x = torch.zeros(20, 1)
    ```

4.  We create our own GAT class with a GAT and linear layers. Note that we use lazy initialization again with the (-1, -1) tuple:

    ```
    class GAT(torch.nn.Module):
        def __init__(self, dim_h, dim_out):
            super().__init__()
    ```

```
        self.conv = GATConv((-1, -1), dim_h, add_self_
loops=False)
        self.linear = nn.Linear(dim_h, dim_out)

    def forward(self, x, edge_index):
        h = self.conv(x, edge_index).relu()
        h = self.linear(h)
        return h
```

5.  We instantiate the model and convert it using to_hetero():

```
model = GAT(dim_h=64, dim_out=4)
model = to_hetero(model, data.metadata(), aggr='sum')
```

6.  We implement the Adam optimizer and store the model and data on a GPU if possible:

```
optimizer = torch.optim.Adam(model.parameters(),
lr=0.001, weight_decay=0.001)
device = torch.device('cuda' if torch.cuda.is_available()
else 'cpu')
data, model = data.to(device), model.to(device)
```

7.  The test process is very similar. This time, we don't need to specify any relation, since the model considers all of them:

```
@torch.no_grad()
def test(mask):
    model.eval()
    pred = model(data.x_dict, data.edge_index_dict)
['author'].argmax(dim=-1)
    acc = (pred[mask] == data['author'].y[mask]).sum() /
mask.sum()
    return float(acc)
```

8.  The same is true for the training loop:

```
for epoch in range(101):
    model.train()
    optimizer.zero_grad()
    out = model(data.x_dict, data.edge_index_dict)
['author']
    mask = data['author'].train_mask
```

```
    loss = F.cross_entropy(out[mask],
data['author'].y[mask])
    loss.backward()
    optimizer.step()

    if epoch % 20 == 0:
        train_acc = test(data['author'].train_mask)
        val_acc = test(data['author'].val_mask)
        print(f'Epoch: {epoch:>3} | Train Loss:
{loss:.4f} | Train Acc: {train_acc*100:.2f}% | Val Acc:
{val_acc*100:.2f}%')
```

9.   We obtain the following test accuracy:

```
test_acc = test(data['author'].test_mask)
print(f'Test accuracy: {test_acc*100:.2f}%')


Test accuracy: 78.42%
```

The heterogeneous GAT obtains a test accuracy of 78.42%. This is a good improvement (+5.13%) over the homogeneous version, but can we do better? In the next section, we will explore an architecture that is specifically designed to process heterogeneous networks.

## Implementing a hierarchical self-attention network

In this section, we will implement a GNN model designed to handle heterogeneous graphs – the **hierarchical self-attention network (HAN)**. This architecture was introduced by Liu et al. in 2021 [5]. HAN uses self-attention at two different levels:

- **Node-level attention** to understand the importance of neighboring nodes in a given meta-path (such as a GAT in a homogeneous setting).

- **Semantic-level attention** to learn the importance of each meta-path. This is the main feature of HAN, allowing us to select the best meta-paths for a given task automatically – for example, the meta-path game-user-game might be more relevant than game-dev-game in some tasks, such as predicting the number of players.

In the following section, we will detail the three main components – node-level attention, semantic-level attention, and the prediction module. This architecture is illustrated in *Figure 12.5*.

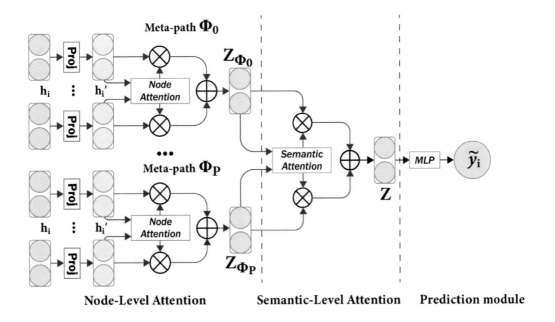

Figure 12.5 – HAN's architecture with its three main modules

Like in a GAT, the first step consists of projecting nodes into a unified feature space for each meta-path. We then calculate the weight of a node pair (concatenation of two projected nodes) in the same meta-path, with a second weight matrix. A nonlinear function is applied to this result, which is then normalized with the softmax function. The normalized attention score (importance) of the $j$ node to the $i$ node is calculated as follows:

$$\alpha_{ij}^{\Phi} = \frac{\exp\left(\sigma(a_{\Phi}^{T}[W_{\Phi}h_i \mid\mid W_{\Phi}h_j])\right)}{\sum_{k \in \mathcal{N}_i^{\Phi}} \exp\left(\sigma(a_{\Phi}^{T}[W_{\Phi}h_i \mid\mid W_{\Phi}h_k])\right)}$$

Here, $h_i$ denotes the features of the $i$ node, $W_{\Phi}$ is a shared weight matrix for the $\Phi$ meta-path, $a_{\Phi}$ is the attention weight matrix for the $\Phi$ meta-path, $\sigma$ is a nonlinear activation function (such as LeakyReLU), and $\mathcal{N}_i^{\Phi}$ is the set of neighbors of the $i$ node (including itself) in the $\Phi$ meta-path.

Multi-head attention is also performed to obtain the final embedding:

$$z_i = \mid\mid_{k=1}^{K} \sigma\left(\sum_{j \in \mathcal{N}_i} \alpha_{ij}^{\Phi} \cdot W_{\Phi}h_j\right)$$

With semantic-level attention, we repeat a similar process for the attention score of every meta-path (denoted $\beta_{\Phi_1}, \beta_{\Phi_2}, \ldots, \beta_{\Phi_P}$). Every node embedding in a given meta-path (denoted as $Z_{\Phi_p}$) is fed to an MLP that applies a nonlinear transformation. We compare this result to a new attention vector, $q$, as a similarity measure. We average this result to calculate the importance of a given meta-path:

$$w_{\Phi_p} = \frac{1}{|V|} \sum_{i \in V} q^T \cdot \tanh\left(W \cdot z_i^{\Phi_p} + b\right)$$

Here, $W$ (the MLP's weight matrix), $b$ (the MLP's bias), and $q$ (the semantic-level attention vector) are shared across the meta-paths.

We must normalize this result to compare the different semantic-level attention scores. We use the softmax function to obtain our final weights:

$$\beta_{\Phi_p} = \frac{\exp\left(w_{\Phi_p}\right)}{\sum_{k=1}^{P} \exp\left(w_{\Phi_k}\right)}$$

The final embedding, $Z$, that combines node-level and semantic-level attention is obtained as follows:

$$Z = \sum_{p=1}^{P} \beta_{\Phi_p} \cdot Z_{\Phi_p}$$

A final layer, like an MLP, is used to fine-tune the model for a particular downstream task, such as node classification or link prediction.

Let's implement this architecture in PyTorch Geometric on the DBLP dataset:

1.  First, we import the HAN layer:

    ```
    from torch_geometric.nn import HANConv
    ```

2.  We load the DBLP dataset and introduce dummy features for conference nodes:

    ```
    dataset = DBLP('.')
    data = dataset[0]
    data['conference'].x = torch.zeros(20, 1)
    ```

3.  We create the HAN class with two layers – a HAN convolution using HANConv and a linear layer for the final classification:

    ```
    class HAN(nn.Module):
        def __init__(self, dim_in, dim_out, dim_h=128,
    heads=8):
            super().__init__()
    ```

```
        self.han = HANConv(dim_in, dim_h, heads=heads,
    dropout=0.6, metadata=data.metadata())
        self.linear = nn.Linear(dim_h, dim_out)
```

4.  In the forward() function, we have to specify that we are interested in the authors:

```
    def forward(self, x_dict, edge_index_dict):
        out = self.han(x_dict, edge_index_dict)
        out = self.linear(out['author'])
        return out
```

5.  We initialize our model with lazy initialization (dim_in=-1), so PyTorch Geometric automatically calculates the input size for each node type:

```
    model = HAN(dim_in=-1, dim_out=4)
```

6.  We choose the Adam optimizer and transfer our data and model to the GPU if possible:

```
    optimizer = torch.optim.Adam(model.parameters(),
    lr=0.001, weight_decay=0.001)
    device = torch.device('cuda' if torch.cuda.is_available()
    else 'cpu')
    data, model = data.to(device), model.to(device)
```

7.  The test() function calculates the accuracy of the classification task:

```
    @torch.no_grad()
    def test(mask):
        model.eval()
        pred = model(data.x_dict, data.edge_index_dict).
    argmax(dim=-1)
        acc = (pred[mask] == data['author'].y[mask]).sum() /
    mask.sum()
        return float(acc)
```

8.  We train the model for 100 epochs. The only difference with a training loop for a homogeneous GNN is that we need to specify we're interested in the author node type:

```
    for epoch in range(101):
        model.train()
        optimizer.zero_grad()
        out = model(data.x_dict, data.edge_index_dict)
        mask = data['author'].train_mask
```

```
    loss = F.cross_entropy(out[mask],
data['author'].y[mask])
    loss.backward()
    optimizer.step()

    if epoch % 20 == 0:
        train_acc = test(data['author'].train_mask)
        val_acc = test(data['author'].val_mask)
        print(f'Epoch: {epoch:>3} | Train Loss:
{loss:.4f} | Train Acc: {train_acc*100:.2f}% | Val Acc:
{val_acc*100:.2f}%')
```

9.    The training gives us the following output:

```
Epoch:    0 | Train Loss: 1.3829 | Train Acc: 49.75% | Val
Acc: 37.75%
Epoch:   20 | Train Loss: 1.1551 | Train Acc: 86.50% | Val
Acc: 60.75%
Epoch:   40 | Train Loss: 0.7695 | Train Acc: 94.00% | Val
Acc: 67.50%
Epoch:   60 | Train Loss: 0.4750 | Train Acc: 97.75% | Val
Acc: 73.75%
Epoch:   80 | Train Loss: 0.3008 | Train Acc: 99.25% | Val
Acc: 78.25%
Epoch:  100 | Train Loss: 0.2247 | Train Acc: 99.50% | Val
Acc: 78.75%
```

10.    Finally, we test our solution on the test set:

```
test_acc = test(data['author'].test_mask)
print(f'Test accuracy: {test_acc*100:.2f}%')
```

```
Test accuracy: 81.58%
```

HAN obtains a test accuracy of 81.58%, which is higher than what we got with the heterogeneous GAT (78.42%) and the classic GAT (73.29%). It shows the importance of building good representations that aggregate different types of nodes and relations. Heterogeneous graphs' techniques are highly application-dependent, but it is worth trying different options, especially when the relationships described in the network are meaningful.

# Summary

In this chapter, we introduced the MPNN framework to generalize GNN layers using three steps – message, aggregate, and update. In the rest of the chapter, we expanded this framework to consider heterogeneous networks, composed of different types of nodes and edges. This particular kind of graph allows us to represent various relations between entities, which are more insightful than a single type of connection.

Moreover, we saw how to transform homogeneous GNNs into heterogeneous ones thanks to PyTorch Geometric. We described the different layers in our heterogeneous GAT, which take node pairs as inputs to model their relations. Finally, we implemented a heterogeneous-specific architecture with HAN and compared the results of three techniques on the DBLP dataset. It proved the importance of exploiting the heterogeneous information that is represented in this kind of network.

In *Chapter 13, Temporal Graph Neural Networks*, we will see how to consider time in GNNs. This chapter will unlock a lot of new applications thanks to temporal graphs, such as traffic forecasting. It will also introduce PyG's extension library called PyTorch Geometric Temporal, which will help us to implement new models specifically designed to handle time.

# Further reading

- [1] J. Gilmer, S. S. Schoenholz, P. F. Riley, O. Vinyals, and G. E. Dahl. *Neural Message Passing for Quantum Chemistry*. arXiv, 2017. DOI: 10.48550/ARXIV.1704.01212. Available: `https://arxiv.org/abs/1704.01212`.

- [2] Jie Tang, Jing Zhang, Limin Yao, Juanzi Li, Li Zhang, and Zhong Su. *ArnetMiner: Extraction and Mining of Academic Social Networks*. In Proceedings of the Fourteenth ACM SIGKDD International Conference on Knowledge Discovery and Data Mining (SIGKDD'2008). pp.990–998. Available: `https://dl.acm.org/doi/abs/10.1145/1401890.1402008`.

- [3] X. Fu, J. Zhang, Z. Meng, and I. King. *MAGNN: Metapath Aggregated Graph Neural Network for Heterogeneous Graph Embedding*. Apr. 2020. DOI: 10.1145/3366423.3380297. Available: `https://arxiv.org/abs/2002.01680`.

- [4] M. Schlichtkrull, T. N. Kipf, P. Bloem, R. van den Berg, I. Titov, and M. Welling. *Modeling Relational Data with Graph Convolutional Networks*. arXiv, 2017. DOI: 10.48550/ARXIV.1703.06103. Available: `https://arxiv.org/abs/1703.06103`.

- [5] J. Liu, Y. Wang, S. Xiang, and C. Pan. *HAN: An Efficient Hierarchical Self-Attention Network for Skeleton-Based Gesture Recognition*. arXiv, 2021. DOI: 10.48550/ARXIV.2106.13391. Available: `https://arxiv.org/abs/2106.13391`.

# 13

# Temporal Graph Neural Networks

In the previous chapters, we have only considered graphs where edges and features do not change. However, in the real world, there are many applications where this is not the case. For instance, in social networks, people follow and unfollow other users, posts go viral, and profiles evolve over time. This dynamicity cannot be represented using the GNN architectures we previously described. Instead, we must embed a new temporal dimension to transform static graphs into dynamic ones. These dynamic networks will then be used as inputs for a new family of GNNs: **Temporal Graph Neural Networks (T-GNNs)**, also called **Spatio-Temporal GNNs**.

In this chapter, we will describe two kinds of **dynamic graphs** that include spatiotemporal information. We will list different applications and focus on time series forecasting, where temporal GNNs are mainly applied. The second section is dedicated to an application we previously looked at: web traffic forecasting. This time, we will exploit temporal information to improve our results and obtain reliable predictions. Finally, we will describe another temporal GNN architecture designed for dynamic graphs. We will apply it to epidemic forecasting to predict the number of cases of COVID-19 in different regions of England.

By the end of this chapter, you will know the difference between the two main types of dynamic graphs. This is particularly useful for modeling your data into the right kind of graph. Moreover, you will learn about the design and architecture of two temporal GNNs and how to implement them using PyTorch Geometric Temporal. This is an essential step to creating your own applications with temporal information.

In this chapter, we will cover the following main topics:

- Introducing dynamic graphs
- Forecasting web traffic
- Predicting cases of COVID-19

# Technical requirements

All the code examples from this chapter can be found on GitHub at `https://github.com/PacktPublishing/Hands-On-Graph-Neural-Networks-Using-Python/tree/main/Chapter13`.

Installation steps required to run the code on your local machine can be found in the *Preface* of this book.

# Introducing dynamic graphs

Dynamic graphs and temporal GNNs unlock a variety of new applications, such as transport and web traffic forecasting, motion classification, epidemiological forecasting, link prediction, power system forecasting, and so on. Time series forecasting is particularly popular with this kind of graph, as we can use historical data to predict the system's future behavior.

In this chapter, we focus on graphs with a temporal component. They can be divided into two categories:

*   **Static graphs with temporal signals**: The underlying graph does not change, but features and labels evolve over time.

*   **Dynamic graphs with temporal signals**: The topology of the graph (the presence of nodes and edges), features, and labels evolve over time.

In the first case, the graph's topology is *static*. For example, it can represent a network of cities within a country for traffic forecasting: features change over time, but the connections stay the same.

In the second option, nodes and/or connections are *dynamic*. It is useful to represent a social network where links between users can appear or disappear over time. This variant is more general, but also harder to learn how to implement.

In the following sections, we will see how to handle these two types of graphs with temporal signals using PyTorch Geometric Temporal.

# Forecasting web traffic

In this section, we will predict the traffic of Wikipedia articles (as an example of a static graph with a temporal signal) using a temporal GNN. This regression task has already been covered in *Chapter 6, Introducing Graph Convolutional Networks*. However, in that version of the task, we performed traffic forecasting using a static dataset without a temporal signal: our model did not have any information about previous instances. This is an issue because it could not understand whether the traffic was currently increasing or decreasing, for example. We can now improve this model to include information about past instances.

We will first introduce the temporal GNN architecture with its two variants and then implement it using PyTorch Geometric Temporal.

## Introducing EvolveGCN

For this task, we will use the **EvolveGCN** architecture. Introduced by Pareja et al. [1] in 2019, it proposes a natural combination of GNNs and **Recurrent Neural Networks (RNNs)**. Previous approaches, such as graph convolutional recurrent networks, applied RNNs with graph convolution operators to calculate node embeddings. By contrast, EvolveGCN applies RNNs to the GCN parameters themselves. As the name implies, the GCN evolves over time to produce relevant temporal node embeddings. The following figure illustrates a high-level view of this process.

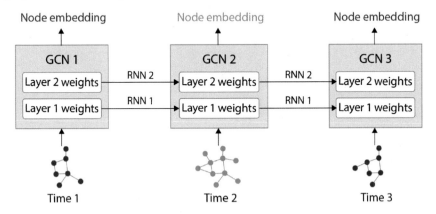

Figure 13.1 – The EvolveGCN's architecture to produce node embeddings
for a static or dynamic graph with temporal signal

This architecture has two variants:

- **EvolveGCN-H**, where the recurrent neural network considers both the previous GCN parameters and the current node embeddings

- **EvolveGCN-O**, where the recurrent neural network only considers the previous GCN parameters

EvolveGCN-H typically uses a **Gated Recurrent Unit (GRU)** instead of a vanilla RNN. The GRU is a streamlined version of the **Long Short-Term Memory (LSTM)** unit that achieves comparable performance with fewer parameters. It is comprised of a reset gate, an update gate, and a cell state. In this architecture, GRU updates the GCN's weight matrix for layer $l$ at time $t$ as follows:

$$W_t^{(l)} = \text{GRU}\,(H_t^{(l)}, W_{t-1}^{(l)})$$

$H_t^{(l)}$ denotes the node embeddings produced at layer $l$ and time $t$, and $W_{t-1}^{(l)}$ is the weight matrix for layer $l$ from the previous time step.

This resulting GCN weight matrix is then used to calculate the next layer's node embeddings:

$$H_t^{(l+1)} = GCN\left(A_t, H_t^{(l)}, W_t^{(t)}\right)$$

$$= \tilde{D}^{-\frac{1}{2}} \tilde{A}^T \tilde{D}^{-\frac{1}{2}} H_t^{(l)} W_t^{(t)T}$$

Here, $\tilde{A}$ is the adjacency matrix, including self-loops, and $\tilde{D}$ is the degree matrix with self-loops.

These steps are summarized in the following figure.

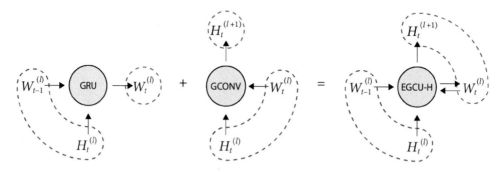

Figure 13.2 – The EvolveGCN-H's architecture with GRU and GNN

EvolveGCN-H can be implemented with a GRU that receives two extensions:

- The inputs and hidden states are matrices instead of vectors to store the GCN weight matrices properly

- The column dimension of the input must match that of the hidden state, which requires summarizing the node embedding matrix $H_t^{(l)}$ to only keep the appropriate number of columns

These extensions are not required for the EvolveGCN-O variant. Indeed, EvolveGCN-O is based on an LSTM network to model the input-output relationship. We do not need to feed a hidden state to the LSTM, as it already includes a cell that remembers previous values. This mechanism simplifies the update step, which can be written as follows:

$$W_t^{(l)} = LSTM\left(W_{t-1}^{(l)}\right)$$

The resulting GCN weight matrix is used in the same way to produce the next layer's node embeddings:

$$H_t^{(l+1)} = GCN\left(A_t, H_t^{(l)}, W_t^{(t)}\right)$$

$$= \tilde{D}^{-\frac{1}{2}} \tilde{A}^T \tilde{D}^{-\frac{1}{2}} H_t^{(l)} W_t^{(t)T}$$

This implementation is simpler since the temporal dimension entirely relies on a vanilla LSTM network. The following figure shows how EvolveGCN-O updates the weight matrix $W_{t-1}^{(l)}$ and calculates node embeddings $H_t^{(l+1)}$:

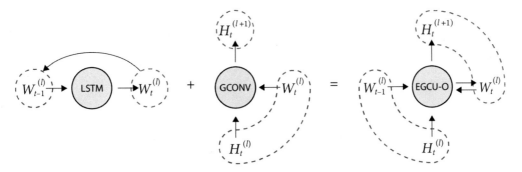

Figure 13.3 – EvolveGCN-O's architecture with LSTM and GCN

So which version should we use? As is often the case in machine learning, the best solution is data-dependent:

- EvolveGCN-H works better when the node features are essential because its RNN explicitly incorporates node embeddings
- EvolveGCN-O works better when the graph structure plays an important role, as it focuses more on topological changes

Note that these remarks are primarily theoretical, which is why it can be helpful to test both variants in your applications. This is what we will do by implementing these models for web traffic forecasting.

## Implementing EvolveGCN

In this section, we want to forecast web traffic on a static graph with a temporal signal. The **WikiMaths** dataset is comprised of 1,068 articles represented as nodes. Node features correspond to the past daily number of visits (eight features by default). Edges are weighted, and weights represent the number of links from the source page to the destination page. We want to predict the daily user visits to these Wikipedia pages between March 16, 2019, and March 15, 2021, which results in 731 snapshots. Each snapshot is a graph describing the state of the system at a certain time.

*Figure 13.4* shows a representation of WikiMaths made with Gephi, where the size and color of the nodes are proportional to their number of connections.

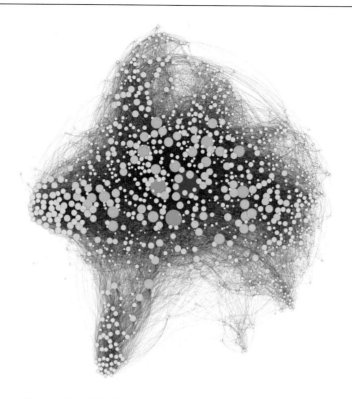

Figure 13.4 – WikiMaths dataset as an unweighted graph (t=0)

PyTorch Geometric does not natively support static or dynamic graphs with a temporal signal. Fortunately, an extension called PyTorch Geometric Temporal [2] fixes this issue and even implements various temporal GNN layers. The WikiMaths dataset was also made public during the development of PyTorch Geometric Temporal. In this chapter, we will use this library to simplify the code and focus on applications:

1.  We need to install this library in an environment containing PyTorch Geometric:

    ```
    pip install torch-geometric-temporal==0.54.0
    ```

2.  We import the WikiMaths dataset, called `WikiMathDatasetLoader`, a temporal-aware train-test split with `temporal_signal_split`, and our GNN layer, `EvolveGCNH`:

    ```
    from torch_geometric_temporal.signal import temporal_
    signal_split
    from torch_geometric_temporal.dataset import
    WikiMathsDatasetLoader
    from torch_geometric_temporal.nn.recurrent import
    EvolveGCNH
    ```

3.   We load the WikiMaths dataset, which is a `StaticGraphTemporalSignal` object. In this object, `dataset[0]` describes the graph (also called a snapshot in this context) at $t = 0$ and `dataset[500]` at $t = 500$. We also create a train-test split with a ratio of $0.5$. The training set is composed of snapshots from the earlier time periods, while the test set regroups snapshots from the later periods:

```
dataset = WikiMathsDatasetLoader().get_dataset() train_
dataset, test_dataset = temporal_signal_split(dataset,
train_ratio=0.5)
dataset[0]
Data(x=[1068, 8], edge_index=[2, 27079], edge_
attr=[27079], y=[1068])
dataset[500]
Data(x=[1068, 8], edge_index=[2, 27079], edge_
attr=[27079], y=[1068])
```

4.   The graph is static, so the node and edge dimensions do not change. However, the values contained in these tensors are different. It is difficult to visualize the values of each of the 1,068 nodes. To better understand this dataset, we can calculate the mean and standard deviation values for each snapshot instead. The moving average is also helpful in smoothing out short-term fluctuations.

```
import pandas as pd
mean_cases = [snapshot.y.mean().item() for snapshot in
dataset]
std_cases = [snapshot.y.std().item() for snapshot in
dataset]
df = pd.DataFrame(mean_cases, columns=['mean'])
df['std'] = pd.DataFrame(std_cases, columns=['std'])
df['rolling'] = df['mean'].rolling(7).mean()
```

5.   We plot these time series with `matplotlib` to visualize our task:

```
plt.figure(figsize=(15,5))
plt.plot(df['mean'], 'k-', label='Mean')
plt.plot(df['rolling'], 'g-', label='Moving average')
plt.grid(linestyle=':')
plt.fill_between(df.index, df['mean']-df['std'],
df['mean']+df['std'], color='r', alpha=0.1)
plt.axvline(x=360, color='b', linestyle='--')
plt.text(360, 1.5, 'Train/test split', rotation=-90,
color='b')
```

```
plt.xlabel('Time (days)')
plt.ylabel('Normalized number of visits')
plt.legend(loc='upper right')
```

This produces *Figure 13.5*.

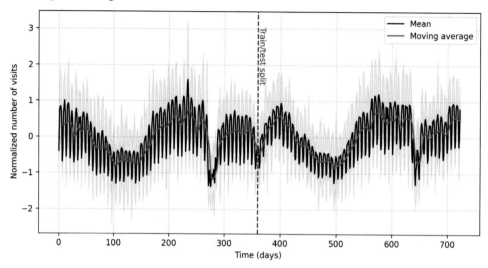

Figure 13.5 – WikiMaths' mean normalized number of visits with moving average

Our data presents periodic patterns that the temporal GNN can hopefully learn. We can now implement it and see how it performs.

6.   The temporal GNN takes two parameters as inputs: the number of nodes (node_count) and the input dimension (dim_in). The GNN only has two layers: an EvolveGCN-H layer and a linear layer that outputs a predicted value for each node:

```
class TemporalGNN(torch.nn.Module):
    def __init__(self, node_count, dim_in):
        super().__init__()
        self.recurrent = EvolveGCNH(node_count, dim_in)
        self.linear = torch.nn.Linear(dim_in, 1)
```

7.   The forward() function applies both layers to the input with a ReLU activation function:

```
    def forward(self, x, edge_index, edge_weight):
        h = self.recurrent(x, edge_index, edge_weight).relu()
        h = self.linear(h)
        return h
```

8.  We create an instance of `TemporalGNN` and give it the number of nodes and input dimension from the WikiMaths dataset. We will train it using the `Adam` optimizer:

```
model = TemporalGNN(dataset[0].x.shape[0],
dataset[0].x.shape[1])
optimizer = torch.optim.Adam(model.parameters(), lr=0.01)
model.train()
```

9.  We can print the model to observe the layers contained in `EvolveGCNH`:

```
model

TemporalGNN(
    (recurrent): EvolveGCNH(
        (pooling_layer): TopKPooling(8,
ratio=0.00749063670411985, multiplier=1.0)
        (recurrent_layer): GRU(8, 8)
        (conv_layer): GCNConv_Fixed_W(8, 8)
    )
    (linear): Linear(in_features=8, out_features=1,
bias=True)
)
```

We see three layers: `TopKPooling`, which summarizes the input matrix in eight columns; GRU, which updates the GCN weight matrix; and `GCNConv`, which produces the new node embedding. Finally, a linear layer outputs a predicted value for every node in the graph.

10. We create a training loop that trains the model on every snapshot from the training set. The loss is backpropagated for every snapshot:

```
for epoch in range(50):
    for i, snapshot in enumerate(train_dataset):
        y_pred = model(snapshot.x, snapshot.edge_index,
snapshot.edge_attr)
        loss = torch.mean((y_pred-snapshot.y)**2)
        loss.backward()
        optimizer.step()
        optimizer.zero_grad()
```

11. Likewise, we evaluate the model on the test set. The MSE is averaged on the entire test set to produce the final score:

```
model.eval()
loss = 0
for i, snapshot in enumerate(test_dataset):
    y_pred = model(snapshot.x, snapshot.edge_index,
snapshot.edge_attr)
    mse = torch.mean((y_pred-snapshot.y)**2)
    loss += mse
loss = loss / (i+1)
print(f'MSE = {loss.item():.4f}')
MSE = 0.7559
```

12. We obtain a loss value of 0.7559. Next, we will plot the mean values predicted by our model on the previous graph to interpret it. The process is straightforward: we must average the predictions and store them in a list. Then, we can add them to the previous plot:

```
y_preds = [model(snapshot.x, snapshot.edge_index,
snapshot.edge_attr).squeeze().detach().numpy().mean() for
snapshot in test_dataset]

plt.figure(figsize=(10,5))
plt.plot(df['mean'], 'k-', label='Mean')
plt.plot(df['rolling'], 'g-', label='Moving average')
plt.plot(range(360,722), y_preds, 'r-',
label='Prediction')
plt.grid(linestyle=':')
plt.fill_between(df.index, df['mean']-df['std'],
df['mean']+df['std'], color='r', alpha=0.1)
plt.axvline(x=360, color='b', linestyle='--')
plt.text(360, 1.5, 'Train/test split', rotation=-90,
color='b')
plt.xlabel('Time (days)')
plt.ylabel('Normalized number of visits')
plt.legend(loc='upper right')
```

That gives us *Figure 13.6*.

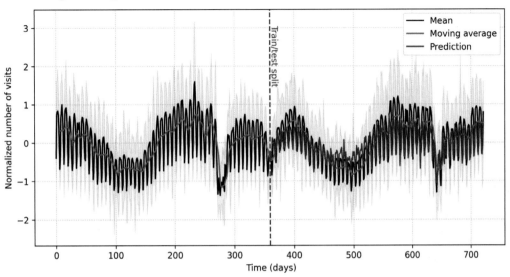

Figure 13.6 – Predicted mean normalized number of visits

We can see that the predicted values follow the general trend in the data. This is an excellent result, considering the limited size of the dataset.

13. Finally, let's create a scatter plot to show how predicted and ground truth values differ for a single snapshot:

```
import seaborn as sns

y_pred = model(test_dataset[0].x, test_dataset[0].edge_
index, test_dataset[0].edge_attr).detach().squeeze().
numpy()
plt.figure(figsize=(10,5))
sns.regplot(x=test_dataset[0].y.numpy(), y=y_pred)
```

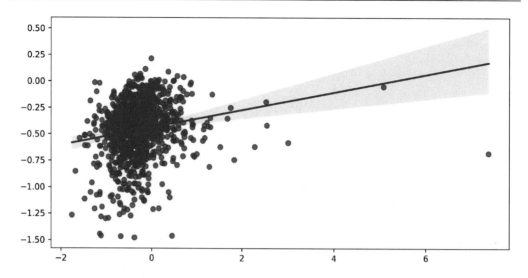

Figure 13.7 – Predicted versus ground truth values for the WikiMaths dataset

We observe a moderate positive correlation between predicted and real values. Our model is not remarkably accurate, but the previous figure showed that it understands the periodic nature of the data very well.

Implementing the EvolveGCN-O variant is very similar. Instead of using the EvolveGCNH layer from PyTorch Geometric Temporal, we replace it with EvolveGCNO. This layer does not require the number of nodes, so we only give it the input dimension. It is implemented as follows:

```
from torch_geometric_temporal.nn.recurrent import EvolveGCNO

class TemporalGNN(torch.nn.Module):
    def __init__(self, dim_in):
        super().__init__()
        self.recurrent = EvolveGCNO(dim_in, 1)
        self.linear = torch.nn.Linear(dim_in, 1)

    def forward(self, x, edge_index, edge_weight):
        h = self.recurrent(x, edge_index, edge_weight).relu()
        h = self.linear(h)
        return h

model = TemporalGNN(dataset[0].x.shape[1])
```

On average, the EvolveGCN-O model obtains similar results with an average MSE of 0.7524. In this case, the use of a GRU or LSTM network does not impact the predictions. This is understandable since both the past numbers of visits contained in node features (EvolveGCN-H) and the connections between pages (EvolveGCN-O) are essential. As a result, this GNN architecture is particularly well-suited to this traffic forecasting task.

Now that we have seen an example of a static graph, let's explore how to process dynamic graphs.

# Predicting cases of COVID-19

This section will focus on a new application with epidemic forecasting. We will use the **England Covid dataset**, a dynamic graph with temporal information introduced by Panagopoulos et al. in 2021 [3]. While nodes are static, connections between and edge weights vary over time. This dataset represents the number of reported cases of COVID-19 in 129 England NUTS 3 regions between March 3 and May 12, 2020. Data was collected from mobile phones that installed the Facebook application and shared their location history. Our goal is to predict the number of cases in each node (region) in 1 day.

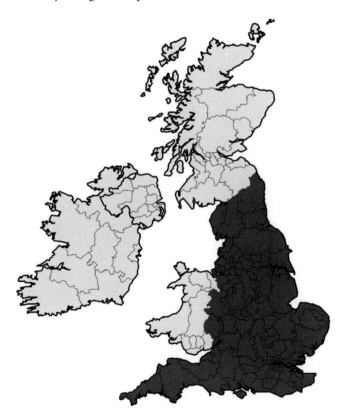

Figure 13.8 – NUTS 3 areas in England are colored in red

This dataset represents England as a graph $G = (V, E)$. Due to the temporal nature of this dataset, it is composed of multiple graphs corresponding to each day of the studied period $G^{(1)}, ..., G^{(T)}$. In these graphs, node features correspond to the number of cases in each of the past $d$ days in this region. Edges are unidirectional and weighted: the weight $w_{v,u}^{(t)}$ of edge $(v, u)$ represents the number of people that moved from region $v$ to region $u$ at time $t$. These graphs also contain self-loops corresponding to people moving within the same region.

This section will introduce a new GNN architecture designed for this task and show how to implement it step by step.

## Introducing MPNN-LSTM

As its name suggests, **MPNN-LSTM** architecture relies on combining an MPNN and an LSTM network. Like the England Covid dataset, it was also introduced by Panagopoulos et al. in 2021 [3].

The input node features with the corresponding edge indexes and weights are fed to a GCN layer. We apply a batch normalization layer and a dropout to this output. This process is repeated a second time with the outcome of the first MPNN. It produces a node embedding matrix $H^{(t)}$. We create a sequence $H^{(1)}, ..., H^{(T)}$ of node embedding representations by applying these MPNNs for each time step. This sequence is fed to a 2-layer LSTM network to capture the temporal information from the graphs. Finally, we apply a linear transformation and a ReLU function to this output to produce a prediction at $t + 1$.

The following figure shows a high-level view of the MPNN-LSTM's architecture.

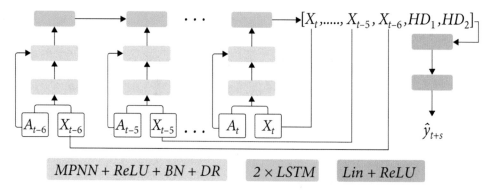

Figure 13.9 – MPNN-LSTM's architecture

The authors of MPNN-LSTM note that it is not the best-performing model on the England Covid dataset (the MPNN with a two-level GNN is). However, it is an interesting approach that could perform better in other scenarios. They also state that it is more suited for long-term forecasting, such as 14 days in the future instead of a single day, as in our version of this dataset. Despite this issue, we use the latter for convenience, as it does not impact the design of the solution.

## Implementing MPNN-LSTM

First, it is important to visualize the number of cases we want to predict. As in the previous section, we will summarize the 129 different time series that composed the dataset by calculating their mean and standard deviation:

1.  We import `pandas`, `matplotlib`, the England Covid dataset, and the temporal train-test split function from PyTorch Geometric Temporal:

    ```
    import pandas as pd
    import matplotlib.pyplot as plt
    from torch_geometric_temporal.dataset import
    EnglandCovidDatasetLoader
    from torch_geometric_temporal.signal import temporal_
    signal_split
    ```

2.  We load the dataset with 14 lags, corresponding to the number of node features:

    ```
    dataset = EnglandCovidDatasetLoader().get_
    dataset(lags=14)
    ```

3.  We perform a temporal signal split with a training ratio of `0.8`:

    ```
    train_dataset, test_dataset = temporal_signal_
    split(dataset, train_ratio=0.8)
    ```

4.  We plot the following graph to show the mean normalized number of reported cases (they are reported approximately every day). The code is available on GitHub and adapts the snippet we used in the last section.

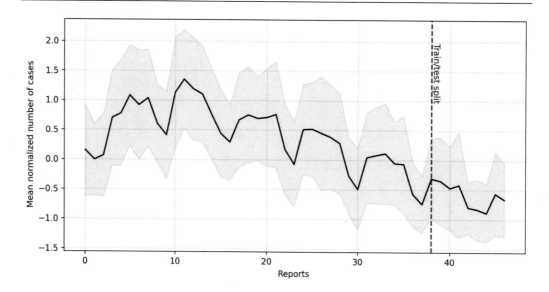

Figure 13.10 – England Covid dataset's mean normalized number of cases

This plot shows a lot of volatility and a low number of snapshots. This is why we use an 80/20 train-test split in this example. Obtaining good performance on such a small dataset might be challenging, nonetheless.

Let's now implement the MPNN-LSTM architecture.

1.  We import the MPNNLSTM layer from PyTorch Geometric Temporal:

```
From torch_geometric_temporal.nn.recurrent import
MPNNLSTM
```

2.  The temporal GNN takes three parameters as inputs: the input dimension, the hidden dimension, and the number of nodes. We declare three layers: the MPNN-LSTM layer, a dropout layer, and a linear layer with the right input dimension:

```
Class TemporalGNN(torch.nn.Module):
    def __init__(self, dim_in, dim_h, num_nodes):
        super().__init__()
        self.recurrent = MPNNLSTM(dim_in, dim_h, num_
nodes, 1, 0.5)
        self.dropout = torch.nn.Dropout(0.5)
        self.linear = torch.nn.Linear(2*dim_h + dim_in,
1)
```

3.  The `forward()` function considers the edge weights, an essential piece of information in this dataset. Note that we are processing a dynamic graph, so a new set of values for `edge_index` and `edge_weight` are provided at each time step. Unlike the original MPNN-LSTM described previously, we replace the final ReLU function with a `tanh` function. The main motivation is that tanh outputs values between -1 and 1, instead of 0 and 1, which is closer to what we observed in the dataset:

```
Def forward(self, x, edge_index, edge_weight):
        h = self.recurrent(x, edge_index, edge_weight).
    relu()
        h = self.dropout(h)
        h = self.linear(h).tanh()
        return h
```

4.  We create our MPNN-LSTM model with a hidden dimension of 64 and print it to observe the different layers:

```
model = TemporalGNN(dataset[0].x.shape[1], 64,
dataset[0].x.shape[0])
print(model)
TemporalGNN(
  (recurrent): MPNNLSTM(
    (_convolution_1): GCNConv(14, 64)
    (_convolution_2): GCNConv(64, 64)
    (_batch_norm_1): BatchNorm1d(64, eps=1e-05,
momentum=0.1, affine=True, track_running_stats=True)
    (_batch_norm_2): BatchNorm1d(64, eps=1e-05,
momentum=0.1, affine=True, track_running_stats=True)
    (_recurrent_1): LSTM(128, 64)
    (_recurrent_2): LSTM(64, 64)
  )
  (dropout): Dropout(p=0.5, inplace=False)
  (linear): Linear(in_features=142, out_features=1,
bias=True)
)
```

We see that the MPNN-LSTM layer contains two GCN, two batch normalization, and two LSTM layers (but no dropout), which corresponds to our previous description.

5.    We train this model for `100` epochs with the Adam optimizer and a learning rate of `0.001`. This time, we backpropagate the loss after every snapshot instead of every instance:

```
optimizer = torch.optim.Adam(model.parameters(),
lr=0.001)
model.train()
for epoch in range(100):
    loss = 0
    for i, snapshot in enumerate(train_dataset):
        y_pred = model(snapshot.x, snapshot.edge_index,
snapshot.edge_attr)
        loss = loss + torch.mean((y_pred-snapshot.y)**2)
    loss = loss / (i+1)
    loss.backward()
    optimizer.step()
    optimizer.zero_grad()
```

6.    We evaluate the trained model on the test set and obtain the following MSE loss:

```
model.eval()
loss = 0
for i, snapshot in enumerate(test_dataset):
    y_pred = model(snapshot.x, snapshot.edge_index,
snapshot.edge_attr)
    mse = torch.mean((y_pred-snapshot.y)**2)
    loss += mse
loss = loss / (i+1)
print(f'MSE: {loss.item():.4f}')
MSE: 1.3722
```

The MPNN-LSTM model obtained an MSE loss of 1.3722, which seems relatively high.

We cannot invert the normalization process that was applied to this dataset, so we will use the normalized numbers of cases instead. First, let's plot the mean normalized number of cases that our model predicted (code available on GitHub).

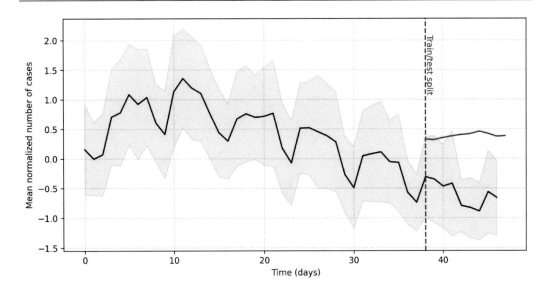

Figure 13.11 – Mean normalized number of cases with true values in black and predicted values in red

As expected, the predicted values do not match the ground truth very well. This is probably due to the lack of data: our model learned an average value that minimizes the MSE loss but cannot fit the curve and understand its periodicity.

Let's inspect the scatter plot corresponding to the test set's first snapshot (code available on GitHub).

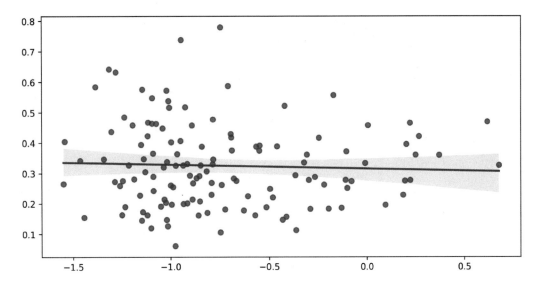

Figure 13.12 – Predicted versus ground truth values for the England Covid dataset

The scatter plot shows a weak correlation. We see that the predictions (y-axis) are mostly centered around 0.35 with little variance. This does not correspond to the ground truth values, spanning from -1.5 to 0.6. As per our experiments, adding a second linear layer did not improve the MPNN-LSTM's predictions.

Several strategies could be implemented to help the model. First, more data points could greatly help because this is a small dataset. Additionally, the time series contains two interesting characteristics: trends (continued increase and decrease over time) and seasonality (predictable pattern). We could add a preprocessing step to remove these characteristics, which add noise to the signal we want to predict.

Beyond recurrent neural networks, self-attention is another popular technique to create temporal GNNs [4]. Attention can be restricted to temporal information or also consider spatial data, typically handled by graph convolution. Finally, temporal GNNs can also be extended to heterogeneous settings described in the previous chapter. Unfortunately, this combination requires even more data and is currently an active area of research.

## Summary

This chapter introduced a new type of graph with spatiotemporal information. This temporal component is helpful in many applications, mostly related to time series forecasting. We described two types of graphs that fit this description: static graphs, where features evolve over time, and dynamic graphs, where features and topology can change. Both of them are handled by PyTorch Geometric Temporal, PyG's extension dedicated to temporal graph neural networks.

Additionally, we covered two applications of temporal GNNs. First, we implemented the EvolveGCN architecture, which uses a GRU or an LSTM network to update the GCN parameters. We applied it by revisiting web traffic forecasting, a task we encountered in *Chapter 6, Introducing Graph Convolutional Networks*, and achieved excellent results with a limited dataset. Secondly, we used the MPNN-LSTM architecture for epidemic forecasting. We applied to the England Covid dataset a dynamic graph with a temporal signal, but its small size did not allow us to obtain comparable results.

In *Chapter 14, Explaining Graph Neural Networks*, we will focus on how to interpret our results. Beyond the different visualizations we have introduced so far, we will see how to apply techniques from **eXplainable Artificial Intelligence (XAI)** to graph neural networks. This field is a key component to build robust AI systems and improve machine learning adoption. In that chapter, we will introduce post hoc explanation methods and new layers to build models that are explainable by design.

## Further reading

- [1] A. Pareja et al., *EvolveGCN: Evolving Graph Convolutional Networks for Dynamic Graphs*. arXiv, 2019. DOI: 10.48550/ARXIV.1902.10191. Available: `https://arxiv.org/abs/1902.10191`

- [2] B. Rozemberczki et al., *PyTorch Geometric Temporal: Spatiotemporal Signal Processing with Neural Machine Learning Models*, in Proceedings of the 30th ACM International Conference on Information and Knowledge Management, 2021, pp. 4564–4573. Available: `https://arxiv.org/abs/2104.07788`

- [3] G. Panagopoulos, G. Nikolentzos, and M. Vazirgiannis. *Transfer Graph Neural Networks for Pandemic Forecasting*. arXiv, 2020. DOI: 10.48550/ARXIV.2009.08388. Available: `https://arxiv.org/abs/2009.08388`

- [4] Guo, S., Lin, Y., Feng, N., Song, C., & Wan, H. (2019). Attention Based Spatial-Temporal Graph Convolutional Networks for Traffic Flow Forecasting. Proceedings of the AAAI Conference on Artificial Intelligence, 33(01), 922-929. `https://doi.org/10.1609/aaai.v33i01.3301922`

# 14

# Explaining Graph Neural Networks

One of the most common criticisms of NNs is that their outputs are difficult to understand. Unfortunately, GNNs are not immune to this limitation: in addition to explaining which features are important, it is necessary to consider neighboring nodes and connections. In response to this issue, the area of **explainability** (in the form of **explainable AI** or **XAI**) has developed many techniques to better understand the reasons behind a prediction or the general behavior of a model. Some of these techniques have been translated to GNNs, while others take advantage of the graph structure to offer more precise explanations.

In this chapter, we will explore some explanation techniques to understand why a given prediction has been made. We will see different families of techniques and focus on two of the most popular: **GNNExplainer** and **integrated gradients**. We will apply the former on a graph classification task using the MUTAG dataset. Then, we will introduce Captum, a Python library that offers many explanation techniques. Finally, using the Twitch social network, we will implement integrated gradients to explain the model's outputs on a node classification task.

By the end of this chapter, you will be able to understand and implement several XAI techniques on GNNs. More specifically, you will learn how to use GNNExplainer and the Captum library (with integrated gradients) for graph and node classification tasks.

In this chapter, we will cover the following main topics:

- Introducing explanation techniques
- Explaining GNNs with GNNExplainer
- Explaining GNNs with Captum

# Technical requirements

All the code examples from this chapter can be found on GitHub at `https://github.com/PacktPublishing/Hands-On-Graph-Neural-Networks-Using-Python/tree/main/Chapter14`.

Installation steps required to run the code on your local machine can be found in the *Preface* of this book.

# Introducing explanation techniques

GNN explanation is a recent field that is heavily inspired by other XAI techniques [1]. We divide it into local explanations on a per-prediction basis and global explanations for entire models. While understanding the behavior of a GNN model is desirable, we will focus on local explanations that are more popular and essential to get insight into a prediction.

In this chapter, we distinguish between "interpretable" and "explainable" models. A model is called "interpretable" if it is human-understandable by design, such as a decision tree. On the other hand, it is "explainable" when it acts as a black box whose predictions can only be retroactively understood using explanation techniques. This is typically the case with NNs: their weights and biases do not provide clear rules like a decision tree, but their results can be explained indirectly.

There are four main categories of local explanation techniques:

- **Gradient-based methods** analyze gradients of the output to estimate attribution scores (for example, **integrated gradients**)

- **Perturbation-based methods** mask or modify input features to measure changes in the output (for example, **GNNExplainer**)

- **Decomposition methods** decompose the model's predictions into several terms to gauge their importance (for example, graph neural network **layer-wise relevance propagation (GNN-LRP)**)

- **Surrogate methods** use a simple and interpretable model to approximate the original model's prediction around an area (for example, **GraphLIME**)

These techniques are complementary: they sometimes disagree on the contribution of edges and features, which can be used to refine the explanation of a prediction further. Explanation techniques are traditionally evaluated using metrics such as the following:

- **Fidelity,** which compares the prediction probabilities of $y_i$ between the original graph $G_i$ and a modified graph $\hat{G}_i$. The modified graph only keeps the most important features (nodes, edges, node features) of $\hat{G}_i$, based on an explanation of $\hat{y}_i$. In other words, fidelity measures the extent to which the features identified as important are sufficient to obtain the correct prediction. It is formally defined as follows:

$$Fidelity = \frac{1}{N} \sum_{i=1}^{N} \left( f(G_i)_{y_i} - f(\hat{G}_i)_{y_i} \right)$$

- **Sparsity**, which measures the fraction of features (nodes, edges, node features) that are considered important. Explanations that are too lengthy are more challenging to understand, which is why sparsity is encouraged. It is computed as follows:

$$Sparsity = \frac{1}{N} \sum_{i=1}^{N} \left( 1 - \frac{|m_i|}{|M_i|} \right)$$

Here, $|m_i|$ is the number of important input features and $|M_i|$ is the total number of features.

In addition to the traditional graphs we saw in previous chapters, explanation techniques are often evaluated on synthetic datasets, such as `BA-Shapes`, `BA-Community`, `Tree-Cycles`, and `Tree-Grid` [2]. These datasets were generated using graph generation algorithms to create specific patterns. We will not use them in this chapter, but they are an interesting alternative that is easy to implement and understand.

In the following sections, we will describe a gradient-based method (integrated gradients) and a perturbation-based technique (GNNExplainer).

## Explaining GNNs with GNNExplainer

In this section, we will introduce our first XAI technique with GNNExplainer. We will use it to understand the predictions produced by a GIN model on the `MUTAG` dataset.

### Introducing GNNExplainer

Introduced in 2019 by Ying et al. [2], GNNExplainer is a GNN architecture designed to explain predictions from another GNN model. With tabular data, we want to know which features are the most important to a prediction. However, this is not enough with graph data: we also need to know which nodes are the most influential. GNNExplainer generates explanations with these two components by providing a subgraph $G_S$ and a subset of node features $X_S$. The following figure illustrates an explanation provided by GNNExplainer for a given node:

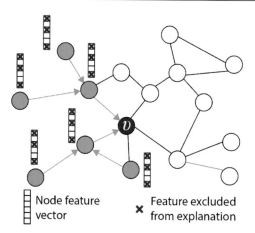

Node feature vector

✗  Feature excluded from explanation

Figure 14.1 – Explanation for node $v$'s label with $G_S$ in green and non-excluded node features $X_S$

To predict $G_S$ and $X_S$, GNNExplainer implements an edge mask (to hide connections) and a feature mask (to hide node features). If a connection or a feature is important, removing it should drastically change the prediction. On the other hand, if the prediction does not change, it means that this information was redundant or simply irrelevant. This principle is at the core of perturbation-based techniques such as GNNExplainer.

In practice, we must carefully craft a loss function to find the best masks possible. GNNExplainer measures the mutual dependence between the predicted label distribution $Y$ and $(G_S, X_S)$, also called **mutual information** (MI). Our goal is to maximize the MI, which is equivalent to minimizing the conditional cross-entropy. GNNExplainer is trained to find the variables $G_S$ and $X_S$ that maximize the probability of a prediction $\hat{y}$.

In addition to this optimization framework, GNNExplainer learns a binary feature mask and implements several regularization techniques. The most important technique is a term used to minimize the size of the explanation (sparsity). It is computed as the sum of all elements of the mask parameters and added to the loss function. It creates more user-friendly and concise explanations that are easier to understand and interpret.

GNNExplainer can be applied to most GNN architectures and different tasks such as node classification, link prediction, or graph classification. It can also generate explanations of a class label or an entire graph. When classifying a graph, the model considers the union of adjacency matrices for all nodes in the graph instead of a single one. In the next section, we will apply it to explain graph classifications.

## Implementing GNNExplainer

In this example, we will explore the MUTAG dataset [3]. Each of the 188 graphs in this dataset represents a chemical compound, where nodes are atoms (seven possible atoms), and edges are chemical bonds (four possible bonds). Node and edge features represent one-hot encodings of the atom and edge types, respectively. The goal is to classify each compound into two classes according to their mutagenic effect on the bacteria *Salmonella typhimurium*.

We will reuse the GIN model introduced in *Chapter 9* for protein classification. In *Chapter 9*, we visualized correct and incorrect classifications made by the model. However, we could not explain the predictions made by the GNN. This time, we'll use GNNExplainer to understand the most important subgraph and node features to explain a classification. In this example, we will ignore the edge features for ease of use. Here are the steps:

1. We import the required classes from PyTorch and PyTorch Geometric:

```
import matplotlib.pyplot as plt
import torch.nn.functional as F
from torch.nn import Linear, Sequential, BatchNorm1d,
ReLU, Dropout
from torch_geometric.datasets import TUDataset
from torch_geometric.loader import DataLoader
from torch_geometric.nn import GINConv, global_add_pool,
GNNExplainer
```

2. We load the MUTAG dataset and shuffle it:

```
dataset = TUDataset(root='.', name='MUTAG').shuffle()
```

3. We create training, validation, and test sets:

```
train_dataset = dataset[:int(len(dataset)*0.8)]
val_dataset    =
dataset[int(len(dataset)*0.8):int(len(dataset)*0.9)]
test_dataset   = dataset[int(len(dataset)*0.9):]
```

4. We create data loaders to implement mini-batching:

```
train_loader = DataLoader(train_dataset, batch_size=64,
shuffle=True)
val_loader   = DataLoader(val_dataset, batch_size=64,
shuffle=True)
test_loader  = DataLoader(test_dataset, batch_size=64,
shuffle=True)
```

5. We create a GIN model with 32 hidden dimensions using code from *Chapter 9*:

```
class GIN(torch.nn.Module):
    ...
model = GIN(dim_h=32)
```

6. We train this model for 100 epochs and test it using code from *Chapter 9*:

```
def train(model, loader):
    ...
model = train(model, train_loader)
test_loss, test_acc = test(model, test_loader)
print(f'Test Loss: {test_loss:.2f} | Test Acc: {test_
acc*100:.2f}%')
Test Loss: 0.48 | Test Acc: 84.21%
```

7. Our GIN model is trained and achieved a high accuracy score (84.21%). Now, let's create a GNNExplainer model using the `GNNExplainer` class from PyTorch Geometric. We will train it for 100 epochs:

```
explainer = GNNExplainer(model, epochs=100, num_hops=1)
```

8. GNNExplainer can be used to explain the prediction made for a node (`.explain_node()`) or an entire graph (`.explain_graph()`). In this case, we will use it on the last graph of the test set:

```
data = dataset[-1]
feature_mask, edge_mask = explainer.explain_graph(data.x,
data.edge_index)
```

9. The last step returned the feature and edge masks. Let's print the feature mask to see the most important values:

```
feature_mask
tensor([0.7401, 0.7375, 0.7203, 0.2692, 0.2587, 0.7516,
0.2872])
```

The values are normalized between 0 (less important) and 1 (more important). These seven values correspond to the seven atoms we find in the dataset in the following order: carbon (C), nitrogen (N), oxygen (O), fluorine (F), iodine (I), chlorine (Cl), and bromine (Br). Features have similar importance: the most useful is the last one, representing bromine (Br), and the least important is the fifth one, representing iodine (I).

10. Instead of printing the edge mask, we can plot it on the graph using the `.visualize_graph()` method. The arrows' opacity represents the importance of each connection:

```
ax, G = explainer.visualize_subgraph(-1, data.edge_index,
edge_mask, y=data.y)
plt.show()
```

This gives us *Figure 14.2*.

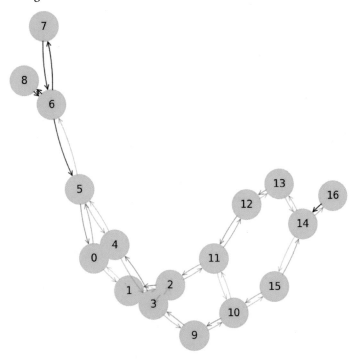

Figure 14.2 – Graph representation of a chemical compound: the edge opacity represents the importance of each connection

The last plot shows the connections that contributed the most to the prediction. In this case, the GIN model correctly classified the graph. We can see that the links between nodes **6**, **7**, and **8** are the most relevant here. The highlighted connections were crucial in the classification of this chemical compound. We can learn more about them by printing `data.edge_attr` to obtain the label associated with their chemical bonds (aromatic, single, double, or triple). In this example, it corresponds to edges **16** to **19**, which all are either single or double bonds.

By printing `data.x`, we can also look at nodes **6**, **7**, and **8** to gain more information. Node **6** represents an atom of nitrogen, while nodes **7** and **8** are two atoms of oxygen. These results should be reported to people with the right domain knowledge to get feedback on our model.

GNNExplainer does not provide precise rules about the decision-making process but gives insights into what the GNN model focused on to make its prediction. Human expertise is still needed to ensure that these ideas are coherent and correspond to traditional domain knowledge.

In the next section, we will use Captum to explain node classifications on a new social network.

# Explaining GNNs with Captum

In this section, we will first introduce Captum and the integrated gradients technique applied to graph data. Then, we will implement it using a PyTorch Geometric model on the Twitch social network.

## Introducing Captum and integrated gradients

Captum (`captum.ai`) is a Python library that implements many state-of-the-art explanation algorithms for PyTorch models. This library is not dedicated to GNNs: it can also be applied to text, images, tabular data, and so on. It is particularly useful because it allows users to quickly test various techniques and compare different explanations for the same prediction. In addition, Captum implements popular algorithms such as LIME and Gradient SHAP for primary, layer, and neuron attributions.

In this section, we will use it to apply a graph version of integrated gradients [4]. This technique aims to assign an attribution score to every input feature. To this end, it uses gradients with respect to the model's inputs. Specifically, it uses an input $x$ and a baseline input $x'$ (all edges have zero weight in our case). It computes the gradients at all points along the path between $x$ and $x'$ and accumulates them.

Formally, the integrated gradient along the $i^{th}$ dimension for an input $x$ is defined as follows:

$$IntegratedGrads_i(x) ::= (x_i - x_i') \times \int_{\alpha=0}^{1} \frac{\partial F(x' + \alpha \times (x - x'))}{\partial x_i} d\alpha$$

In practice, instead of directly calculating this integral, we approximate it with a discrete sum.

Integrated gradients is model-agnostic and based on two axioms:

- **Sensitivity**: Every input contributing to the prediction must receive a nonzero attribution

- **Implementation invariance**: Two NNs whose outputs are equal for all inputs (these networks are called functionally equivalent) must have identical attributions

The graph version we will employ is slightly different: it considers nodes and edges *instead of* features. As a result, you can see that the output differs from GNNExplainer, which considers node features *and* edges. This is why these two approaches can be complementary.

Let's now implement this technique and visualize the results.

# Implementing integrated gradients

We will implement integrated gradients on a new dataset: the Twitch social networks dataset (English version) [5]. It represents a user-user graph, where nodes correspond to Twitch streamers and connections to mutual friendships. The 128 node features represent information such as streaming habits, location, games liked, and so on. The goal is to determine whether a streamer uses explicit language (binary classification).

We will implement a simple two-layer GCN with PyTorch Geometric for this task. We will then convert our model to Captum to use the integrated gradients algorithm and explain our results. Here are the steps:

1.  We install the `captum` library:

    ```
    !pip install captum
    ```

2.  We import the required libraries:

    ```
    import numpy as np
    import matplotlib.pyplot as plt
    import torch.nn.functional as F
    from captum.attr import IntegratedGradients

    import torch_geometric.transforms as T
    from torch_geometric.datasets import Twitch
    from torch_geometric.nn import Explainer, GCNConv, to_
    captum
    ```

3.  Let's fix the random seeds to make computations deterministic:

    ```
    torch.manual_seed(0)
    np.random.seed(0)
    ```

4.  We load the Twitch gamer network dataset (English version):

    ```
    dataset = Twitch('.', name="EN")
    data = dataset[0]
    ```

5.  This time, we will use a simple two-layer GCN with `dropout`:

    ```
    class GCN(torch.nn.Module):
        def __init__(self, dim_h):
            super().__init__()
    ```

```
        self.conv1 = GCNConv(dataset.num_features, dim_h)
        self.conv2 = GCNConv(dim_h, dataset.num_classes)


    def forward(self, x, edge_index):
        h = self.conv1(x, edge_index).relu()
        h = F.dropout(h, p=0.5, training=self.training)
        h = self.conv2(h, edge_index)
        return F.log_softmax(h, dim=1)
```

6.  We try to train the model on a GPU—if one is available—using the Adam optimizer:

```
device = torch.device('cuda' if torch.cuda.is_available()
else 'cpu')
model = GCN(64).to(device)
data = data.to(device)
optimizer = torch.optim.Adam(model.parameters(), lr=0.01,
weight_decay=5e-4)
```

7.  We train the model for 200 epochs using the negative log-likelihood loss function:

```
for epoch in range(200):
    model.train()
    optimizer.zero_grad()
    log_logits = model(data.x, data.edge_index)
    loss = F.nll_loss(log_logits, data.y)
    loss.backward()
    optimizer.step()
```

8.  We test the trained model. Note that we did not specify any test, so we will evaluate the GCN's accuracy on the training set in this case:

```
def accuracy(pred_y, y):
    return ((pred_y == y).sum() / len(y)).item()
@torch.no_grad()
def test(model, data):
    model.eval()
    out = model(data.x, data.edge_index)
    acc = accuracy(out.argmax(dim=1), data.y)
    return acc
acc = test(model, data)
```

```
print(f'Accuracy: {acc*100:.2f}%')
Accuracy: 79.75%
```

The model achieved an accuracy score of 79.75%, which is relatively low considering that it was evaluated on the training set.

9.  We can now start implementing the explanation method we chose: the integrated gradients. First, we must specify the node we want to explain (node 0 in this example) and convert the PyTorch Geometric model to Captum. Here, we also specify we want to use a feature and an edge mask with mask_type=node_and_feature:

```
node_idx = 0
captum_model = to_captum(model, mask_type='node_and_
edge', output_idx=node_idx)
```

10. Let's create the integrated gradients object using Captum. We give it the result of the previous step as input:

```
ig = IntegratedGradients(captum_model)
```

11. We already have the node mask we need to pass to Captum (data.x), but we need to create a tensor for the edge mask. In this example, we want to consider every edge in the graph, so initialize a tensor of ones with size data.num_edges:

```
edge_mask = torch.ones(data.num_edges, requires_
grad=True, device=device)
```

12. The .attribute() method takes a specific format of inputs for the node and edge masks (hence the use of .unsqueeze(0) to reformat these tensors). The target corresponds to the class of our target node. Finally, we pass the adjacency matrix (data.edge_index) as an additional forward argument:

```
attr_node, attr_edge = ig.attribute(
    (data.x.unsqueeze(0), edge_mask.unsqueeze(0)),
    target=int(data.y[node_idx]),
    additional_forward_args=(data.edge_index),
    internal_batch_size=1)
```

13. We scale the attribution scores between 0 and 1:

```
attr_node = attr_node.squeeze(0).abs().sum(dim=1)
attr_node /= attr_node.max()
attr_edge = attr_edge.squeeze(0).abs()
attr_edge /= attr_edge.max()
```

14. Using PyTorch Geometric's `Explainer` class, we visualize a graph representation of these attributions:

```
explainer = Explainer(model)
ax, G = explainer.visualize_subgraph(node_idx, data.edge_
index, attr_edge, node_alpha=attr_node, y=data.y)
plt.show()
```

This gives us the following output:

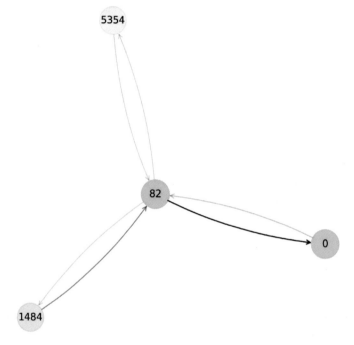

Figure 14.3 – Explanation for node 0's classification with edge and node
attribution scores represented with different opacity values

Node 0's subgraph comprises blue nodes, which share the same class. We can see that node **82** is the most important node (other than 0) and the connection between these two nodes is the most critical edge. This is a straightforward explanation: we have a group of four streamers using the same language. The mutual friendship between nodes **0** and **82** is a good argument for this prediction.

Let's now look at another graph illustrated in *Figure 14.4*, the explanation for node **101**'s classification:

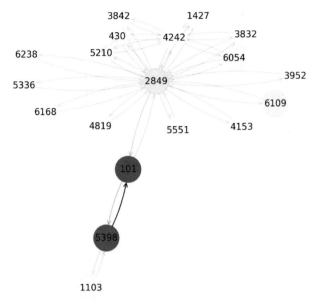

Figure 14.4 – Explanation for node 101's classification with edge and node
attribution scores represented with different opacity values

In this case, our target node is connected to neighbors with different classes (nodes **5398** and **2849**). Integrated gradients give greater importance to the node that shares the same class as node **101**. We also see that their connection is the one that contributed the most to this classification. This subgraph is richer; you can see that even two-hop neighbors contribute a little.

However, these explanations should not be considered a silver bullet. Explainability in AI is a rich topic that often involves people with different backgrounds. Thus, communicating the results and getting regular feedback is particularly important. Knowing the importance of edges, nodes, and features is essential, but it should only be the start of a discussion. Experts from other fields can exploit or refine these explanations, and even find issues that can lead to architectural changes.

## Summary

In this chapter, we explored the field of XAI applied to GNNs. Explainability is a key component in many areas and can help us to build better models. We saw different techniques to provide local explanations and focused on GNNExplainer (a perturbation-based method) and integrated gradients (a gradient-based method). We implemented them on two different datasets using PyTorch Geometric and Captum to obtain explanations for graph and node classification. Finally, we visualized and discussed the results of these techniques.

In *Chapter 15, Forecasting Traffic Using A3T-GCN*, we will revisit temporal GNNs to predict future traffic on a road network. In this practical application, we will see how to translate roads into graphs and apply a recent GNN architecture to forecast short-term traffic accurately.

## Further reading

- [1] H. Yuan, H. Yu, S. Gui, and S. Ji. *Explainability in Graph Neural Networks: A Taxonomic Survey*. arXiv, 2020. DOI: 10.48550/ARXIV.2012.15445. Available at `https://arxiv.org/abs/2012.15445`.

- [2] R. Ying, D. Bourgeois, J. You, M. Zitnik, and J. Leskovec. *GNNExplainer: Generating Explanations for Graph Neural Networks*. arXiv, 2019. DOI: 10.48550/ARXIV.1903.03894. Available at `https://arxiv.org/abs/1903.03894`.

- [3] Debnath, A. K., Lopez de Compadre, R. L., Debnath, G., Shusterman, A. J., and Hansch, C. (1991). *Structure-activity relationship of mutagenic aromatic and heteroaromatic nitro compounds. Correlation with molecular orbital energies and hydrophobicity.* DOI: 10.1021/jm00106a046. *Journal of Medicinal Chemistry*, 34(2), 786–797. Available at `https://doi.org/10.1021/jm00106a046`.

- [4] M. Sundararajan, A. Taly, and Q. Yan. *Axiomatic Attribution for Deep Networks*. arXiv, 2017. DOI: 10.48550/ARXIV.1703.01365. Available at `https://arxiv.org/abs/1703.01365`.

- [5] B. Rozemberczki, C. Allen, and R. Sarkar. *Multi-Scale Attributed Node Embedding. arXiv, 2019.* DOI: 10.48550/ARXIV.1909.13021. Available at `https://arxiv.org/pdf/1909.13021.pdf`.

# Part 4:
# Applications

In this fourth and final part of the book, we delve into the development of comprehensive applications that utilize real-world data. Our focus will be on encompassing aspects previously omitted in previous chapters, such as exploratory data analysis and data processing. We aim to provide an exhaustive overview of the machine learning pipeline, from raw data to model output analysis. We will also highlight the strengths and limitations of the techniques discussed.

The projects in this section have been designed to be adaptable and customizable, enabling readers to apply them to other datasets and tasks with ease. This makes it an ideal resource for readers who wish to build a portfolio of applications and showcase their work on GitHub.

By the end of this part, you will know how to implement GNNs for traffic forecasting, anomaly detection, and recommender systems. These projects have been selected to demonstrate the versatility and potential of GNNs in solving real-world problems. The knowledge and skills gained from these projects will prepare readers for developing their own applications and contributing to the field of graph learning.

This part comprises the following chapters:

- *Chapter 15, Forecasting Traffic Using A3T-GCN*
- *Chapter 16, Detecting Anomalies Using Heterogeneous Graph Neural Networks*
- *Chapter 17, Recommending Books Using LightGCN*
- *Chapter 18, Unlocking the Potential of Graph Neural Networks for Real-Word Applications*

# 15
# Forecasting Traffic Using A3T-GCN

We introduced T-GNNs in *Chapter 13*, but we did not elaborate on their main application: **traffic forecasting**. In recent years, the concept of smart cities has become increasingly popular. This idea refers to cities where data is used to manage and improve operations and services. In this context, one of the main sources of appeal is the creation of intelligent transportation systems. Accurate traffic forecasts can help traffic managers to optimize traffic signals, plan infrastructure, and reduce congestion. However, traffic forecasting is a challenging problem due to complex spatial and temporal dependencies.

In this chapter, we will apply T-GNNs to a particular case of traffic forecasting. First, we will explore and process a new dataset to create a temporal graph from raw CSV files. We will then apply a new type of T-GNN to predict future traffic speed. Finally, we will visualize and compare the results to a baseline solution to verify that our architecture is relevant.

By the end of this chapter, you will know how to create a temporal graph dataset from tabular data. In particular, we will see how to create a weighted adjacency matrix that will provide us with edge weights. Finally, you will learn how to apply a T-GNN to a traffic forecasting task and evaluate the results.

In this chapter, we will cover the following main topics:

- Exploring the PeMS-M dataset
- Processing the dataset
- Implementing a temporal GNN

# Technical requirements

All the code examples from this chapter can be found on GitHub at `https://github.com/PacktPublishing/Hands-On-Graph-Neural-Networks-Using-Python/tree/main/Chapter15`.

Installation steps required to run the code on your local machine can be found in the *Preface* of this book. This chapter requires a large amount of GPU. You can lower it by decreasing the size of the training set in the code.

# Exploring the PeMS-M dataset

In this section, we will explore our dataset to find patterns and get insights that will be useful to the task of interest.

The dataset we will use for this application is the medium variant of the `PeMSD7` dataset [1]. The original dataset was obtained by collecting traffic speed from 39,000 sensor stations on the weekdays of May and June 2012 using the Caltrans **Performance Measurement System (PeMS)**. We will only consider 228 stations across District 7 of California in the medium variant. These stations output 30-second speed measurements that are aggregated into 5-minute intervals in this dataset. For example, the following figure shows the Caltrans PeMS (`pems.dot.ca.gov`) with various traffic speeds:

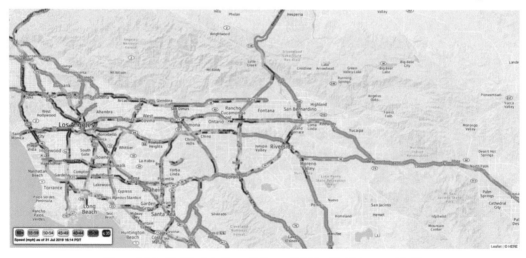

Figure 15.1 – Traffic data from Caltrans PeMS with high speed (>60 mph) in green and low speed (<35 mph) in red

We can directly load the dataset from GitHub and unzip it:

```
from io import BytesIO
```

```
from urllib.request import urlopen
from zipfile import ZipFile

url = 'https://github.com/VeritasYin/STGCN_IJCAI-18/raw/master/
data_loader/PeMSD7_Full.zip'
with urlopen(url) as zurl:
    with ZipFile(BytesIO(zurl.read())) as zfile:
        zfile.extractall('.')
```

The resulting folder contains two files: V_228.csv and W_228.csv. The V_228.csv file contains the traffic speed collected by the 228 sensor stations, and W_228.csv stores the distances between these stations.

Let's load them using pandas. We will rename the columns using range() for easy access:

```
import pandas as pd
speeds = pd.read_csv('PeMSD7_V_228.csv', names=range(0,228))
distances = pd.read_csv('PeMSD7_W_228.csv.csv',
names=range(0,228))
```

The first thing we want to do with this dataset is to visualize the evolution of traffic speed. This is a classic in time series forecasting since characteristics such as seasonality can be extremely helpful. On the other hand, non-stationary time series might need further processing before they can be used.

Let's plot the traffic speed over time using matplotlib:

1. We import NumPy and matplotlib:

    ```
    import numpy as np
    import matplotlib.pyplot as plt
    ```

2. We use plt.plot() to create a line plot for every row in our DataFrame:

    ```
    plt.figure(figsize=(10,5))
    plt.plot(speeds)
    plt.grid(linestyle=':')
    plt.xlabel('Time (5 min)')
    plt.ylabel('Traffic speed')
    ```

3.   We obtain the following plot:

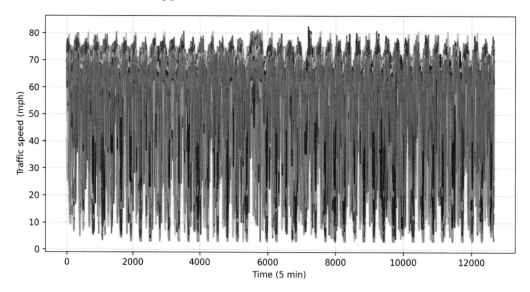

Figure 15.2 – Traffic speed over time for each of the 228 sensor stations

Unfortunately, the data is too noisy to give us any insight using this approach. Instead, we could plot the data corresponding to a few sensor stations. However, it might not be representative of the entire dataset. There is another option: we can plot the mean traffic speed with standard deviation. That way, we can visualize a summary of the dataset.

In practice, we would use both approaches, but let's try the second option now:

1.   We calculate the mean traffic speed with the corresponding standard deviation for each column (time step):

```
mean = speeds.mean(axis=1)
std = speeds.std(axis=1)
```

2.   We plot the mean values in black with a solid line:

```
plt.plot(mean, 'k-')
```

3.   We plot the standard deviation around the mean values using `plt.fill_between()` in light red:

```
plt.fill_between(mean.index, mean-std, mean+std,
color='r', alpha=0.1)
plt.grid(linestyle=':')
```

```
plt.xlabel('Time (5 min)')
plt.ylabel('Traffic speed')
```

4.  The code generates the following plot:

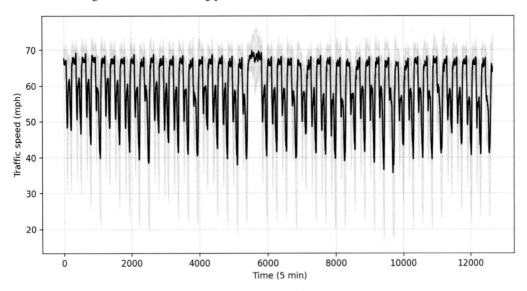

Figure 15.3 – Mean traffic speed over time with a standard deviation

This figure is much more comprehensible. We can see a clear seasonality (pattern) in the time series data, except around the 5,800[th] data sample. The traffic speed has a lot of variability with important spikes. This is understandable because the sensor stations are spread throughout District 7 of California: traffic might be jammed for some sensors but not for others.

We can verify that by plotting the correlation between the speed values from every sensor. In addition to that, we can compare it with the distances between each station. Stations close to each other should display similar values more often than distant ones.

Let's compare these two plots on the same figure:

1.  We create a figure with two horizontal subplots and some padding between them:

    ```
    fig, (ax1, ax2) = plt.subplots(1, 2, figsize=(8, 8))
    fig.tight_layout(pad=3.0)
    ```

2.  First, we use the matshow() function to plot the distance matrix:

    ```
    ax1.matshow(distances)
    ax1.set_xlabel("Sensor station")
    ```

```
ax1.set_ylabel("Sensor station")
ax1.title.set_text("Distance matrix")
```

3.  Then, we calculate the Pearson correlation coefficients for each sensor station. We must transpose the speed matrix or we will get the correlation coefficients for each time step instead. Finally, we invert them, so the two plots are easier to compare:

```
ax2.matshow(-np.corrcoef(speeds.T))
ax2.set_xlabel("Sensor station")
ax2.set_ylabel("Sensor station")
ax2.title.set_text("Correlation matrix")
```

4.  We obtain the following plot:

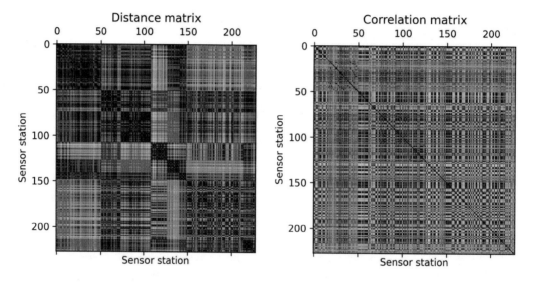

Figure 15.4 – Distance and correlation matrices with darker colors representing short distances and high correlation, while brighter colors represent long distances and low correlation

Interestingly, long distances between stations do not mean they are not highly correlated (and vice versa). This is particularly important if we only consider a subset of this dataset: close stations might have very different outputs, making traffic forecasting more difficult. In this chapter, we will take into account every sensor station in the dataset.

# Processing the dataset

Now that we have more information about this dataset, it is time to process it before we can feed it to a T-GNN.

The first step consists of transforming the tabular dataset into a temporal graph. So, first, we need to create a graph from the raw data. In other words, we must connect the different sensor stations in a meaningful way. Fortunately, we have access to the distance matrix, which should be a good way to connect the stations.

There are several options to compute the adjacency matrix from the distance matrix. For example, we could assign a link when the distance between two stations is inferior to the mean distance. Instead, we will perform a more advanced processing introduced in [2] to calculate a weighted adjacency matrix. Instead of binary values, we calculate weights between 0 (no connection) and 1 (strong connection) using the following formula:

$$w_{ij} = \{exp\left(-\frac{d_{ij}^2}{\sigma^2}\right), i \neq j \text{ and } exp\left(-\frac{d_{ij}^2}{\sigma^2}\right) \geq \epsilon \; 0, otherwise.$$

Here, $W_{ij}$ represents the weight of the edge from node $i$ to node $j$, $d_{ij}$ is the distance between these two nodes, and $\sigma^2$ and $\epsilon$ are two thresholds to control the distribution and sparsity of the adjacency matrix. The official implementation of [2] is available on GitHub (https://github.com/VeritasYin/STGCN_IJCAI-18). We will reuse the same threshold values $\sigma^2 = 0.1$ and $\epsilon = 0.5$.

Let's implement it in Python and plot the resulting adjacency matrix:

1.  We create a function to compute the adjacency matrix that takes three parameters: the distance matrix and the two thresholds $\sigma^2$ and $\epsilon$. Like in the official implementation, we divide the distances by 10,000 and calculate $d^2$:

    ```
    def compute_adj(distances, sigma2=0.1, epsilon=0.5):
        d = distances.to_numpy() / 10000.
        d2 = d * d
    ```

2.  Here, we want weights when their values are greater than or equal to $\epsilon$ (otherwise, they should be equal to zero). When we test whether the weights are greater than or equal to $\epsilon$, the results are True or False statements. This is why we need a mask of ones (w_mask) to convert it back into 0 and 1 values. We multiply it a second time so that we only obtain the real values of weights that are greater than or equal to $\epsilon$:

    ```
    n = distances.shape[0]
    w_mask = np.ones([n, n]) - np.identity(n)
    return np.exp(-d2 / sigma2) * (np.exp(-d2 / sigma2)
    >= epsilon) * w_mask
    ```

3.  Let's compute our adjacency matrix and print the result for one line:

```
adj = compute_adj(distances)
adj[0]
array([0.        , 0.        , 0.        , 0.        , 0.        ,
       0.        , 0.        , 0.61266012, 0.        , ...
```

We can see a value of 0.61266012, representing the weight of the edge from node 1 to node 2.

4.  A more efficient way to visualize this matrix is to use `matplotlib`'s `matshow` again:

```
plt.figure(figsize=(8, 8))
cax = plt.matshow(adj, False)
plt.colorbar(cax)
plt.xlabel("Sensor station")
plt.ylabel("Sensor station")
```

We get the following figure:

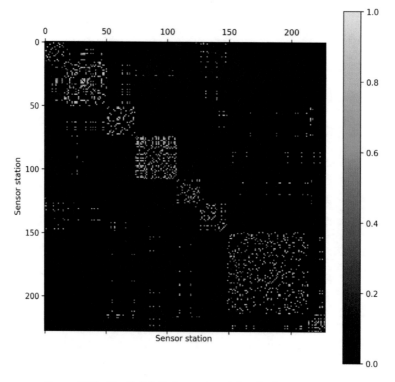

Figure 15.5 – The PeMS-M dataset's weighted adjacency matrix

This is a great way to summarize this first processing step. We can compare it to the distance matrix we previously plotted to find similarities.

5.  We can also directly plot it as a graph using `networkx`. In this case, connections are binary, so we can simply consider every weight higher than 0. We could display these values using edge labels, but the graph would be extremely difficult to read:

```
import networkx as nx

def plot_graph(adj):
    plt.figure(figsize=(10,5))
    rows, cols = np.where(adj > 0)
    edges = zip(rows.tolist(), cols.tolist())
    G = nx.Graph()
    G.add_edges_from(edges)
    nx.draw(G, with_labels=True)
    plt.show()
```

6.  Even without labels, the resulting graph is not easy to read:

```
plot_graph(adj)
```

It gives us the following output:

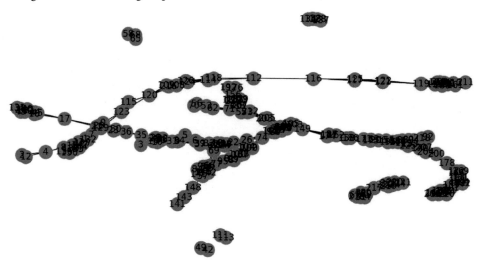

Figure 15.6 – The PeMS-M dataset as a graph (every node represents a sensor station)

Indeed, many nodes are interconnected because they are very close to each other. Yet, despite that, we can distinguish several branches that could correspond to actual roads.

Now that we have a graph, we can focus on the time series aspect of this problem. The first step consists of normalizing the speed values so they can be fed to a neural network. In the traffic forecasting literature, many authors choose a z-score normalization (or standardization), which we will implement here:

1. We create a function to calculate z-scores:

```
def zscore(x, mean, std):
    return (x - mean) / std
```

2. We apply it to our dataset to create a normalized version of it:

```
speeds_norm = zscore(speeds, speeds.mean(axis=0), speeds.
std(axis=0))
```

3. We can check the result:

```
speeds_norm.head(1)
```

We get the following output:

| 0 | 1 | 2 | 3 | 4 | 5 | 6 | ... |
|---|---|---|---|---|---|---|-----|
| 0 | 0.950754 | 0.548255 | 0.502211 | 0.831672 | 0.793696 | 1.193806 | ... |

Figure 15.7 – An example of standardized speed values

These values are correctly standardized. Now, we can use them to create time series for each node. We want $n$ input data samples at each time step, $t$, to predict the speed value at $t + h$. A high number of input data samples also increases the memory footprint of the dataset. The value for $h$, also called the horizon, depends on the task we want to perform: short-term or long-term traffic forecasting.

In this example, let's take a high value of 48 to predict the traffic speed in 4 hours:

1. We initialize the variables: the number of lags (number of input data samples), horizon, the input matrix, and the ground-truth matrix:

```
lags = 24
horizon = 48
xs = []
ys = []
```

2.  For each time step $t$, we store the 12 (lags) previous values in xs and the value at $t + h$ in ys:

```
for i in range(lags, speeds_norm.shape[0]-horizon):
    xs.append(speeds_norm.to_numpy()[i-lags:i].T)
    ys.append(speeds_norm.to_numpy()[i+horizon-1])
```

3.  Finally, we can create the temporal graph using PyTorch Geometric Temporal. We need to give the edge index in COO format and the edge weight from the weighted adjacency matrix:

```
from torch_geometric_temporal.signal import
StaticGraphTemporalSignal
edge_index = (np.array(adj) > 0).nonzero()
edge_weight = adj[adj > 0]
dataset = StaticGraphTemporalSignal(edge_index, adj[adj >
0], xs, ys)
```

4.  Let's print information about the first graph to see whether everything looks good:

```
dataset[0]
Data(x=[228, 12], edge_index=[2, 1664], edge_attr=[1664],
y=[228])
```

5.  Let's not forget the train/test split to finalize our dataset:

```
from torch_geometric_temporal.signal import temporal_
signal_split
train_dataset, test_dataset = temporal_signal_
split(dataset, train_ratio=0.8)
```

The final temporal graph has 228 nodes with 12 values and 1,664 connections. We are now ready to apply a T-GNN to predict traffic.

# Implementing the A3T-GCN architecture

In this section, we will train an **Attention Temporal Graph Convolutional Network** (A3T-GCN), designed for traffic forecasting. This architecture allows us to consider complex spatial and temporal dependencies:

- Spatial dependencies refer to the fact that the traffic condition of a location can be influenced by the traffic condition of nearby locations. For example, traffic jams often spread to neighboring roads.

- Temporal dependencies refer to the fact that the traffic condition of a location at a time can be influenced by the traffic condition of the same location at previous times. For example, if a road is congested during the morning peak, it is likely to remain congested until the evening peak.

A3T-GCN is an improvement over the **temporal GCN** (**TGCN**) architecture. The TGCN is a combination of a GCN and GRU that produces hidden vectors from each input time series. The combination of these two layers captures spatial and temporal information from the input. An attention model is then used to calculate weights and output a context vector. The final prediction is based on the resulting context vector. The addition of this attention model is motivated by the need to understand global trends.

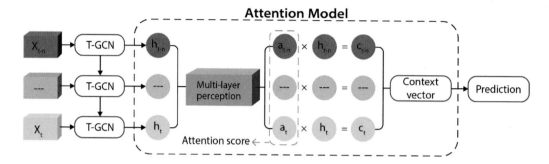

Figure 15.8 – The A3T-GCN framework

We will now implement it using the PyTorch Geometric Temporal library:

1. First, we import the required libraries:

```
import torch
from torch_geometric_temporal.nn.recurrent import A3TGCN
```

2. We create a T-GNN with an A3TGCN layer and a linear layer with 32 hidden dimensions. The edge_attr parameter will store our edge weights:

```
class TemporalGNN(torch.nn.Module):
    def __init__(self, dim_in, periods):
        super().__init__()
        self.tgnn = A3TGCN(in_channels=dim_in, out_
channels=32, periods=periods)
        self.linear = torch.nn.Linear(32, periods)

    def forward(self, x, edge_index, edge_attr):
        h = self.tgnn(x, edge_index, edge_attr).relu()
        h = self.linear(h)
        return h
```

3.  We instantiate the T-GNN and the Adam optimizer with a learning rate of $0.005$. Due to implementation details, we will train this model using a CPU instead of a GPU, which is faster in this case:

```
model = TemporalGNN(lags, 1).to('cpu')
optimizer = torch.optim.Adam(model.parameters(),
lr=0.005)
```

4.  We train the model for 30 epochs using the **Mean Squared Error** (**MSE**) as the `loss` function. The `loss` value is backpropagated after each epoch:

```
model.train()
for epoch in range(30):
    loss = 0
    step = 0
    for i, snapshot in enumerate(train_dataset):
        y_pred = model(snapshot.x.unsqueeze(2), snapshot.
edge_index, snapshot.edge_attr)
        loss += torch.mean((y_pred-snapshot.y)**2)
        step += 1
    loss = loss / (step + 1)
    loss.backward()
    optimizer.step()
    optimizer.zero_grad()
    if epoch % 10 == 0:
        print(f"Epoch {epoch+1:>2} | Train MSE:
{loss:.4f}")
```

5.  We obtain the following output:

```
Epoch  1 | Train MSE: 1.0209
Epoch 10 | Train MSE: 0.9625
Epoch 20 | Train MSE: 0.9143
Epoch 30 | Train MSE: 0.8905
```

Now that our model is trained, we have to evaluate it. Beyond classic metrics such as **Root Mean Squared Error** (**RMSE**) and **Mean Absolute Error** (**MAE**), it is particularly helpful to compare our model to a baseline solution with time series data. In the following list, we will introduce two methods:

- Using **Random Walk** (**RW**) as a naïve forecaster. In this case, RW refers to using the last observation as the predicted value. In other words, the value at $t$ is the same one as at $t + h$.

- Using **Historical Average** (**HA**) as a slightly more evolved solution. In this case, we calculate the mean traffic speed of $k$ previous samples as the value at $t + h$. In this example, we will use the number of lags as our $k$ value, but we could also take the overall historical average.

Let's start by evaluating the model's predictions on the test set:

1. We create a function to invert the z-score and get back to the original values:

```
def inverse_zscore(x, mean, std):
    return x * std + mean
```

2. We use it to recalculate the speeds we want to predict from their normalized values. The following loop is not very efficient, but it is clearer to understand than more optimized code:

```
y_test = []
for snapshot in test_dataset:
    y_hat = snapshot.y.numpy()
    y_hat = inverse_zscore(y_hat, speeds.mean(axis=0),
speeds.std(axis=0))
    y_test = np.append(y_test, y_hat)
```

3. We apply the same strategy to the predictions made by the GNN:

```
gnn_pred = []
model.eval()
for snapshot in test_dataset:
    y_hat = model(snapshot.x.unsqueeze(2), snapshot.edge_
index, snapshot.edge_weight).squeeze().detach().numpy()
    y_hat = inverse_zscore(y_hat, speeds.mean(axis=0),
speeds.std(axis=0))
    gnn_pred = np.append(gnn_pred, y_hat)
```

4. We do the same thing for the RW and HA techniques:

```
rw_pred = []
for snapshot in test_dataset:
    y_hat = snapshot.x[:,-1].squeeze().detach().numpy()
```

```
        y_hat = inverse_zscore(y_hat, speeds.mean(axis=0),
    speeds.std(axis=0))
        rw_pred = np.append(rw_pred, y_hat)


    ha_pred = []
    for i in range(lags, speeds_norm.shape[0]-horizon):
        y_hat = speeds_norm.to_numpy()
    [i-lags:i].T.mean(axis=1)
        y_hat = inverse_zscore(y_hat, speeds.mean(axis=0),
    speeds.std(axis=0))
        ha_pred.append(y_hat)
    ha_pred = np.array(ha_pred).flatten()[-len(y_test):]
```

5.  We create functions to calculate the MAE, RMSE, and the **Mean Absolute Percentage Error (MAPE)**:

```
    def MAE(real, pred):
        return np.mean(np.abs(pred - real))


    def RMSE(real, pred):
        return np.sqrt(np.mean((pred - real) ** 2))


    def MAPE(real, pred):
        return np.mean(np.abs(pred - real) / (real + 1e-5))
```

6.  We evaluate the GNN's predictions in the following block and repeat this process for every technique:

```
    print(f'GNN MAE  = {MAE(gnn_pred, y_test):.4f}')
    print(f'GNN RMSE = {RMSE(gnn_pred, y_test):.4f}')
    print(f'GNN MAPE = {MAPE(gnn_pred, y_test):.4f}')
```

In the end, we obtain the following table:

|  | RMSE | MAE | MAPE |
|---|---|---|---|
| A3T-GCN | **11.9396** | **8.3293** | **14.95%** |
| Random Walk | 17.6501 | 11.0469 | 29.99% |
| Historical Average | 17.9009 | 11.7308 | 28.93% |

Figure 15.9 – Output table of predictions

We see that the baseline techniques are outperformed by the A3T-GCN model in every metric. This is an important result because baselines can often be difficult to beat. It would be interesting to compare these metrics to the predictions provided by LSTM or GRU networks to measure the importance of the topological information.

Finally, we can plot the mean predictions to obtain a visualization that is similar to *Figure 15.3*:

1.  We obtain the mean predictions using a list comprehension that is a little faster than the previous method (but harder to read):

```
y_preds = [inverse_zscore(model(snapshot.x.unsqueeze(2),
snapshot.edge_index, snapshot.edge_weight).squeeze().
detach().numpy(), speeds.mean(axis=0), speeds.
std(axis=0)).mean() for snapshot in test_dataset]
```

2.  We calculate the mean and standard deviation of the original dataset:

```
mean = speeds.mean(axis=1)
std = speeds.std(axis=1)
```

3.  We plot the mean traffic speed with standard deviation and compare it to the predicted values ($t + 4$ hours):

```
plt.figure(figsize=(10,5), dpi=300)
plt.plot(mean, 'k-', label='Mean')
plt.plot(range(len(speeds)-len(y_preds), len(speeds)), y_
preds, 'r-', label='Prediction')
plt.grid(linestyle=':')
plt.fill_between(mean.index, mean-std, mean+std,
color='r', alpha=0.1)
plt.axvline(x=len(speeds)-len(y_preds), color='b',
linestyle='--')
plt.xlabel('Time (5 min)')
plt.ylabel('Traffic speed to predict')
plt.legend(loc='upper right')
```

We obtain the following figure:

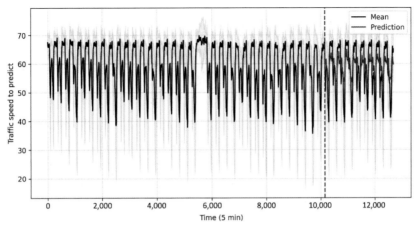

Figure 15.10 – Mean traffic speeds predicted by the A3T-GCN model on the test set

The T-GNN correctly predicts spikes and follows the general trend. However, the predicted speeds are closer to the overall average value, as it is more costly for the model to make serious mistakes due to the MSE loss. Despite that, the GNN is quite accurate and could be fine-tuned to output more extreme values.

## Summary

This chapter focused on a traffic forecasting task using T-GNNs. First, we explored the PeMS-M dataset and converted it from tabular data into a static graph dataset with a temporal signal. In practice, we created a weighted adjacency matrix based on the input distance matrix and converted the traffic speeds into time series. Finally, we implemented an A3T-GCN model, a T-GNN designed for traffic forecasting. We compared the results to two baselines and validated the predictions made by our model.

In *Chapter 16, Building a Recommender System Using LightGCN*, we will see the most popular application of GNNs. We will implement a lightweight GNN on a massive dataset and evaluate it using techniques from recommender systems.

## Further reading

- [1] B. Yu, H. Yin, and Z. Zhu. *Spatio-Temporal Graph Convolutional Networks: A Deep Learning Framework for Traffic Forecasting*. Jul. 2018. doi: 10.24963/ijcai.2018/505. Available at https://arxiv.org/abs/1709.04875.

- [2] Y. Li, R. Yu, C. Shahabi, and Y. Liu. *Diffusion Convolutional Recurrent Neural Network: Data-Driven Traffic Forecasting*. arXiv, 2017. doi: 10.48550/ARXIV.1707.01926. Available at https://arxiv.org/abs/1707.01926.

# 16
# Detecting Anomalies Using Heterogeneous GNNs

In machine learning, anomaly detection is a popular task that aims to identify patterns or observations in data that deviate from the expected behavior. This is a fundamental problem that arises in many real-world applications, such as detecting fraud in financial transactions, identifying defective products in a manufacturing process, and detecting cyber attacks in a computer network.

GNNs can be trained to learn the normal behavior of a network and then identify nodes or patterns that deviate from that behavior. Indeed, their ability to understand complex relationships makes them particularly appropriate to detect weak signals. Additionally, GNNs can be scaled to large datasets, making them an efficient tool for processing large amounts of data.

In this chapter, we will build a GNN application for anomaly detection in computer networks. First, we will introduce the `CIDDS-001` dataset, which contains attacks and benign traffic in a computer network. Next, we will process the dataset, preparing it for input into GNNs. We will then move on to implementing a heterogenous GNN to handle different types of nodes and edges. Finally, we will train the network using the processed dataset and evaluate the results to see how well it detects anomalies in the network traffic.

By the end of this chapter, you will know how to implement a GNN for intrusion detection. In addition, you will know how to build relevant features to detect attacks and process them to feed them to a GNN. Finally, you will learn how to implement and evaluate a heterogenous GNN to detect rare attacks.

In this chapter, we will cover the following main topics:

* Exploring the CIDDS-001 dataset
* Preprocessing the CIDDS-001 dataset
* Implementing a heterogeneous GNN

# Technical requirements

All the code examples from this chapter can be found on GitHub at `https://github.com/PacktPublishing/Hands-On-Graph-Neural-Networks-Using-Python/tree/main/Chapter16`.

The installation steps required to run the code on your local machine can be found in the *Preface* of this book. This chapter requires a large amount of GPU. You can lower it by decreasing the size of the training set in the code.

# Exploring the CIDDS-001 dataset

This section will explore the dataset and get more insights about feature importance and scaling.

The `CIDDS-001` dataset [1] is designed to train and evaluate anomaly-based network intrusion detection systems. It provides realistic traffic that includes up-to-date attacks to assess these systems. It was created by collecting and labeling 8,451,520 traffic flows in a virtual environment using OpenStack. Precisely, each row corresponds to a NetFlow connection, describing **Internet Protocol (IP)** traffic statistics, such as the number of bytes exchanged.

The following figure provides an overview of the simulated network environment in `CIDDS-001`.

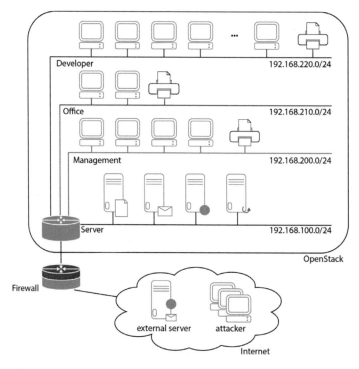

Figure 16.1 – Overview of the virtual network simulated by CIDDS-001

We see four different subnets (developer, office, management, and server) with their respective IP address ranges. All these subnets are linked to a single server connected to the internet through a firewall. An external server is also present and provides two services: a file synchronization service and a web server. Finally, attackers are represented outside of the local network.

Connections in CIDDS-001 were collected from the local and external servers. The goal of this dataset is to correctly classify these connections into five categories: benign (no attack), brute-force, denial of service, ping scan, and port scan.

Let's download the CIDDS-001 dataset and explore its input features:

1.  We download CIDDS-001:

```python
from io import BytesIO
from urllib.request import urlopen
from zipfile import ZipFile

url = 'https://www.hs-coburg.de/fileadmin/hscoburg/
WISENT-CIDDS-001.zip'
with urlopen(url) as zurl:
    with ZipFile(BytesIO(zurl.read())) as zfile:
        zfile.extractall('.')
```

2.  We import the required libraries:

```python
import numpy as np
import pandas as pd
import matplotlib.pyplot as plt
import itertools
from sklearn.model_selection import train_test_split
from sklearn.preprocessing import PowerTransformer
from sklearn.metrics import f1_score, classification_
report, confusion_matrix
from torch_geometric.loader import DataLoader
from torch_geometric.data import HeteroData
from torch.nn import functional as F
from torch.optim import Adam
from torch import nn
import torch
```

3.  We load the dataset using `pandas`:

```
df = pd.read_csv("CIDDS-001/traffic/OpenStack/CIDDS-001-
internal-week1.csv")
```

4.  Let's look at the data corresponding to the first five connections:

```
df.head(5)
```

```
Date first seen Duration Proto Src IP Addr Src Pt Dst
IP Addr Dst Pt Packets Bytes Flows Flags Tos class
attackType attackID attackDescription
2017-03-15 00:01:16.632 0.000 TCP 192.168.100.5 445
192.168.220.16 58844.0 1 108 1 .AP... 0 normal --- ---
---
2017-03-15 00:01:16.552 0.000 TCP 192.168.100.5 445
192.168.220.15 48888.0 1 108 1 .AP... 0 normal --- ---
---
2017-03-15 00:01:16.551 0.004 TCP 192.168.220.15 48888
192.168.100.5 445.0 2 174 1 .AP... 0 normal --- --- ---
2017-03-15 00:01:16.631 0.004 TCP 192.168.220.16 58844
192.168.100.5 445.0 2 174 1 .AP... 0 normal --- --- ---
2017-03-15 00:01:16.552 0.000 TCP 192.168.100.5 445
192.168.220.15 48888.0 1 108 1 .AP... 0 normal --- ---
---
```

There are a few interesting features we can use for our model:

- The date first seen is a timestamp we can process to extract information about the day of the week and the time of day. In general, network traffic is seasonal, and connections that occur at night or on unusual days are suspicious.

- IP addresses (such as 192.168.100.5) are notoriously difficult to process because they are not numerical values and follow a complex set of rules. We could bin them into a few categories since we know how our local network is set up. Another popular and more generalizable solution is to convert them into a binary representation ("192" becomes "11000000").

- Duration, the number of packets, and the number of bytes are features that usually display heavy-tailed distributions. Therefore, they will require special processing if that is the case.

Let's check this last point and look closely at the distribution of attacks in this dataset:

1. We start by removing features we will not consider in this project: ports, the number of flows, type of service, class, attack ID, and attack description:

```
df = df.drop(columns=['Src Pt', 'Dst Pt', 'Flows', 'Tos',
'class', 'attackID', 'attackDescription'])
```

2. We rename the benign class and convert the "date first seen" feature into the timestamp data type:

```
df['attackType'] = df['attackType'].replace('---',
'benign')
df['Date first seen'] = pd.to_datetime(df['Date first
seen'])
```

3. We count the labels and make a pie chart with the three most represented classes (the two others are under 0.1%):

```
count_labels = df['attackType'].value_counts() / len(df)
* 100
plt.pie(count_labels[:3], labels=df['attackType'].
unique()[:3], autopct='%.0f%%')
```

4. We obtain the following plot:

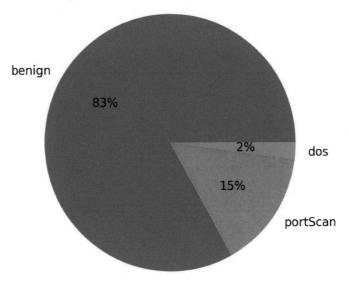

Figure 16.2 – Proportion of each class in the CIDDS-001 dataset

As you can see, benign traffic represents the immense majority of this dataset. On the contrary, brute-force attacks and ping scans have very few samples in comparison. This imbalanced learning setting could negatively impact the model's performance when dealing with rare classes.

5.  Finally, we can display the duration distribution, number of packets, and number of bytes. This allows us to see whether they really need a specific rescaling process:

```
fig, ((ax1, ax2, ax3)) = plt.subplots(1, 3,
figsize=(20,5))
df['Duration'].hist(ax=ax1)
ax1.set_xlabel("Duration")
df['Packets'].hist(ax=ax2)
ax2.set_xlabel("Number of packets")
pd.to_numeric(df['Bytes'], errors='coerce').hist(ax=ax3)
ax3.set_xlabel("Number of bytes")
plt.show()
```

It outputs the following figure:

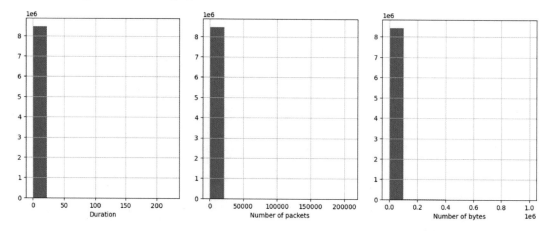

Figure 16.3 – Distributions of duration, the number of packets, and number of bytes

We can see that most values are close to zero, but there is also a long tail of rare values stretching along the *x* axes. We will use a power transform to make these features more Gaussian-like, which should help the model during training.

Now that we have explored the main characteristics of the CIDDS-001 dataset, we can move on to the preprocessing stage.

# Preprocessing the CIDDS-001 dataset

In the last section, we identified some issues with the dataset we need to address to improve the accuracy of our model.

The `CIDDS-001` dataset includes diverse types of data: we have numerical values such as duration, categorical features such as protocols (TCP, UDP, ICMP, and IGMP), and others such as timestamps or IP addresses. In the following exercise, we will choose how to represent these data types based on the information from the previous section and expert knowledge:

1. First, we can one-hot-encode the day of the week by retrieving this information from the timestamp. We will rename the resulting columns to make them more readable:

   ```
   df['weekday'] = df['Date first seen'].dt.weekday
   df = pd.get_dummies(df, columns=['weekday']).
   rename(columns = {'weekday_0': 'Monday','weekday_1':
   'Tuesday','weekday_2': 'Wednesday', 'weekday_3':
   'Thursday','weekday_4': 'Friday','weekday_5':
   'Saturday','weekday_6': 'Sunday',})
   ```

2. Another important type of information we can get using timestamps is the time of day. We also normalize it between 0 and 1:

   ```
   df['daytime'] = (df['Date first seen'].dt.second
   +df['Date first seen'].dt.minute*60 + df['Date first
   seen'].dt.hour*60*60)/(24*60*60)
   ```

3. We have not talked about TCP flags yet. Each flag indicates a particular state during a TCP connection. For example, F or FIN signifies that the TCP peer has finished sending data. We can extract each flag, and one-hot-encode them as follows:

   ```
   df = df.reset_index(drop=True)
   ohe_flags = one_hot_flags(df['Flags'].to_numpy())
   ohe_flags = df['Flags'].apply(one_hot_flags).to_list()
   df[['ACK', 'PSH', 'RST', 'SYN', 'FIN']] =
   pd.DataFrame(ohe_flags, columns=['ACK', 'PSH', 'RST',
   'SYN', 'FIN'])
   ```

4.  Let's now process the IP addresses. In this example, we will use binary encoding. Instead of taking 32 bits to encode the complete IPv4 address, we will only keep the last 16 bits, which are the most significant here. Indeed, the 16 first bits either correspond to `192.168` if the host belongs to the internal network or another value if it's external:

```python
temp = pd.DataFrame()
temp['SrcIP'] = df['Src IP Addr'].astype(str)
temp['SrcIP'][~temp['SrcIP'].str.contains('\d{1,3}\.',
regex=True)] = '0.0.0.0'
temp = temp['SrcIP'].str.split('.', expand=True).
rename(columns = {2: 'ipsrc3', 3: 'ipsrc4'}).astype(int)
[['ipsrc3', 'ipsrc4']]
temp['ipsrc'] = temp['ipsrc3'].apply(lambda x: format(x,
"b").zfill(8)) + temp['ipsrc4'].apply(lambda x: format(x,
"b").zfill(8))
df = df.join(temp['ipsrc'].str.split('', expand=True)
            .drop(columns=[0, 17])
            .rename(columns=dict(enumerate([f'ipsrc_{i}'
for i in range(17)])))
            .astype('int32'))
```

5.  We repeat this process for destination IP addresses:

```python
temp = pd.DataFrame()
temp['DstIP'] = df['Dst IP Addr'].astype(str)
temp['DstIP'][~temp['DstIP'].str.contains('\d{1,3}\.',
regex=True)] = '0.0.0.0'
temp = temp['DstIP'].str.split('.', expand=True).
rename(columns = {2: 'ipdst3', 3: 'ipdst4'}).astype(int)
[['ipdst3', 'ipdst4']]
temp['ipdst'] = temp['ipdst3'].apply(lambda x: format(x,
"b").zfill(8)) + temp['ipdst4'].apply(lambda x: format(x,
"b").zfill(8))
df = df.join(temp['ipdst'].str.split('', expand=True)
            .drop(columns=[0, 17])
            .rename(columns=dict(enumerate([f'ipdst_{i}'
for i in range(17)])))
            .astype('int32'))
```

6.  There is an issue with the 'Bytes' feature: millions are represented as m instead of a numerical value. We can fix it by multiplying the numerical part of these non-numerical values by one million:

```
m_index = df[pd.to_numeric(df['Bytes'], errors='coerce').
isnull() == True].index
df['Bytes'].loc[m_index] = df['Bytes'].loc[m_index].
apply(lambda x: 10e6 * float(x.strip().split()[0]))
df['Bytes'] = pd.to_numeric(df['Bytes'], errors='coerce',
downcast='integer')
```

7.  The last features we need to encode are the easiest ones: categorical features such as protocols and attack types. We use the get_dummies() function from pandas:

```
df = pd.get_dummies(df, prefix='', prefix_sep='',
columns=['Proto', 'attackType'])
```

8.  We create a train/validation/test split with 80/10/10 ratios:

```
labels = ['benign', 'bruteForce', 'dos', 'pingScan',
'portScan']
df_train, df_test = train_test_split(df, random_state=0,
test_size=0.2, stratify=df[labels])
df_val, df_test = train_test_split(df_test, random_
state=0, test_size=0.5, stratify=df_test[labels])
```

9.  Finally, we need to address the scaling of three features: duration, the number of packets, and the number of bytes. We use PowerTransformer() from scikit-learn to modify their distributions:

```
scaler = PowerTransformer()
df_train[['Duration', 'Packets', 'Bytes']] = scaler.fit_
transform(df_train[['Duration', 'Packets', 'Bytes']])
df_val[['Duration', 'Packets', 'Bytes']] = scaler.
transform(df_val[['Duration', 'Packets', 'Bytes']])
df_test[['Duration', 'Packets', 'Bytes']] = scaler.
transform(df_test[['Duration', 'Packets', 'Bytes']])
```

10. Let's plot the new distributions to see how they compare:

```
fig, ((ax1, ax2, ax3)) = plt.subplots(1, 3,
figsize=(15,5))
df_train['Duration'].hist(ax=ax1)
ax1.set_xlabel("Duration")
```

```
df_train['Packets'].hist(ax=ax2)
ax2.set_xlabel("Number of packets")
df_train['Bytes'].hist(ax=ax3)
ax3.set_xlabel("Number of bytes")
plt.show()
```

We obtain the following figure:

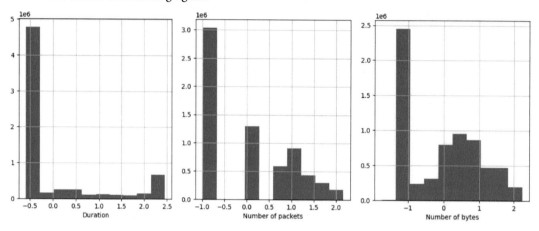

Figure 16.4 – Rescaled distributions of duration, the number of packets, and the number of bytes

These new distributions are not Gaussian, but the values are more spread out, which should help the model.

Note that the dataset we processed is purely tabular. We still need to convert it into a graph dataset before we can feed it to a GNN. In our case, there is no obvious way of converting our traffic flows into nodes. Ideally, flows between the same computers should be connected. This can be achieved using a heterogeneous graph with two types of nodes:

- **Hosts**, which correspond to computers and use IP addresses as features. If we had more information, we could add other computer-related features, such as logs or CPU utilization.

- **Flows**, which correspond to connections between two hosts. They consider all the other features from the dataset. They also have the label we want to predict (a benign or malicious flow).

In this example, flows are unidirectional, which is why we also define two types of edges: host-to-flow (source), and flow-to-host (destination). A single graph would require too much memory, so we will divide it into subgraphs and place them into data loaders:

1. We define the batch size and the features we want to consider for host and flow nodes:

```
BATCH_SIZE = 16
features_host = [f'ipsrc_{i}' for i in range(1, 17)] +
[f'ipdst_{i}' for i in range(1, 17)]
features_flow = ['daytime', 'Monday', 'Tuesday',
'Wednesday', 'Thursday', 'Friday', 'Duration', 'Packets',
'Bytes', 'ACK', 'PSH', 'RST', 'SYN', 'FIN', 'ICMP ',
'IGMP ', 'TCP  ', 'UDP  ']
```

2. We define the function that will create our data loaders. It takes two parameters: the tabular DataFrame we created, and the subgraph size (1024 nodes in this example):

```
def create_dataloader(df, subgraph_size=1024):
```

3. We initialize a list called data to store our subgraphs, and we count the number of subgraphs we will create:

```
data = []
n_subgraphs = len(df) // subgraph_size
```

4. For each subgraph, we retrieve the corresponding samples in the DataFrame, the list of source IP addresses, and the list of destination IP addresses:

```
for i in range(1, n_batches+1):
        subgraph = df[(i-1)*subgraph_size:i*subgraph_
size]
        src_ip = subgraph['Src IP Addr'].to_numpy()
        dst_ip = subgraph['Dst IP Addr'].to_numpy()
```

5. We create a dictionary that maps the IP addresses to a node index:

```
ip_map = {ip:index for index, ip in enumerate(np.
unique(np.append(src_ip, dst_ip)))}
```

6. This dictionary will help us to create the edge index from the host to the flow and vice versa. We use a function called get_connections(), which we will create after this one.

```
host_to_flow, flow_to_host = get_connections(ip_map, src_
ip, dst_ip)
```

7.  We use all the data we have collected so far to create a heterogeneous graph for each subgraph and append it to the list:

```
batch = HeteroData()
batch['host'].x = torch.Tensor(subgraph[features_
host].to_numpy()).float()
batch['flow'].x = torch.Tensor(subgraph[features_
flow].to_numpy()).float()
batch['flow'].y = torch.Tensor(subgraph[labels].
to_numpy()).float()
batch['host','flow'].edge_index = host_to_flow
batch['flow','host'].edge_index = flow_to_host
data.append(batch)
```

8.  Finally, we return the data loader with the appropriate batch size:

```
return DataLoader(data, batch_size=BATCH_SIZE)
```

9.  There is one function we still need to implement – get_connections() – which calculates two edge indices from the list of source and destination IP addresses and their corresponding map:

```
def get_connections(ip_map, src_ip, dst_ip):
```

10. We get indexes from the IP addresses (both source and destination) and stack them:

```
src1 = [ip_map[ip] for ip in src_ip]
src2 = [ip_map[ip] for ip in dst_ip]
src = np.column_stack((src1, src2)).flatten()
```

11. The connections are unique, so we can easily index them with the appropriate range of numbers:

```
dst = list(range(len(src_ip)))
dst = np.column_stack((dst, dst)).flatten()
```

12. Finally, we return the two following edge indexes:

```
return torch.Tensor([src, dst]).int(), torch.Tensor([dst,
src]).int()
```

13. Now that we have everything we need, we can call the first function to create the training, validation, and test data loaders:

```
train_loader = create_dataloader(df_train)
val_loader = create_dataloader(df_val)
test_loader = create_dataloader(df_test)
```

14. We now have three data loaders corresponding to our training, validation, and test sets. The next step consists of implementing the GNN model.

## Implementing a heterogeneous GNN

In this section, we will implement a heterogeneous GNN using a GraphSAGE operator. This architecture will allow us to consider both node types (hosts and flows) to build better embeddings. This is done by duplicating and sharing messages across different layers, as shown in the following figure.

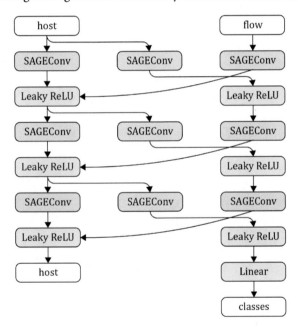

Figure 16.5 – Architecture of the heterogeneous GNN

We will implement three layers of SAGEConv with LeakyRELU for each node type. Finally, a linear layer will output a five-dimensional vector, where each dimension corresponds to a class. Furthermore, we will train this model in a supervised way using the cross-entropy loss and the Adam optimizer:

1.  We import the relevant neural network layers from PyTorch Geometric:

    ```
    import torch_geometric.transforms as T
    from torch_geometric.nn import Linear, HeteroConv,
    SAGEConv
    ```

2.  We define the heterogeneous GNN with three parameters: the number of hidden dimensions, the number of output dimensions, and the number of layers:

    ```
    class HeteroGNN(torch.nn.Module):
        def __init__(self, dim_h, dim_out, num_layers):
            super().__init__()
    ```

3.  We define a heterogenous version of the GraphSAGE operator for each layer and edge type. Here, we could apply a different GNN layer to each edge type, such as GCNConv or GATConv. The HeteroConv() wrapper manages the messages between layers, as shown in *Figure 16.5*:

    ```
            self.convs = torch.nn.ModuleList()
            for _ in range(num_layers):
                conv = HeteroConv({
                    ('host', 'to', 'flow'): SAGEConv((-1,-1),
    dim_h, add_self_loops=False),
                    ('flow', 'to', 'host'): SAGEConv((-1,-1),
    dim_h, add_self_loops=False),
                }, aggr='sum')
                self.convs.append(conv)
    ```

4.  We define a linear layer that will output the final classification:

    ```
            self.lin = Linear(dim_h, dim_out)
    ```

5.  We create the forward() method, which computes embeddings for host and flow nodes (stored in the x_dict dictionary). The flow embeddings are then used to predict a class:

    ```
        def forward(self, x_dict, edge_index_dict):
            for conv in self.convs:
                x_dict = conv(x_dict, edge_index_dict)
    ```

```
            x_dict = {key: F.leaky_relu(x) for key, x in
x_dict.items()}
            return self.lin(x_dict['flow'])
```

6. We instantiate the heterogeneous GNN with 64 hidden dimensions, 5 outputs (our 5 classes), and 3 layers. If available, we place it on a GPU and create an Adam optimizer with a learning rate of 0.001:

```
device = torch.device('cuda' if torch.cuda.is_available()
else 'cpu')
model = HeteroGNN(dim_h=64, dim_out=5, num_layers=3).
to(device)
optimizer = Adam(model.parameters(), lr=0.001)
```

7. We define the test() function and create arrays to store predictions and true labels. We also want to count the number of subgraphs and the total loss, so we create the corresponding variables:

```
@torch.no_grad()
def test(loader):
    model.eval()
    y_pred = []
    y_true = []
    n_subgraphs = 0
    total_loss = 0
```

8. We get the model's prediction for each batch and compute the cross-entropy loss:

```
    for batch in loader:
        batch.to(device)
        out = model(batch.x_dict, batch.edge_index_dict)
        loss = F.cross_entropy(out,
batch['flow'].y.float())
```

9. We append the predicted class to the list of predictions and do the same with the true labels:

```
        y_pred.append(out.argmax(dim=1))
        y_true.append(batch['flow'].y.argmax(dim=1))
```

10. We count the number of subgraphs and the total loss as follows:

```
        n_subgraphs += BATCH_SIZE
        total_loss += float(loss) * BATCH_SIZE
```

11. Now that the batch loop is over, we compute the F1 score (macro) using the prediction and true label lists. The macro-averaged F1 score is a good metric in this imbalanced learning setting because it treats all classes equally regardless of the number of samples:

```
y_pred = torch.cat(y_pred).cpu()
y_true = torch.cat(y_true).cpu()
f1score = f1_score(y_true, y_pred, average='macro')
```

12. We return the final loss, the macro-averaged F1 score, the list of predictions, and the list of true labels:

```
    return total_loss/n_subgraphs, f1score, y_pred, y_
true
```

13. We create the training loop to train the model for 101 epochs:

```
model.train()
for epoch in range(101):
    n_subgraphs = 0
    total_loss = 0
```

14. We train the heterogenous GNN on each batch using the cross-entropy loss:

```
    for batch in train_loader:
        optimizer.zero_grad()
        batch.to(device)
        out = model(batch.x_dict, batch.edge_index_dict)
        loss = F.cross_entropy(out,
batch['flow'].y.float())
        loss.backward()
        optimizer.step()
        n_subgraphs += BATCH_SIZE
        total_loss += float(loss) * BATCH_SIZE
```

15. Every 10 epochs, we evaluate the model on the validation set and display relevant metrics (the training loss, validation loss, and validation macro-averaged F1 score):

```
    if epoch % 10 == 0:
        val_loss, f1score, _, _ = test(val_loader)
        print(f'Epoch {epoch} | Loss: {total_loss/n_
subgraphs:.4f} | Val loss: {val_loss:.4f} | Val F1 score:
{f1score:.4f}')
```

We obtain the following output during training:

```
Epoch 0 | Loss: 0.1006 | Val loss: 0.0072 | Val F1 score:
0.6044
Epoch 10 | Loss: 0.0020 | Val loss: 0.0021 | Val
F1-score: 0.8899
Epoch 20 | Loss: 0.0015 | Val loss: 0.0015 | Val
F1-score: 0.9211

...

Epoch 90 | Loss: 0.0004 | Val loss: 0.0008 | Val
F1-score: 0.9753
Epoch 100 | Loss: 0.0004 | Val loss: 0.0009 | Val
F1-score: 0.9785
```

16. Finally, we evaluate the model on the test set. We also print scikit-learn's classification report, which includes the macro-averaged F1 score:

```
_, _, y_pred, y_true = test(test_loader)
print(classification_report(y_true, y_pred, target_
names=labels, digits=4))
```

|  | precision | recall | f1-score | support |
|---|---|---|---|---|
| benign | 0.9999 | 0.9999 | 0.9999 | 700791 |
| bruteForce | 0.9811 | 0.9630 | 0.9720 | 162 |
| dos | 1.0000 | 1.0000 | 1.0000 | 125164 |
| pingScan | 0.9413 | 0.9554 | 0.9483 | 336 |
| portScan | 0.9947 | 0.9955 | 0.9951 | 18347 |
| accuracy |  |  | 0.9998 | 844800 |
| macro avg | 0.9834 | 0.9827 | 0.9831 | 844800 |
| weighted avg | 0.9998 | 0.9998 | 0.9998 | 844800 |

We obtained a macro-averaged F1 score of 0.9831. This excellent result shows that our model has learned to predict each class reliably.

The approach we adopted would be even more relevant if we could access more host-related features, but it shows how you can expand it to fit your needs. The other main advantage of GNNs is their ability to process large amounts of data. This approach makes even more sense when dealing with millions of flows. To finish this project, let's plot the model's errors to see how we could improve it.

We create a dataframe to store the predictions (y_pred) and the true labels (y_true). We use this new dataframe to plot the proportion of misclassified samples:

```
df_pred = pd.DataFrame([y_pred.numpy(), y_true.numpy()]).T
df_pred.columns = ['pred', 'true']
plt.pie(df_pred['true'][df_pred['pred'] != df_pred['true']].
value_counts(), labels=labels, autopct='%.0f%%')
```

This gives us the following chart:

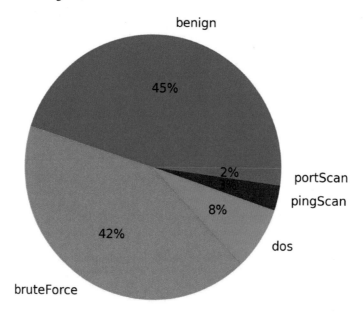

Figure 16.6 – Proportion of each misclassified class

If we compare this pie chart to the original proportions in the dataset, we see that the model performs better for the majority classes. This is not surprising since minority classes are harder to learn (fewer samples), and not detecting them is less penalizing (with 700,000 benign flows versus 336 ping scans). Port and ping scan detection could be improved with techniques such as oversampling and introducing class weights during training.

We can gather even more information by looking at the confusion matrix (the code can be found on GitHub).

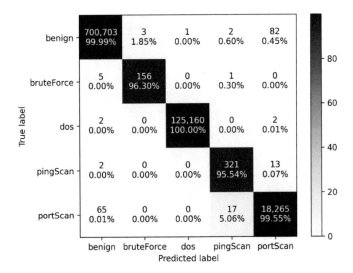

Figure 16.7 – Confusion matrix for multi-class flow classification

This confusion matrix displays interesting results, such as a bias toward the benign class or errors between ping and port scans. These errors can be attributed to the similarity between these attacks. Engineering additional features could help the model distinguish these classes.

## Summary

In this chapter, we explored the use of GNNs for detecting anomalies in a new dataset, the `CIDDS-001` dataset. First, we preprocessed the dataset and converted it into a graph representation, allowing us to capture the complex relationships between the different components of the network. We then implemented a heterogeneous GNN with `GraphSAGE` operators. It captured the heterogeneity of the graph and allowed us to classify the flows as benign or malicious.

The application of GNNs in network security has shown promising results and opened up new avenues for research. As technology continues to advance and the amount of network data increases, GNNs will become an increasingly important tool for detecting and preventing security breaches.

In *Chapter 17, Recommending Books Using LightGCN*, we will explore the most popular application of GNNs with recommender systems. We will implement a lightweight GNN on a large dataset and produce book recommendations for given users.

## Further reading

- [1] M. Ring, S. Wunderlich, D. Grüdl, D. Landes, and A. Hotho, *Flow-based benchmark data sets for intrusion detection*, in *Proceedings of the 16th European Conference on Cyber Warfare and Security* (ECCWS), ACPI, 2017, pp. 361–369.

# 17

# Building a Recommender System Using LightGCN

Recommender systems have become an integral part of modern online platforms, with the goal of providing personalized recommendations to users based on their interests and past interactions. These systems can be found in a variety of applications, including suggesting products to purchase on e-commerce websites, recommending content to watch on streaming services, and suggesting connections to make on social media platforms.

Recommendation systems are one of the main applications of GNNs. Indeed, they can effectively incorporate the complex relationships between users, items, and their interactions into a unified model. In addition, the graph structure allows for the incorporation of side information, such as user and item metadata, into the recommendation process.

In this chapter, we will introduce a new GNN architecture called **LightGCN**, specifically designed for recommender systems. We will also introduce a new dataset, the `Book-Crossing` dataset, which contains users, books, and over a million ratings. Using this dataset, we will build a book recommender system with collaborative filtering and apply it to get recommendations for a specific user. Through this process, we will demonstrate how to use the LightGCN architecture to build a practical recommendation system.

By the end of this chapter, you will be able to create your own recommender system using LightGCN. You will learn how to process any dataset with users, items, and scores for a collaborative filtering approach. Finally, you will learn how to implement and evaluate this architecture and get recommendations for individual users.

In this chapter, we will cover the following main topics:

- Exploring the Book-Crossing dataset
- Preprocessing the Book-Crossing dataset
- Implementing the LightGCN architecture

# Technical requirements

All the code examples from this chapter can be found on GitHub at `https://github.com/PacktPublishing/Hands-On-Graph-Neural-Networks-Using-Python/tree/main/Chapter17`. The installation steps required to run the code on your local machine can be found in the *Preface* of this book.

This chapter requires a large amount of GPU. You can lower it by decreasing the size of the training set in the code.

# Exploring the Book-Crossing dataset

In this section, we will perform exploratory data analysis on a new dataset and visualize its main characteristics.

The `Book-Crossing` dataset [1] is a collection of book ratings provided by 278,858 users in the *BookCrossing community* (`www.bookcrossing.com`). The ratings, which are both explicit (rating between 1 and 10) and implicit (users interacted with the book), total 1,149,780 and pertain to 271,379 books. The dataset was collected by Cai-Nicolas Ziegler during a four-week crawl in August and September 2004. We will use the `Book-Crossing` dataset to build a book recommender system in this chapter.

Let's download the dataset and unzip it with the following commands:

```
from io import BytesIO
from urllib.request import urlopen
from zipfile import ZipFile

url = 'http://www2.informatik.uni-freiburg.de/~cziegler/BX/BX-
CSV-Dump.zip'
with urlopen(url) as zurl:
    with ZipFile(BytesIO(zurl.read())) as zfile:
        zfile.extractall('.')
```

This will unzip three files:

- The `BX-Users.csv` file contains data on individual BookCrossing users. User IDs have been anonymized and are represented as integers. Demographic information, such as location and age, is also included for some users. If this information is not available, the corresponding fields contain `NULL` values.

- The `BX-Books.csv` file contains data on the books included in the dataset, identified by their ISBN. Invalid ISBNs have been removed from the dataset. In addition to content-based information, such as the book title, author, year of publication, and publisher. This file also includes URLs linking to cover images of the books of three different sizes.

- The BX-Book-Ratings.csv file includes information on the ratings given to books in the dataset. Ratings are either explicit, given on a scale from 1-10 with higher values indicating a greater appreciation, or implicit, indicated by a rating of 0.

The following figure is a graph representation made with Gephi using a subsample of this dataset.

Figure 17.1 – Graph representation of the Book-Crossing dataset, with books represented as blue nodes and users represented as red nodes

The size of the nodes is proportional to the number of connections (degree) in the graph. We can see popular books such as **The Da Vinci Code** that act like hubs thanks to their high number of connections.

Now, let's explore the dataset to get more insight:

1.  We import pandas and load every file with the ; separator and the latin-1 encoding for compatibility issues. BX-Books.csv also requires the error_bad_lines parameter:

```
import pandas as pd
ratings = pd.read_csv('BX-Book-Ratings.csv', sep=';',
encoding='latin-1')
```

```
users = pd.read_csv('BX-Users.csv', sep=';',
encoding='latin-1')
books = pd.read_csv('BX-Books.csv', sep=';',
encoding='latin-1', error_bad_lines=False)
```

2.  Let's print these DataFrames to see the columns and the number of rows:

```
ratings
```

|         | User-ID | ISBN       | Book-Rating |
|---------|---------|------------|-------------|
| 0       | 276725  | 034545104X | 0           |
| 1       | 276726  | 0155061224 | 5           |
| ...     | ...     | ...        | ...         |
| 1149777 | 276709  | 0515107662 | 10          |
| 1149778 | 276721  | 0590442449 | 10          |
| 1149779 | 276723  | 05162443314 | 8          |

```
1149780 rows × 3 columns
```

3.  Let's repeat the process with the `users` DataFrame:

```
users
```

| User-ID |        | Location                        | Age   |
|---------|--------|---------------------------------|-------|
| 0       | 1      | nyc, new york, usa              | NaN   |
| 1       | 2      | stockton, california, usa       | 18.0  |
| 2       | 3      | moscow, yukon territory, russia | NaN   |
| ...     | ...    | ...                             | ...   |
| 278855  | 278856 | brampton, ontario, canada       | NaN   |
| 278856  | 278857 | knoxville, tennessee, usa    NaN |      |
| 278857  | 278858 | dublin, n/a, ireland    NaN     |       |

```
278858 rows × 3 columns
```

4.  Finally, the `books` DataFrame has too many columns to be printed like the two others. Let's print the column names instead:

```
list(books.columns)
```

```
['ISBN', 'Book-Title', 'Book-Author', 'Year-Of-
Publication', 'Publisher', 'Image-URL-S', 'Image-URL-M',
'Image-URL-L']
```

The `ratings` DataFrame links the `users` and `books` DataFrames using `User-ID` and `ISBN` information and includes a rating, which could be considered a weight. The `users` DataFrame includes demographic information, such as location and age, for each user when available. The `books` DataFrame includes content-related information about the books, such as the title, author, year of publication, publisher, and URLs linking to cover images of three different sizes.

5.  Let's visualize the rating distribution to see whether we can use this information. We can plot it using `matplotlib` and `seaborn` as follows:

```
import matplotlib.pyplot as plt
import seaborn as sns

sns.countplot(x=ratings['Book-Rating'])
```

6.  This gives us the following plot:

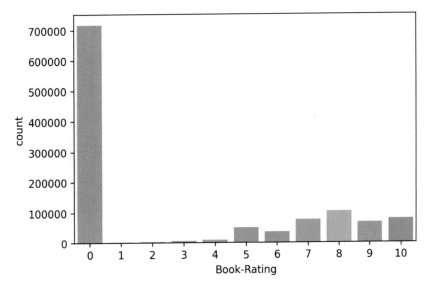

Figure 17.2 – Rating distribution (interaction with a book is represented as a rating of zero, while ratings between 1 and 10 are real ratings)

7.  Do these ratings correspond to the data we have in the `books` and `users` DataFrames? We can compare the number of unique `User-ID` and `ISBN` entries in `ratings` to the number of rows in these DataFrames as a quick check:

```
print(len(ratings['User-ID'].unique()))
print(len(ratings['ISBN'].unique()))
```

```
105283
340556
```

Interestingly, there are fewer unique users in `ratings` compared to `users` (105,283 versus 278,858) but more unique ISBNs compared to `books` (340,556 versus 271,379). This means that our database is missing a lot of values, so we will need to be careful when joining tables.

8.  Let's finish by plotting the number of books that have been rated only once, twice, and so on. First, we calculate the number of times each ISBN appears in the `ratings` DataFrame using the `groupby()` and `size()` functions:

```
isbn_counts = ratings.groupby('ISBN').size()
```

This creates a new DataFrame, `isbn_counts`, which contains the count of each unique ISBN in the `ratings` DataFrame.

9.  We calculate the number of occurrences of each count value using the `value_counts()` function. This new DataFrame will contain the count of occurrences of each count value in `isbn_counts`:

```
count_occurrences = isbn_counts.value_counts()
```

10.  Finally, we can plot the distribution using pandas' `.plot()` method. In this case, we will only plot the first 15 values:

```
count_occurrences[:15].plot(kind='bar')
plt.xlabel("Number of occurrences of an ISBN number")
plt.ylabel("Count")
```

11. We obtain the following plot:

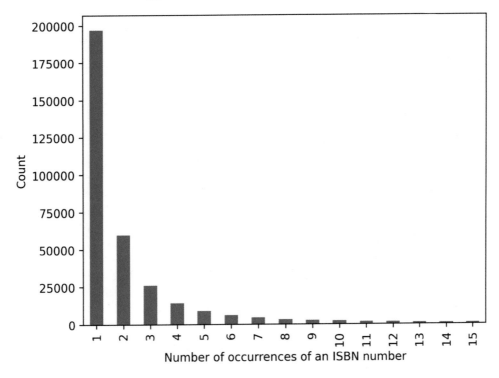

Figure 17.3 – Distribution of the number of times each book (ISBN) appears in ratings (15 first values)

We see that a lot of books have only been rated once or twice. It is very rare to see books with a lot of ratings, which makes things more difficult for us since we rely on these connections.

12. We repeat the same process to obtain the distribution of the number of times each user (User-ID) appears in `ratings`:

```
userid_counts = ratings.groupby('User-ID').size()
count_occurrences = userid_counts.value_counts()
count_occurrences[:15].plot(kind='bar')
plt.xlabel("Number of occurrences of a User-ID")
plt.ylabel("Count")
```

13.  We obtain a similar distribution:

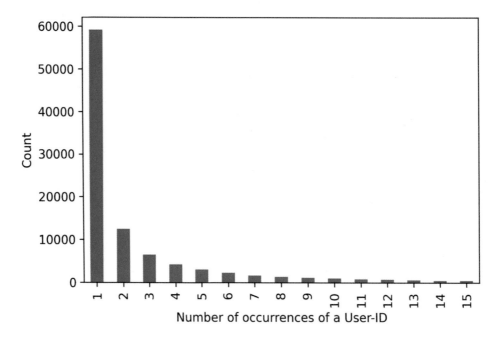

Figure 17.4 – Distribution of the number of times each user (User-ID) appears in ratings (15 first values)

This also means that most users only rate one or two books, but a few of them rate a lot of books.

There are different issues with this dataset, such as mistakes in the year of publication or the name of the publishers, and other missing or incorrect values. However, we will not directly use metadata from the books and users DataFrames in this chapter. We will rely on the connections between User-ID and ISBN values, which is why we don't need to clean the dataset here.

In the next section, we will see how to process the dataset to prepare it before feeding it to the LightGCN.

## Preprocessing the Book-Crossing dataset

We want to process the dataset for a particular task: recommending items, and more specifically using a **collaborative filtering** approach. Collaborative filtering is a technique used to make personalized recommendations to users. It is based on the idea that users who have similar preferences or behaviors are more likely to have similar interests. Collaborative filtering algorithms use this information to identify patterns and make recommendations to users based on the preferences of similar users.

This is different from content-based filtering, which is a recommendation approach that relies on the features of the items being recommended. It generates recommendations by identifying the characteristics of an item and matching them to the characteristics of other items that have been liked by the user in the past. **Content-based filtering** approaches are typically based on the idea that if a user likes an item with certain characteristics, they will also like items with similar characteristics.

In this chapter, we will focus on collaborative filtering. Our objective is to determine which book to recommend to a user based on the preferences of other users. This problem can be represented as a bipartite graph as in the following figure.

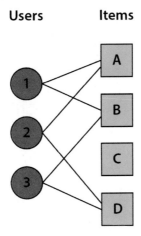

Figure 17.5 – Example of a user-item bipartite graph

Knowing that user **1** liked items **A** and **B**, and user **3** liked items **B** and **D**, we should probably recommend item **B** to user **2**, who also enjoyed items **A** and **D**.

This is the type of graph we want to build from the `Book-Crossing` dataset. More precisely, we also want to include negative samples. In this context, negative samples refer to items that have not been rated by a given user. Items that have been rated by a particular user are also referred to as positive items. We will explain why we use this negative sampling technique when we implement the `loss` function.

In the rest of the chapter, the `LightGCN` code is mostly based on the official implementation and the excellent work of Hotta and Zhou [2] and Li et al. [3] on a different dataset:

1.  We import the following libraries:

    ```
    import numpy as np
    from sklearn.model_selection import train_test_split

    import torch
    ```

```
import torch.nn.functional as F
from torch import nn, optim, Tensor

from torch_geometric.utils import structured_negative_
sampling
from torch_geometric.nn.conv.gcn_conv import gcn_norm
from torch_geometric.nn import LGConv
```

2.  We re-load the datasets:

```
df = pd.read_csv('BX-Book-Ratings.csv', sep=';',
encoding='latin-1')
users = pd.read_csv('BX-Users.csv', sep=';',
encoding='latin-1')
books = pd.read_csv('BX-Books.csv', sep=';',
encoding='latin-1', error_bad_lines=False)
```

3.  We only keep rows where ISBN information can be found in the books DataFrame and User-ID information can be found in the users DataFrame:

```
df = df.loc[df['ISBN'].isin(books['ISBN'].unique()) &
df['User-ID'].isin(users['User-ID'].unique())]
```

4.  We only keep high ratings (>= 8/10) so the connections we create correspond to books that were liked by users. Then, we filter out even more samples and keep a limited number of rows (100,000) to speed up training:

```
df = df[df['Book-Rating'] >= 8].iloc[:100000]
```

5.  We create mappings from user and item identifiers to integer indices:

```
user_mapping = {userid: i for i, userid in
enumerate(df['User-ID'].unique())}
item_mapping = {isbn: i for i, isbn in
enumerate(df['ISBN'].unique())}
```

6.  We count the number of users, items, and total entities in the dataset:

```
num_users = len(user_mapping)
num_items = len(item_mapping)
num_total = num_users + num_items
```

7.  We create a tensor of `user` and `item` indices based on the user ratings in the dataset. The `edge_index` tensor is created by stacking these two tensors:

```
user_ids = torch.LongTensor([user_mapping[i] for i in
df['User-ID']])
item_ids = torch.LongTensor([item_mapping[i] for i in
df['ISBN']])
edge_index = torch.stack((user_ids, item_ids))
```

8.  We split `edge_index` into training, validation, and test sets using the `train_test_split()` function from `scikit-learn`:

```
train_index, test_index = train_test_
split(range(len(df)), test_size=0.2, random_state=0)
val_index, test_index = train_test_split(test_index,
test_size=0.5, random_state=0)
```

9.  We generate a batch of random indices using the `np.random.choice()` function. This generates BATCH_SIZE random indices from a range of 0 to `edge_index.shape[1]-1`. These indices will be used to select rows from the `edge_index` tensor:

```
def sample_mini_batch(edge_index):
    index = np.random.choice(range(edge_index.shape[1]),
size=BATCH_SIZE)
```

10. We generate negative samples using the `structured_negative_sampling()` function from PyTorch Geometric. Negative samples are items with which the corresponding user has not interacted. We use the `torch.stack()` function to add a dimension at the beginning:

```
edge_index = structured_negative_sampling(edge_index)
edge_index = torch.stack(edge_index, dim=0)
```

11. We select the user, positive item, and negative item indices for the batch using the `index` array and the `edge_index` tensor:

```
user_index = edge_index[0, index]
pos_item_index = edge_index[1, index]
neg_item_index = edge_index[2, index]


return user_index, pos_item_index, neg_item_index
```

The `user_index` tensor contains the user indices for the batch, the `pos_item_index` tensor contains the positive item indices for the batch, and the `neg_item_index` tensor contains the negative item indices for the batch.

We now have three sets and a function to return mini-batches. The next step is to understand and implement the LightGCN architecture.

## Implementing the LightGCN architecture

The LightGCN [4] architecture aims to learn representations for nodes by smoothing features over the graph. It iteratively performs graph convolution, where neighboring nodes' features are aggregated as the new representation of a target node. The entire architecture is summarized in *Figure 17.6*.

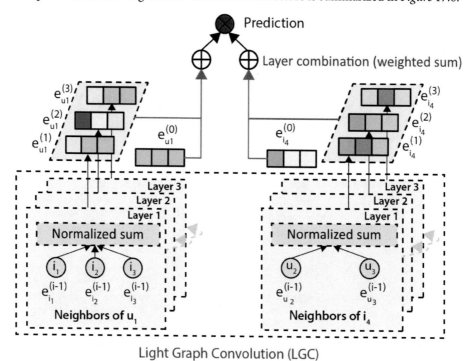

Figure 17.6 – LightGCN model architecture with convolution and layer combination

However, `LightGCN` adopts a simple weighted sum aggregator rather than using feature transformation or nonlinear activation as seen in other models such as the GCN or GAT. The light graph convolution operation calculates the $k + 1$-th user and item embedding $\mathbf{e}_u^{(k+1)}$ and $\mathbf{e}_i^{(k+1)}$ as follows:

$$\mathbf{e}_u^{(k+1)} = \sum_{i \in \mathcal{N}_u} \frac{1}{\sqrt{|\mathcal{N}_u|}\sqrt{|\mathcal{N}_i|}} \mathbf{e}_i^{(k)}$$

$$e_i^{(k+1)} = \sum_{u \in \mathcal{N}_i} \frac{1}{\sqrt{|\mathcal{N}_i|}\sqrt{|\mathcal{N}_u|}} e_u^{(k)}$$

The symmetric normalization term ensures that the scale of embeddings does not increase with graph convolution operations. In contrast to other models, `LightGCN` only aggregates the connected neighbors and does not include self-connections.

Indeed, it achieves the same effect by using a layer combination operation. This mechanism consists of a weighted sum using user and item embeddings at each layer. It produces the final embeddings $e_u$ and $e_i$ with the following equations:

$$e_u = \sum_{k=0}^{K} \alpha_k e_u^{(k)}$$

$$e_i = \sum_{k=0}^{K} \alpha_k e_i^{(k)}$$

Here, the contribution of $k$-th layer is weighted by the variable $\alpha_k \geq 0$. The authors of `LightGCN` recommend setting it to $1/(K + 1)$.

The prediction shown in *Figure 17.6* corresponds to ratings or ranking scores. It is obtained using the inner product of user and item final representations:

$$\hat{y}_{ui} = e_u^T e_i$$

Let's now implement this architecture in PyTorch Geometric:

1. We create a `LightGCN` class with four arguments: `num_users`, `num_items`, `num_layers`, and `dim_h`. The `num_users` and `num_items` arguments specify the number of users and items in the dataset, respectively. `num_layers` indicates the number of `LightGCN` layers that will be used, and the `dim_h` argument specifies the size of the embedding vectors (for the users and items):

```
class LightGCN(nn.Module):
    def __init__(self, num_users, num_items, num_
layers=4, dim_h=64):
        super().__init__()
```

2.  We store the number of users and items and create user and item embedding layers. The shape of the emb_users or $\mathbf{e}_u^{(0)}$ is (*num_users, dim_h*) and the shape of the emb_items or $\mathbf{e}_i^{(0)}$ is (*num_items, dim_h*):

```
self.num_users = num_users
self.num_items = num_items
self.emb_users = nn.Embedding(num_
embeddings=self.num_users, embedding_dim=dim_h)
self.emb_items = nn.Embedding(num_
embeddings=self.num_items, embedding_dim=dim_h)
```

3.  We create a list of num_layers (previously called $K$) LightGCN layers using PyTorch Geometric's LGConv(). This will be used to perform the light graph convolution operations:

```
self.convs = nn.ModuleList(LGConv() for _ in
range(num_layers))
```

4.  We initialize the user and item embedding layers with normal distributions with a standard deviation of 0.01. This helps to prevent the model from getting stuck in poor local optima when it is trained:

```
nn.init.normal_(self.emb_users.weight, std=0.01)
nn.init.normal_(self.emb_items.weight, std=0.01)
```

5.  The forward() method takes in an edge index tensor and returns the final user and item embedding vectors, $\mathbf{e}_u^{(K)}$ and $\mathbf{e}_i^{(K)}$. It starts by concatenating the user and item embedding layers and storing the result in the emb tensor. It then creates a list, embs, with emb as its first element:

```
def forward(self, edge_index):
    emb = torch.cat([self.emb_users.weight, self.emb_
items.weight])
    embs = [emb]
```

6.  We then apply the LightGCN layers in a loop and store the output of each layer in the embs list:

```
for conv in self.convs:
    emb = conv(x=emb, edge_index=edge_index)
    embs.append(emb)
```

7.  We perform layer combination by calculating the final embedding vectors by taking the mean of the tensors in the embs list along the second dimension:

```
emb_final = torch.mean(torch.stack(embs, dim=1), dim=1)
```

8.  We split emb_final into user and item embedding vectors ($\mathbf{e}_u$ and $\mathbf{e}_i$) and return them along with $\mathbf{e}_u^{(0)}$ and $\mathbf{e}_i^{(0)}$:

```
        emb_users_final, emb_items_final = torch.
    split(emb_final, [self.num_users, self.num_items])


        return emb_users_final, self.emb_users.weight,
    emb_items_final, self.emb_items.weight
```

9.  Finally, the model is created by calling the LightGCN() class with the appropriate arguments:

```
    model = LightGCN(num_users, num_items)
```

Before we can train the model, we need a loss function. The LightGCN architecture employs **Bayesian Personalized Ranking** (**BPR**) loss, which optimizes the model's ability to rank positive items higher than negative items for a given user. It is implemented as follows:

$$L_{BPR} = -\sum_{u=1}^{M} \sum_{i \in \mathcal{N}_u} \sum_{j \notin \mathcal{N}_u} \ln \sigma \left( \hat{y}_{ui} - \hat{y}_{uj} \right) + \lambda \left\| \mathbf{E}^{(0)} \right\|^2$$

Here, $\mathbf{E}^{(0)}$ is the 0th-layer embedding matrix (concatenation of the initial user and item embeddings), $\lambda$ weighs the regularization strength, $\hat{y}_{ui}$ corresponds to the predicted rating of a positive item, and $\hat{y}_{uj}$ represents the predicted rating of a negative item.

We implement it in PyTorch with the following function:

1.  We calculate the regularization loss based on the embeddings that are stored in the LightGCN model:

```
def bpr_loss(emb_users_final, emb_users, emb_pos_items_
final, emb_pos_items, emb_neg_items_final, emb_neg_
items):
    reg_loss = LAMBDA * (emb_users.norm().pow(2) +
                         emb_pos_items.norm().pow(2) +
                         emb_neg_items.norm().pow(2))
```

2.  We calculate the ratings for the positive and negative items as the dot product between the user and item embeddings:

```
    pos_ratings = torch.mul(emb_users_final, emb_pos_
items_final).sum(dim=-1)
    neg_ratings = torch.mul(emb_users_final, emb_neg_
items_final).sum(dim=-1)
```

3.  Unlike the log sigmoid in the previous equation, we calculate the BPR loss as the mean of the `softplus` function applied to the difference between the positive and negative scores. This variant was chosen because it gave better experimental results:

```
bpr_loss = torch.mean(torch.nn.functional.
softplus(pos_ratings - neg_ratings))
```

4.  We return the BPR loss and the regularization loss as follows:

```
return -bpr_loss + reg_loss
```

On top of the BPR loss, we use two metrics to evaluate the performance of our model:

-   **Recall@k** is the proportion of relevant recommended items in top $k$ among all possible relevant items. However, this metric does not consider the order of relevant items in top $k$:

$$Precision@K = \frac{\#\ of\ relevant\ recommended\ items}{\#\ of\ all\ the\ possible\ relevant\ items}$$

-   **Normalized Discounted Cumulative Gain** (**NDGC**) measures the effectiveness of the system's ranking of the recommendations, taking into account the relevance of the items, where relevance is usually represented by a score or a binary relevance (relevant or not).

The implementation is not included in this chapter for improved readability. However, it can be found in the GitHub repository along with the rest of the code.

We can now create a training loop and start training the `LightGCN` model:

1.  We define the following constants. They can be tuned as hyperparameters to improve the performance of the model:

```
K = 20
LAMBDA = 1e-6
BATCH_SIZE = 1024
```

2.  We try to select a GPU if one is available. Otherwise, we use a CPU instead. The model and data are moved to this device:

```
device = torch.device('cuda' if torch.cuda.is_available()
else 'cpu')
model = model.to(device)
edge_index = edge_index.to(device)
train_edge_index = train_edge_index.to(device)
val_edge_index = val_edge_index.to(device)
```

3. We create an Adam optimizer with a learning rate of 0.001:

```
optimizer = optim.Adam(model.parameters(), lr=0.001)
```

4. Let's start the training loop. First, we calculate num_batch, the number of BATCH_SIZE batches in an epoch. Then, we create two loops: one of 31 epochs, and a second one the length of num_batch:

```
num_batch = int(len(train_index)/BATCH_SIZE)
for epoch in range(31):
    model.train()
    for _ in range(num_batch):
```

5. The model is run on the training data and returns the initial and final user and item embeddings:

```
        optimizer.zero_grad()
        emb_users_final, emb_users, emb_items_final, emb_
items = model.forward(train_edge_index)
```

6. The training data is then sampled in mini-batches using the sample_mini_batch() function, which returns the indices of the sampled user, positive item, and negative item embeddings:

```
        user_indices, pos_item_indices, neg_item_indices
= sample_mini_batch(train_edge_index)
```

7. The embeddings for the sampled users, positive items, and negative items are then retrieved:

```
        emb_users_final, emb_users = emb_users_final[user_
indices], emb_users[user_indices]
        emb_pos_items_final, emb_pos_items = emb_items_
final[pos_item_indices], emb_items[pos_item_indices]
        emb_neg_items_final, emb_neg_items = emb_items_
final[neg_item_indices], emb_items[neg_item_indices]
```

8. The loss is then computed using the bpr_loss() function:

```
        train_loss = bpr_loss(emb_users_final, emb_users,
emb_pos_items_final, emb_pos_items, emb_neg_items_final,
emb_neg_items)
```

9. The optimizer is then used to perform the backward pass and update the model parameters:

```
        train_loss.backward()
        optimizer.step()
```

10. The model's performance is evaluated every 250 epochs on the validation set using the `test()` function. The evaluation metrics are printed:

```
if epoch % 5 == 0:
    model.eval()
    val_loss, recall, ndcg = test(model, val_edge_
index, [train_edge_index])
    print(f"Epoch {epoch} | Train loss: {train_loss.
item():.5f} | Val loss: {val_loss:.5f} | Val recall@{K}:
{recall:.5f} | Val ndcg@{K}: {ndcg:.5f}")
```

11. This gives us the following output:

```
Epoch 0 | Train loss: -0.69320 | Val loss: -0.69302 | Val
recall@20: 0.00700 | Val ndcg@20: 0.00388
Epoch 5 | Train loss: -0.70283 | Val loss: -0.68329 | Val
recall@20: 0.01159 | Val ndcg@20: 0.00631
Epoch 10 | Train loss: -0.73299 | Val loss: -0.64598 |
Val recall@20: 0.01341 | Val ndcg@20: 0.00999
...
Epoch 25 | Train loss: -1.53056 | Val loss: -0.19498 |
Val recall@20: 0.01507 | Val ndcg@20: 0.01016
Epoch 30 | Train loss: -1.95703 | Val loss: 0.06340 | Val
recall@20: 0.01410 | Val ndcg@20: 0.00950
```

12. We evaluate the model's performance on the test set as follows:

```
test_loss, test_recall, test_ndcg = test(model, test_
edge_index.to(device), [train_edge_index, val_edge_
index])
print(f"Test loss: {test_loss:.5f} | Test recall@{K}:
{test_recall:.5f} | Test ndcg@{K}: {test_ndcg:.5f}")
Test loss: 0.06827 | Test recall@20: 0.01936 | Test
ndcg@20: 0.01119
```

We obtain a `recall@20` value of `0.01936` and an `ndcg@20` value of `0.01119`, which is close to the results obtained by the authors of `LightGCN` on other datasets.

Now that the model is trained, we want to get recommendations for a given user. The recommendation function we want to create has two components:

1. First, we want to retrieve a list of books the user liked. This will help us to contextualize the recommendations for our own understanding.

2.  Secondly, we want to generate a list of recommendations. These recommendations cannot be books the user has already rated (it cannot be a positive item).

Let's write this function step by step:

1.  We create a function called `recommend` that takes in two arguments: `user_id` (the identifier for a user), and `num_recs` (the number of recommendations we want to generate):

```
def recommend(user_id, num_recs):
```

2.  We create the `user` variable by looking up the user's identifier in the `user_mapping` dictionary, which maps user IDs to integer indices:

```
user = user_mapping[user_id]
```

3.  We retrieve the `dim_h` dim vector learned by the `LightGCN` model for this particular user:

```
emb_user = model.emb_users.weight[user]
```

4.  We can use it to calculate the corresponding ratings. As seen previously, we use the dot product of the embeddings for all items stored in the `LightGCN`'s `emb_items` attribute and the `emb_user` variable:

```
ratings = model.emb_items.weight @ emb_user
```

5.  We apply the `topk()` function to the `ratings` tensor, which returns the top 100 values (scores calculated by the model) and their corresponding indices:

```
values, indices = torch.topk(ratings, k=100)
```

6.  Let's get a list of this user's favorite books. We create a new list of indices by filtering the `indices` list to only include those that are present in the `user_items` dictionary for the given user. In other words, we only keep books that this user rated. This list is then sliced to keep the first `num_recs` items:

```
ids = [index.cpu().item() for index in indices if
index in user_items[user]][:num_recs]
```

7.  We convert these book IDs into ISBNs:

```
item_isbns = [list(item_mapping.keys())[list(item_
mapping.values()).index(book)] for book in ids]
```

8.    We can now use these ISBNs to retrieve more information about the books. Here, we want to obtain the titles and the authors so that we can print them:

```
titles = [bookid_title[id] for id in item_isbns]
authors = [bookid_author[id] for id in item_isbns]
```

9.    We print this information as follows:

```
print(f'Favorite books from user n°{user_id}:')
for i in range(len(item_isbns)):
    print(f'- {titles[i]}, by {authors[i]}')
```

10.   We repeat this process, but with IDs of books that were not rated by the user (not in user_pos_items[user]):

```
ids = [index.cpu().item() for index in indices if
index not in user_pos_items[user]][:num_recs]
item_isbns = [list(item_mapping.keys())[list(item_
mapping.values()).index(book)] for book in ids]
titles = [bookid_title[id] for id in item_isbns]
authors = [bookid_author[id] for id in item_isbns]

print(f'\nRecommended books for user n°{user_id}')
for i in range(num_recs):
    print(f'- {titles[i]}, by {authors[i]}')
```

11.   Let's get 5 recommendations for a user in our database. Let's use 277427:

```
recommend(277427, 5)
```

12.   This is the output we obtain:

```
Favorite books from user n°277427:
- The Da Vinci Code, by Dan Brown
- Lord of the Flies, by William Gerald Golding
- The Cardinal of the Kremlin (Jack Ryan Novels), by Tom
Clancy
- Into the Wild, by Jon Krakauer

Recommended books for user n°277427
- The Lovely Bones: A Novel, by Alice Sebold
- The Secret Life of Bees, by Sue Monk Kidd
```

```
  - The Red Tent (Bestselling Backlist), by Anita Diamant
  - Harry Potter and the Sorcerer's Stone (Harry Potter
  (Paperback)), by J. K. Rowling
  - To Kill a Mockingbird, by Harper Lee
```

We can now generate recommendations for any user from the original `df` DataFrame. You can test other IDs and explore how that changes the recommendations.

## Summary

This chapter presented a detailed exploration of using `LightGCN` for book recommendation tasks. We used the `Book-Crossing` dataset, preprocessed it to form a bipartite graph, and implemented a `LightGCN` model with BPR loss. We trained the model and evaluated it using the `recall@20` and `ndcg@20` metrics. We demonstrated the effectiveness of the model by generating recommendations for a given user.

Overall, this chapter has provided valuable insight into the usage of `LightGCN` models in recommendation tasks. It is a state-of-the-art architecture that performs better than more complex models. You can expand this project by trying other techniques we discussed in previous chapters, such as matrix factorization and `node2vec`.

## Further reading

- [1] C.-N. Ziegler, S. M. McNee, J. A. Konstan, and G. Lausen, *Improving Recommendation Lists through Topic Diversification*, in *Proceedings of the 14th International Conference on World Wide Web*, 2005, pp. 22–32. doi: 10.1145/1060745.1060754. Available: `https://dl.acm.org/doi/10.1145/1060745.1060754`

- [2] D. Li, P. Maldonado, A. Sbaih, *Recommender Systems with GNNs in PyG, Stanford CS224W GraphML Tutorials*, 2022. Available: `https://medium.com/stanford-cs224w/recommender-systems-with-gnns-in-pyg-d8301178e377`

- [3] X. He, K. Deng, X. Wang, Y. Li, Y. Zhang, and M. Wang, *LightGCN: Simplifying and Powering Graph Convolution Network for Recommendation*. arXiv, 2020. doi: 10.48550/ARXIV.2002.02126. Available: `https://arxiv.org/abs/2002.02126`

- [4] H. Hotta and A. Zhou, *LightGCN with PyTorch Geometric. Stanford CS224W GraphML Tutorials*, 2022. Available: `https://medium.com/stanford-cs224w/lightgcn-with-pytorch-geometric-91bab836471e`

# 18
# Unlocking the Potential of Graph Neural Networks for Real-World Applications

Thank you for taking the time to read *Hands-On Graph Neural Networks Using Python*. We hope that it has provided you with valuable insights into the world of graph neural networks and their applications.

As we conclude this book, we would like to leave you with some final pieces of advice on how to effectively use GNNs. GNNs can be incredibly performant in the right conditions, but they suffer from the same pros and cons as other deep learning techniques. Knowing when and where to apply these models is a crucial skill to master, as over-engineered solutions can result in poor performance.

First, GNNs are especially effective when a large amount of data is available for training. This is because deep learning algorithms require a lot of data to learn complex patterns and relationships effectively. With a large enough dataset, GNNs can achieve high levels of accuracy and generalization.

For similar reasons, GNNs are most valuable when dealing with complex, high-dimensional data (node and edge features). They can automatically learn intricate patterns and relationships between features that would be difficult or impossible for humans to identify. Traditional machine learning algorithms, such as linear regression or decision trees, rely on handcrafted features that are often limited in their ability to capture the complexity of real-world data.

Finally, when working with GNNs, it is important to ensure that the graph representation adds value to the features. This is particularly applicable when the graph is an artificially constructed representation rather than a natural one, such as social networks or protein structures. The connections between nodes should not be arbitrary but represent meaningful relationships between the nodes.

You might notice that some examples in this book did not follow the previous rules. This is mostly due to the technical limitation of being able to run the code in Google Colab, and a general lack of high-quality datasets. However, this is also reflective of real-life datasets, which can be messy and difficult to obtain in large quantities. Most of this data also tends to be tabular, where excellent tree-based models such as XGBoost are difficult to beat.

More generally, sound baseline solutions are crucial, as they can be challenging to outperform, even in the right conditions. A powerful strategy when working with GNNs is to implement multiple types of GNNs and compare their performance. For example, a convolutional-based GNN such as GCN (*Chapter 6*) might work well for certain types of graphs, while an attention-based GNN such as GAT (*Chapter 7*) might be better suited for others. Additionally, a message-passing GNN such as MPNN (*Chapter 12*) might excel in certain contexts. Note how each approach is more expressive than the previous one, and each has different strengths and weaknesses.

If you're working on a more specific problem, there are several GNN approaches covered in this book that may be more appropriate. For example, if you're dealing with small graph data that lacks node and edge features, you may want to consider using Node2Vec (*Chapter 4*). On the contrary, if you're dealing with large graphs, GraphSAGE and LightGCN can help manage the computational time and memory storage requirements (*Chapters 8* and *17*).

Additionally, GIN and global pooling layers may be suitable for graph classification tasks (*Chapter 9*), while Variational Graph Autoencoders and SEAL can be used for link prediction (*Chapter 10*). For generating new graphs, you can explore GraphRNN and MolGAN (*Chapter 11*). If you're working with heterogeneous graphs, you may want to consider one of the many flavors of heterogeneous GNNs (*Chapters 12* and *16*). For spatio-temporal graphs, Graph WaveNet, STGraph, and other temporal GNNs can be useful (*Chapters 13* and *15*). Finally, if you need to explain the predictions made by your GNN, you can turn to the graph explainability techniques covered in *Chapter 14*.

By reading this book, you will have gained a deep understanding of GNNs and how they can be applied to solve real-world problems. As you continue to work in this field, we encourage you to put this knowledge into practice, experiment with new approaches, and continue to grow your expertise. The field of machine learning is constantly evolving, and your skills will only become more valuable as time goes on. We hope that you will apply what you have learned to tackle challenges and have a positive impact on the world. Thank you again for reading this book, and we wish you all the best in your future endeavors.

# Index

www.packtpub.com

Subscribe to our online digital library for full access to over 7,000 books and videos, as well as industry leading tools to help you plan your personal development and advance your career. For more information, please visit our website.

## Why subscribe?

- Spend less time learning and more time coding with practical eBooks and Videos from over 4,000 industry professionals

- Improve your learning with Skill Plans built especially for you

- Get a free eBook or video every month

- Fully searchable for easy access to vital information

- Copy and paste, print, and bookmark content

Did you know that Packt offers eBook versions of every book published, with PDF and ePub files available? You can upgrade to the eBook version at www.packtpub.com and as a print book customer, you are entitled to a discount on the eBook copy. Get in touch with us at customercare@packtpub.com for more details.

At www.packtpub.com, you can also read a collection of free technical articles, sign up for a range of free newsletters, and receive exclusive discounts and offers on Packt books and eBooks.

# Other Books You May Enjoy

If you enjoyed this book, you may be interested in these other books by Packt:

**Network Science with Python**

David Knickerbocker

ISBN: 9781801073691

- Explore NLP, network science, and social network analysis
- Apply the tech stack used for NLP, network science, and analysis
- Extract insights from NLP and network data
- Generate personalized NLP and network projects
- Authenticate and scrape tweets, connections, the web, and data streams
- Discover the use of network data in machine learning projects

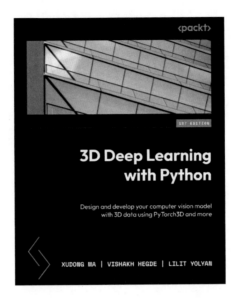

**3D Deep Learning with Python**

Xudong Ma, Vishakh Hegde, Lilit Yolyan

ISBN: 9781803247823

- Develop 3D computer vision models for interacting with the environment
- Get to grips with 3D data handling with point clouds, meshes, ply, and obj file format
- Work with 3D geometry, camera models, and coordination and convert between them
- Understand concepts of rendering, shading, and more with ease
- Implement differential rendering for many 3D deep learning models
- Advanced state-of-the-art 3D deep learning models like Nerf, synsin, mesh RCNN

## Packt is searching for authors like you

If you're interested in becoming an author for Packt, please visit `authors.packtpub.com` and apply today. We have worked with thousands of developers and tech professionals, just like you, to help them share their insight with the global tech community. You can make a general application, apply for a specific hot topic that we are recruiting an author for, or submit your own idea.

## Share your thoughts

Now you've finished *Hands-On Graph Neural Networks Using Python*, we'd love to hear your thoughts! Scan the QR code below to go straight to the Amazon review page for this book and share your feedback or leave a review on the site that you purchased it from.

https://packt.link/r/1-804-61752-0

Your review is important to us and the tech community and will help us make sure we're delivering excellent quality content.

# Download a free PDF copy of this book

Thanks for purchasing this book!

Do you like to read on the go but are unable to carry your print books everywhere?

Is your eBook purchase not compatible with the device of your choice?

Don't worry, now with every Packt book you get a DRM-free PDF version of that book at no cost.

Read anywhere, any place, on any device. Search, copy, and paste code from your favorite technical books directly into your application.

The perks don't stop there, you can get exclusive access to discounts, newsletters, and great free content in your inbox daily

Follow these simple steps to get the benefits:

1.  Scan the QR code or visit the link below

https://packt.link/free-ebook/9781804617526

2.  Submit your proof of purchase
3.  That's it! We'll send your free PDF and other benefits to your email directly